RYA National Sailing Scheme Instructor Handbook

© RYA
Third Edition 2021
The Royal Yachting Association
RYA House, Ensign Way,
Hamble, Southampton,
Hampshire SO31 4YA

Tel: 02380 604 100

Web: www.rya.org.uk

We welcome feedback on our publications at publications@rya.org.uk

You can check content updates for RYA publications at
www.rya.org.uk/bookschangelog

ISBN 978-1-910017302
RYA Order Code G14

Reprinted April 2022, December 2022, March 2024, November 2025

All rights reserved. No part of this publication may be reproduced, stored in a retrieval system, or transmitted, in any form or by any means, electronic, mechanical, photocopying, recording or otherwise, without prior permission in writing from the publishers.
A CIP record of this book is available from the British Library.

Note: While all reasonable care has been taken in the preparation of this book, the publisher takes no responsibility for the use of the methods or products or contracts described in this book.

Cover design: Pete Galvin
Illustrations: Pete Galvin
Photographic credits: Laurence West, Paul Wyeth, Minorca Sailing, RS Sailing
Acknowledgements: Clive Grant, David Mellor, Laurence West
Typesetting and design: Velveo Design
Proofreading and indexing: Matthew Gale
Printed in the UK

CONTENTS

FOREWORD	4
THE RYA NATIONAL SAILING SCHEME	5
RYA YOUTH SAILING SCHEME	6
RYA INSTRUCTOR TRAINING AWARDS	7
TECHNIQUES FOR INSTRUCTING & COACHING	30
THE RYA TEACHING METHOD	65
THE RYA DOUBLE-HANDED TEACHING METHOD	69
THE RYA SINGLE-HANDED TEACHING METHOD	92
THE RYA TEACHING METHOD: FURTHER SESSIONS	110
BACKGROUND KNOWLEDGE & INFORMATION	161
GLOSSARY	180
INDEX	182
INSTRUCTOR LOG	186

FOREWORD

Welcome to the RYA National Sailing Scheme Instructor Handbook. The RYA is thrilled that you are looking to become an RYA Instructor and assist in the delivery of RYA training courses to the many individuals who participate across the world.

Sailing is a wonderfully diverse sport with many types of boats to suit everyone regardless of age or ability. The RYA National Sailing and Youth Sailing Schemes offer one of the best ways into the sport, while also providing a route that enables sailors to develop their skills.

As an RYA Instructor you play an important role in enabling participants to progress quickly from beginner to expert in a controlled, safe, and fun environment.

The assumption is that you are already a competent sailor who would like to become involved in an RYA Recognised Training Centre teaching dinghy, multihull, or keelboat sailing.

The training schemes are for those working or volunteering as Instructors, Senior Instructors, and Coaches within the RYA National Sailing Scheme and Youth Sailing Scheme. It provides an outline of the RYA teaching methods, who can teach the scheme and where, the various Instructor qualifications and appointments on the RYA pathway, and how to be an effective Instructor and Coach.

Thank you for making the decision to become an RYA Instructor. You really will make a difference to people by introducing them to the exciting world of sailing. Get out on the water and I hope you enjoy your journey into instructing as much as I have.

Liz McMaster

RYA Chief Instructor – Dinghy, Wing & Windsurfing

THE RYA NATIONAL SAILING SCHEME

Overview

The aim of the RYA National Sailing Scheme (NSS) is to introduce and promote the sport of sailing in a safe, enjoyable, and informative way.

Participants can choose to learn in dinghies, (single- and double-handed) multihulls, or small keelboats offering a level of activity and adrenaline to suit any taste, with both the youth and the adult schemes offering parallel routes to learning the basics before embarking on the more advanced courses.

The RYA Youth Sailing Scheme is closely aligned to the adult National Sailing Scheme, but with even more emphasis on fun and games in the early stages.

At the end of their course, students should understand the content covered, while possibly still making mistakes in their performance. However, this should not prevent them from being awarded a certificate.

For example, and as a guide, if a student 'can', during 'picking up a mooring', use the correct speed, angle, and sail-setting in their approach, but still miss picking up the buoy, they should still have the section signed off in their logbook.

Conversely, if a student makes a lee-shore landing at full speed under full sail and crashes into the beach or pontoon, this indicates that they haven't fully understood what is required of the manoeuvre, and will need further practice and input before they can be signed off.

For further information on each stage and syllabus detail, refer to the latest edition of G4 RYA National Sailing Scheme Syllabus & Logbook.

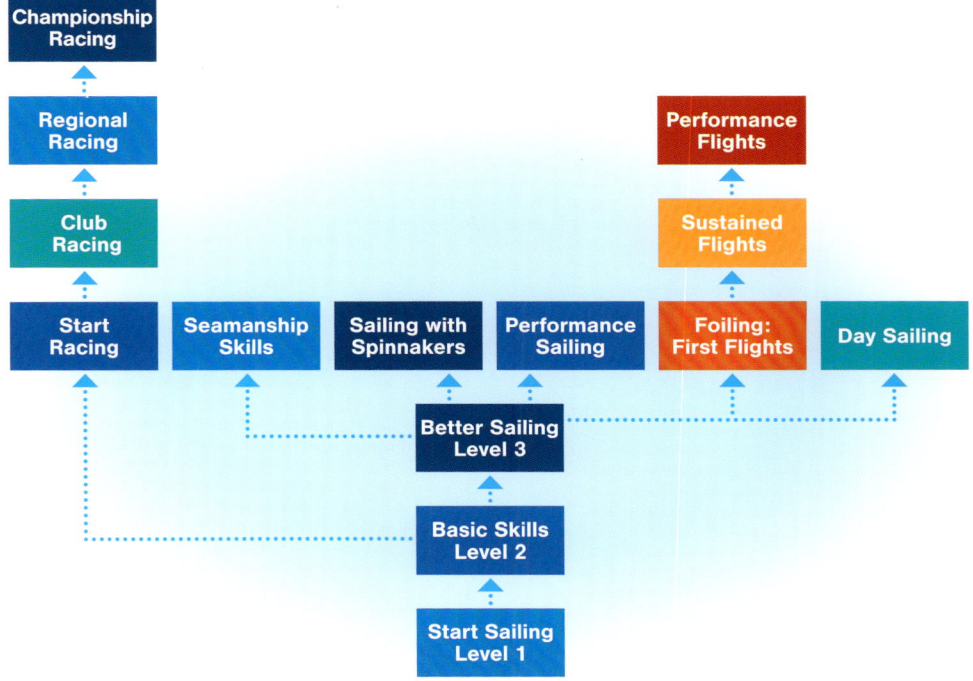

RYA YOUTH SAILING SCHEME

Overview

The syllabi for each of the four stages of the RYA Youth Sailing Scheme (YSS) are clearly expressed in terms of competencies. When the student can do each item it can be signed off.

There is provision for some guidance and help to be given within the Youth Sailing Scheme. When all items for a particular award are complete, the certificate or sticker may be given. On any course it is possible that some students will complete some extra items from the next stages, in which case those items can also be signed off.

For further information on each stage and syllabus detail, refer to the latest edition of G11 RYA Youth Sailing Scheme Syllabus & Logbook.

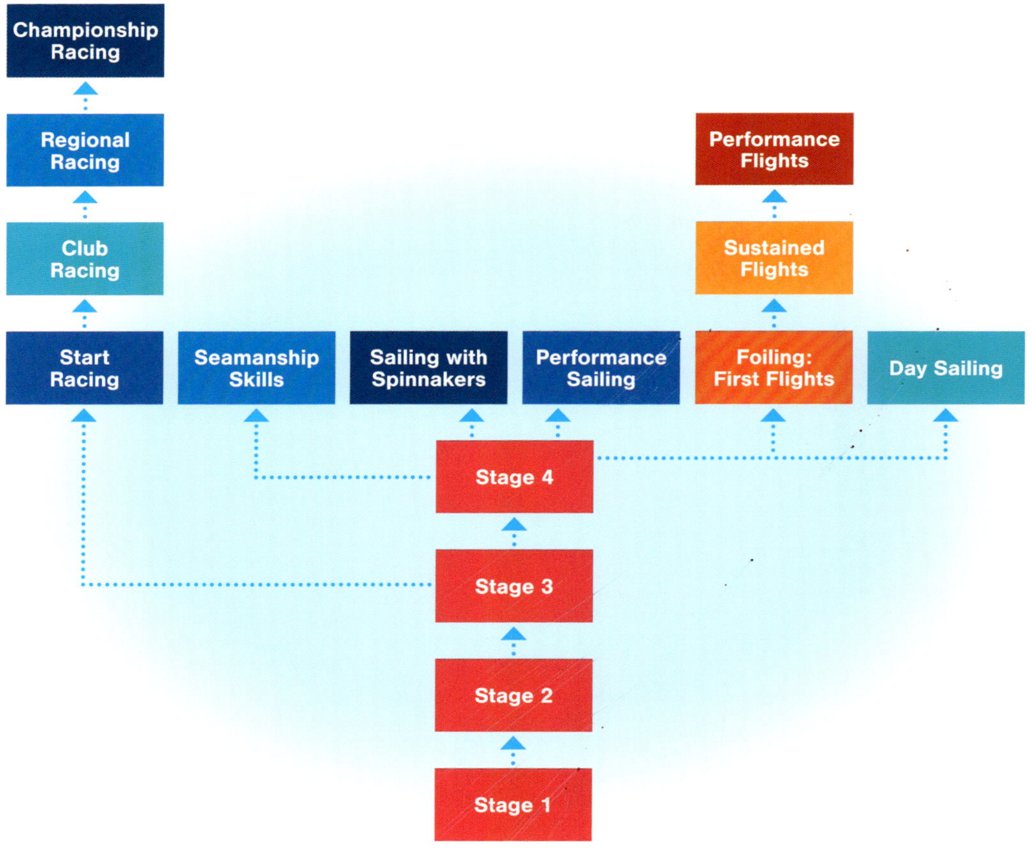

RYA INSTRUCTOR TRAINING AWARDS

The RYA Instructor pathway is progressive, enabling participants to choose their preferred class, such as multihull, dinghy, or keelboat, or become qualified to teach in all. The RYA teaching methods have been developed over many years and are world renowned.

The following section helps to explain the progression from one qualification to the next, as well as outlining the prerequisites and experience necessary at each level.

Once qualified, RYA Instructors can enhance their coaching through short two-day endorsement courses enabling them to teach a wider range of RYA training courses, such as racing, foiling, or advanced skills.

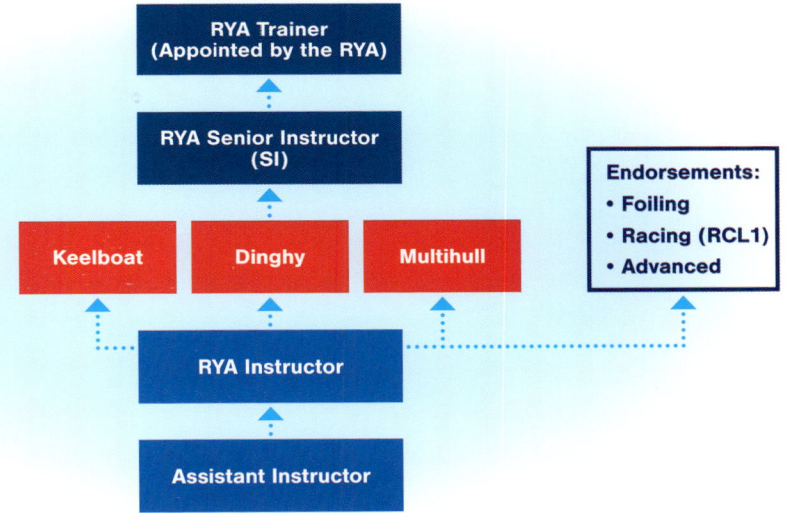

Below is a list of useful RYA publications available to assist Instructors:
- G3 RYA Start Sailing
- G4 RYA National Sailing Scheme Syllabus & Logbook
- G11 RYA Youth Sailing Scheme Syllabus & Logbook
- G12 RYA Advanced Sailing
- E-G101 RYA Race Coaching Handbook
- G110 RYA Foiling

RYA Assistant Instructor

The Assistant Instructor (AI) is trained to assist qualified Instructors to teach beginners up to the standard of the National Sailing Scheme Level 2 and the Youth Sailing Scheme Stage 3.

Role

- Assists RYA Instructors
- The award is centre specific
- Instructs up to National Sailing Certificate Level 2 and Youth Sailing Scheme Stage 3
- Must only work under the supervision of a Senior Instructor

Eligibility for the Training Course

- Sailing standard – pass one of the National Sailing Scheme Advanced Modules
- Recommendation by Principal of training centre

Training

Training will cover the centre's safe-operating procedures, and the teaching points related to teaching beginners in double- and single-handed boats shown in the RYA teaching methods within this book.

Training is approximately 20 hours in duration, run as either two days or as modular sessions. It can also be run as 1:1 'on-the-job' training over a similar period.

Training is primarily afloat, covering teaching points from each session based around the centre's main fleet (double or single handers). If double handers, the AI will helm initially then hand over to the students as quickly as possible. If single handers, the AI will mainly be a helper, rigger, catcher etc.

Assessment

After training, AI candidates will be assessed on their ability to teach beginners effectively. Successful candidates will be awarded an RYA Assistant Instructor certificate by their Principal.

Certificate Validity

The Assistant Instructor certificate is valid for five years, at which point it is encouraged that AIs progress on to taking the RYA Dinghy Instructor training.

Important Note

The AI does not need to hold a first aid or powerboat certificate. Therefore AIs must always work with direct supervision.

The award is centre specific. Thus, if an Assistant Instructor moves from one training centre to another, the new Principal will be required to deliver centre-specific training and issue a new Assistant Instructor certificate.

RYA Dinghy/Keelboat/Multihull Instructor

The National Sailing Scheme course can be taught in dinghies, keelboats, or multihulls. Therefore Instructors teaching the scheme must be qualified for the type of boat in which they will be teaching, i.e. only RYA Dinghy Instructors can teach in dinghies and only RYA Keelboat Instructors can teach in keelboats. However, Dinghy Instructors can broaden their qualification to include keelboats and vice versa, with the Instructor certificate endorsed accordingly.

The Instructor training course comprises of three sections:

1. Course prerequisites, including Safe & Fun online course, First Aid, and Powerboat Level 2.
2. Pre-entry sailing assessment.
3. Five-day training course.

Role

- Competent, experienced sailor able to sail in strong winds
- Can teach in dinghies, keelboats, or multihulls depending on previous experience and training
- Can teach RYA National Sailing Scheme Levels 1, 2, 3, Seamanship Skills, Day Sailing, Sailing with Spinnakers (where appropriately experienced and approved by the Principal) and Youth Sailing Scheme Stages 1–4

Eligibility for the Training Course

- Minimum age 16 (no candidates will be accepted for training under this age)
- A valid RYA First Aid certificate, or another acceptable first aid qualification
- RYA Safe & Fun online certificate
- RYA Powerboat Level 2 certificate
- RYA membership
- Pre-entry sailing assessment completed within one year prior to the Instructor training course

Certificate Validity

Instructor certificates are valid for five years from date of issue when supported by a valid first aid certificate.

Certificates can be revalidated by completing the online revalidation form, accompanied by evidence of a minimum of 30 hours' teaching experience in an RYA Recognised Training Centre, valid first aid certificate, and valid RYA membership.

Little or no logged experience may require a reassessment to ensure the Instructor is still up to date.

Pre-entry Sailing Assessment

Before being accepted on to an Instructor training course, candidates need to pass a 'Pre-entry sailing assessment' conducted by an RYA Trainer not more than one year in advance of their proposed course.

It is recommended that, prior to taking the assessment, candidates satisfy themselves they can sail confidently and to the standard detailed below. They should also have the appropriate background knowledge and understanding of requirements.

The assessment will be conducted in a training dinghy of the RYA Trainer's choice.

When the pre-entry assessment is conducted for a keelboat or multihull Instructor the rudderless sailing section should be omitted.

The candidate should be able to complete the sailing tasks listed below, while sailing at all times with an awareness of the Five Essentials, i.e. sail setting, balance, trim, centerboard, and course sailed.

The Trainer will be seeking to confirm that the candidate can sail in a controlled and competent manner considering preparation, communication, approach, and execution for each exercise, including an escape route if required.

Pre-entry Sailing Tasks

1. **Sail around a triangular course**
- Each leg of the course will be a minimum of 100 metres
- Use all the boat's equipment to best advantage including spinnaker if carried

2. **Sail a tight circular course**
- Circle less than three boat lengths' radius around a stationary (free floating) boat
- Make only one tack and one gybe.
- Sail trim and boat balance/trim suited to the manoeuvre. The circle should be as small as you can safely make it, but the Trainer will accept that in doing this you might have to leave the centreboard in one position.

3. **Sail a follow-my-leader course**
- On all points of sailing
- Speeding up/slowing down (up and downwind)
- Maintain a constant distance (one–two boat lengths)

4. **Pick up a man-overboard dummy**
- Boat must be stopped when you pick up the dummy
- Pick up at the windward shroud
- Should remain on the same tack while you pull it aboard

You may also be asked to complete some of the following, paying attention to the Five Essentials, control, and communication:

1. **Sail rudderless,** or with rudder in place and the tiller on loose elastic (class dependent)
   - Sail a course using all points of sail
   - Modifications to sail area, sheeting purchase, and centreboard setting are permitted during the exercise
   - Consider other water users and apply the 'rules of the road'

2. **Lee-shore landing and departure**
   - Use correct sail plan for landing
   - Land in a controlled fashion
   - On departure, clear the shore on favoured tack successfully in a controlled way

3. **Pick up a mooring or anchor**
   - Correct plan/approach considering wind and/or tide
   - Boat should be stopped next to the buoy and secured using correct knot
   - When secured, the boat should remain under control
   - Anchoring to take place in the area designated by the Trainer
   - After the anchor has held, the boat should remain under control
   - Recovery and sail away should be controlled

4. **Come alongside a moored boat**
   - Approach under control
   - Stop alongside on the correct side once committed
   - Remain in control thereafter
   - Depart under control

5. **Recover a capsized dinghy and sail away**
   - No external help required
   - The recovery should be controlled in a seamanlike manner

RYA Instructor Training Course

During the course you will be introduced to many techniques which have become standardised, as it is important that RYA instruction should follow broadly the same pattern in every training centre.

It is equally important, however, that you should not follow certain drills slavishly without considering that certain boats will require variations of the 'method'. Without scope for minor variations there would be no room for development and improvement.

Staffed by RYA Trainers, the training includes teaching techniques both ashore and afloat:

- Course duration is typically 50 hours/five-day week but could be modular over a number of weekends or single days. This approach may actually take longer
- The structure and content of the National Sailing Scheme and Youth Sailing Scheme
- Training in RYA teaching methods to the Seamanship Skills module including teaching those with special needs
- Instructing techniques for adults and children
- Preparation and presentation of a theory lesson
- Short discussion/presentation
- Preparation and use of visual aids
- The assessment of students' abilities
- The use of powered craft in a teaching environment
- Safeguarding, child protection, health & safety, and cold-water shock

Throughout the course, and during the moderation, evidence of competence in these areas will be noted by the Trainer in charge.

Afloat

- The ability to plan and deliver a safe session
- A friendly, supportive manner
- Good briefing and debriefing skills
- The boat rigged according to weather conditions and the abilities of your students
- Teaching according to the methods outlined on your course and in this book
- Correct positioning of Instructor and students
- Successful demonstrations and clear explanations
- Correct diagnosis and tactful correction of students' faults
- Use of lying-to position for crew changes and briefings

Ashore: Land Drills

- Use of the whole-part-whole method
- Simulator is safe
- A brief explanation of why drills are used
- Adequate preparation (and explanation) of equipment
- Good positioning of students

- Clear and accurate demonstrations both at normal speed and slowly with commentary, then again at normal speed
- Ability to identify and correct students' faults

Moderation & Course Outcome

Instructor courses are moderated by an outside moderator (Trainer) who has usually not been involved in the training.

The moderator's task is to add further training and confirm that all RYA standards expected on the course have been upheld, and they will do this by observing the candidates delivering teaching in as realistic conditions as possible.

Moderation elements may include practical teaching afloat, a teaching session ashore, teaching a land drill, and the moderator may also ask for the delivery of a short five-minute discussion or presentation.

In the unlikely event that a candidate is not considered ready to be moderated, a separate time for moderation will be suggested, along with an agreed action plan.

Trainers will review performance with candidates individually. This will help the moderator to take into account any particular circumstances on the day and to confirm whether or not candidates have proved their competence. The final decisions and course outcome will be delivered by the Trainer.

If for some reason a candidate is not entirely successful in a particular area, an action plan will be provided to help develop the candidate and overcome any gaps in knowledge or ability.

The content of an action plan will vary from individual to individual, depending on the reasons and shortfalls for which it is being issued. However, it is generally areas identified as requiring further development using SMART (Specific Measurable Achievable Realistic Timely) to create clear action, progression, and development. For example:

- Assist/shadow/be shadowed by an experienced Instructor in the delivery of a given number of specific courses. This may be required to develop further the candidate's confidence in a 'real' teaching environment, or if more time is needed to develop the candidate's knowledge of certain aspects of the RYA teaching methods
- Attend a future moderation. If a candidate is felt to have understood the teaching methods, but either did not show this during moderation or is felt to need more time, they may be asked to attend a future moderation
- Evidence of prerequisites. In most cases only RYA membership and first aid will be action-planned. All others must be in place prior to attending the course

If you disagree with the decision, the RYA Trainer will discuss the possibility of a reassessment or the procedure for appeal to the RYA.

Once qualified as an Instructor, they should feel confident in the following areas:

- Awareness of safety throughout
- Enthusiasm for the sport
- Confidence in the subject
- Teaching in a supportive manner
- Anticipation of changes in environment

RYA Instructor Endorsements

An RYA Instructor can teach students Level 1 Start Sailing to Level 3 Better Sailing, and Seamanship Skills from the National Sailing Scheme, as well as the Youth Sailing Scheme up to Stage 4.

Instructors can also teach Sailing with Spinnakers with the approval of the Principal, and Day Sailing under the supervision of an appropriately experienced Senior Instructor.

The following endorsements are designed to extend the scope of an Instructor's ability and will increase their value to the Principal of a training centre.

Dinghy, Keelboat, or Multihull Endorsement

Instructors who completed their initial training course and assessment in one boat discipline such as dinghies, but who subsequently want to instruct in another, such as multihulls or keelboats, should obtain these endorsements for their Instructor qualification.

Training/Assessment

- Training will be given by an authorised RYA Trainer
- Attend a two-day training/continuous assessment course during which they will be asked to demonstrate pre-entry skills and teaching techniques in the new discipline
- A certificate will be issued by the RYA upon successful completion

Advanced Instructor Endorsement

Candidates must have the background knowledge, technical ability, and skills to demonstrate any of the Sailing with Spinnakers or Performance Sailing techniques.

Teaching people how to sail performance boats requires a subtle change in the attitude of the Instructor, and there are many different skills to learn from a coaching point of view.

While students will have and understand the basic skills, Instructors have to be able to analyse their performance, identify areas for improvement, provide positive feedback, and coach them progressively.

Advanced Instructors must be confident sailing the boats in which they are coaching so they can provide effective demonstrations.

Eligibility

- Candidates will hold the RYA Instructor certificate
- Have at least one season's teaching experience at an RYA Recognised Training Centre
- Possess skills to at least the Performance Sailing and Sailing with Spinnakers modules

Training/Assessment

A two-day training course covering the following content:

- Performance-boat techniques
- Spinnaker techniques
- Application in coaching the Five Essentials at advanced level
- Use of powerboats in an advanced coaching environment
- Continuous assessment through the two days
- A certificate will be issued by the RYA upon successful completion

RYA Foiling Endorsement

An experienced Instructor with a good sail-foiling personal ability and background knowledge may wish to progress on to becoming a Foiling Instructor.

Eligibility

- Candidates will hold the RYA Dinghy Instructor certificate
- Minimum age 17
- Have at least one season's teaching experience at an RYA Recognised Training Centre
- Hold an RYA Sustained Flights certificate or above
- A valid RYA First Aid certificate, or another acceptable first aid qualification
- RYA membership

Training/Assessment

A four-day training course covering the following content:

- Foiling boats and required background knowledge: specific and adapted
- Foiling boat techniques
- Use of powerboats in a foiling boat coaching environment
- Continuous assessment through the four days
- A certificate will be issued by the RYA upon successful completion

This endorsement enables Instructors to teach the 'First Flights' course from the RYA National Sailing Scheme, or higher (personal foiling level dependent).

RYA Race Coach Level 1 (RCL1)

The Race Coach Level 1 course (previously known as the Racing Instructor endorsement) is designed to enable Race Coaches to introduce relatively inexperienced sailors to entry-level dinghy racing.

This endorsement can be obtained by Race Coaches with experience of club racing who wish to teach racing skills through the Start Racing module of the RYA National and Youth Sailing Schemes.

Race Coaches with sufficient personal racing experience will also be permitted to teach the Club Racing course at their Principal or Chief Instructor's discretion.

Eligibility

It may be possible for RYA Race Coaches who have experience of club racing to qualify as a Race Coach during their RCL1 training course.

Alternatively, qualified Race Coaches may undertake further training at a later date with a Trainer.

Training/Assessment

The one-day course will include the organisation of club racing, preparation, management of the Start Racing course, and instructional techniques afloat (at least half of the day), including the use of race-training exercises.

Assessment is continuous and on successful completion a record card will be completed by an RYA Trainer and sent to the RYA.

The course should include the following characteristics:

- An emphasis on racing as an enjoyable pastime
- Ensuring the students have a basic understanding of starting and some fundamental racing rules
- The provision of enough information for Level 2/3 standard sailors to compete in a club racing course safely without presenting a hazard to other sailors
- Encouraging sailors to start racing, join a club, and progress within the sport

RYA Race Coach Level 2 (RCL2)

A course for a competent racer with personal racing knowledge of club and/or regional racing. The aim of the course is to provide candidates with skills and techniques to coach racing to youth and adult sailors.

Level 2 Race Coaches are able to deliver Start, Club, and Regional Racing (where appropriate) coaching at affiliated clubs or Recognised Training Centres.

Eligibility

- Appropriate racing experience (guide = competent club racer)
- Appropriate current racing knowledge (classes/pathways/Racing Rules of Sailing)
- RYA Powerboat Level 2 certificate
- A valid RYA First Aid certificate, or another acceptable first aid qualification
- Minimum age 16. Level 2 Coaches aged under 18 should be appropriately supervised by an adult who is either a Senior Instructor or a Racing Coach Level 2 or above
- Previous instructing experience is preferred but is not essential if the candidate has suitable alternative experience
- RYA membership
- RYA Safe & Fun online course

Training/Assessment

The RYA Race Coach Level 2 is an intensive two-day course (three day in keelboats) looking at the theory of coaching and applying it through a series of practical on-the-water exercises. The focus is on how to create positive learning environments through the delivery of effective and capable coaching.

Each candidate will be expected to run a number of sessions, including providing an exercise brief, delivering on-the-water coaching with feedback, and facilitating a learning review. Assessment is continuous throughout the course.

Revalidation

Race Coaches are requested to revalidate every five years to ensure their continued effectiveness. They need to:

- Complete the Race Coaches Revalidation Form
- Provide a copy of a valid first aid certificate

RYA Senior Instructor

Prior to considering and attending the Senior Instructor (SI) course it is important for an RYA Instructor to understand and appreciate the varied roles an RYA Senior Instructor may play within an RYA Recognised Training Centre. An Instructor must understand the difference in role and the importance of the SI to the RYA, their centre (or club), students, and other Instructors.

The role is diverse and dependent on the individual club or centre. An SI might be a volunteer or employee, part of a small team or larger workforce, or a mixture! These circumstances will influence and dictate what type of role an SI takes on, whether they develop into more of a manager and role model, while remaining an active Instructor.

Background Knowledge

An RYA Recognised Dinghy/Keelboat/Multihull Training Centre must have a current Senior Instructor as its Principal or Chief Instructor.

The Principal may themselves be a Senior Instructor or they may appoint a Senior Instructor to act as Sailing Chief Instructor, who would then oversee and manage the dinghy scheme delivery and ensure that sailing tuition is organised according to RYA methods and standards.

It is the Principal of an RYA Recognised Training Centre who carries the formal responsibility for ensuring that all training complies with RYA guidelines laid down in the current Guidance Notes for inspection of RYA Recognised Training Centres.

Qualities and Abilities

An SI has a great deal of responsibility: relying on resourcefulness to solve problems as they arise, directing the work of Instructors, and assisting and supporting their team, particularly if and when they need advice. Some of the many qualities a Senior Instructor requires are:

- **Soft skills:** Patience, resourcefulness, and having the ability to deal with students and Instructors in an appropriate manner
- **Organiser:** Organisational ability to ensure courses are safe, enjoyable, and informative
- **A manager:** Capable of managing and supervising one or more groups ashore or afloat and ensuring each group is taught by an appropriately qualified Instructor
- **To support and supervise:** Assist and support their Instructor team, particularly when they need advice and mentoring
- **Knowledge of the RYA:** Understand the full requirements of RYA Training Centre Recognition and where necessary put in place all the systems and documentation. This may well include carrying out or revising a risk assessment and specifying and recording safety procedures

Apart from problems caused by deteriorating weather conditions, issues generally arise from poor planning, expectations, or a lack of communication between the SI, Instructors, and students.

Senior Instructor Training Course

Role

The SI is a special type of role and leans more towards management than a coaching qualification.

The role of an SI is challenging and rewarding, and may be the last formal course an RYA Instructor attends. As mentioned above, the most important part of the Senior Instructor's role is day-to-day organisation of each course. Every course has four elements:

1. The students
2. The Instructors
3. The fleet/teaching facilities
4. Session delivery, considering relevant syllabus

Eligibility

Those wishing to apply for an SI course should contact their Regional Development Officer, Regional Trainer, or, if overseas, RYA Training, who will have information where courses are being run in their particular region.

Once confirmed on a course a candidate will receive the 'SI Workbook', which must be completed prior to the course, as well as any preparation set by the Trainers. Failure to do so may have a direct effect on the outcome.

Candidates must first be an RYA Dinghy/Keelboat/Multihull Instructor and must fulfil the following criteria before taking part in the Senior Instructor training course:

- Minimum age 18
- Two years' intermittent, or one year full-time, instructing since qualifying as a Dinghy Instructor
- RYA Safety Boat certificate
- A valid RYA First Aid certificate, or another acceptable first aid certificate
- RYA Safe & Fun online course (within 12 months of the course), or previous course which has been taken within the last three years
- Signed recommendation from either the RYA Chief Instructor or Principal, RYA Regional Development Officer/Regional Trainer, or RYA-appointed Trainer
- Candidates must have sailing ability to at least the standard of RYA Pre-entry, as listed on pages 10–11

Training

- Staffed by two RYA Trainers
- Courses require a minimum of six candidates
- Four days' duration, which can be spread over two weekends which may take longer
- SI courses may also be organised on a regional basis

Due to the diverse skills and knowledge an SI requires, the course covers a wide range of different, but equally as important, aspects through the following areas and delivery:

- Development of briefing and debriefing skills facilitated through a variety of tasks/sessions
- Organisation and management skills
- Course planning and organisation
- A number of short on-water sessions planned, led, and debriefed by the candidates on a wide range of the syllabus, encouraging fresh input to candidates' skills
- Session planning. Before each practical session the SI must be confident each of their Instructors has a clear idea of the aim and purpose of that session, so they can confirm that the aims will be met during the debriefing
- Shorebased teaching sessions
- Candidate-led workshops/discussions
- Training tasks led by specialist Coaches
- Personal sailing to at least pre-entry level, including use of spinnakers
- Safeguarding children and vulnerable adults
- Knowledge of centre administration and RYA inspections
- Group control ashore and afloat
- Safe slipway and launching procedures
- Correct teaching ratios
- Safe and effective use of safety boats (including 'role-model' standard of driving at all times) and their allocation
- An awareness of weather conditions and calling a halt to on-water activities
- Alternative teaching programme (high/no wind)

Course Evaluation

Throughout the SI course candidates will be assessed on their ability to plan, organise, and run practical sessions, as well as their input to shorebased sessions such as group discussions.

By the end of the SI training course, the Trainers are looking in particular for SIs who can clearly identify and provide feedback to their Instructors on the following areas:

- Safety was maintained
- Aims were clearly stated (did the session have clear objectives?)
- Briefing was complete and clear (did the group know what was required?)
- Sailing area was identified
- Whether the whole group was involved
- Enthusiasm was maintained
- Problems were solved
- Signals (two-way) were established
- Effective on-water coaching took place for the group and individuals
- Group control was maintained (no unnecessary delays) ashore and afloat
- Each student was carefully debriefed and problems discussed and solved
- Students' questions were answered clearly and correctly
- The follow-on session was described
- Maintained good relationships with others

Throughout the course, Trainers will provide feedback to the candidates regarding their knowledge and experience of the RYA scheme and sessions run. At the end of the training, if the Trainers are unable to confirm whether the candidates have successfully completed the course, they will outline the reasons for that decision and agree a suitable action plan for future success.

Certificate Validity and Revalidation

- Valid for five years from date of issue when supported by a valid first aid certificate
- Certificates can be revalidated by using the online revalidation form, with evidence of logged teaching experience at an RYA Recognised Training Centre, valid first aid certificate, and valid RYA membership.
- Little or no logged experience may require a reassessment to ensure that the Instructor is still up to date

RYA Trainer

An RYA Trainer is an experienced RYA Senior Instructor who has been selected and trained as competent to train and assess Instructors. They represent the RYA and act as an ambassador for the RYA training schemes.

The RYA requires that Trainers have sensitivity to individuals' needs, in addition to being a strong role model. Enthusiasm and a commitment to the RYA training schemes are essential, as is having an approachable and friendly attitude.

RYA Trainers need to be competent and experienced sailors with good teaching and coaching skills, motivational and leadership skills, a positive and enthusiastic approach, and good communication skills. The role is broad and candidates must be willing to involve themselves in all aspects of the RYA National and Youth Sailing Schemes.

RYA Trainers are appointed by the RYA Chief Instructor on an annual basis, and are required to attend a practical revalidation every five years.

Eligibility

The RYA Trainer process is through application and selection. The RYA Chief Instructor is looking for Senior Instructors with proven ability and extensive experience of the National and Youth Sailing Schemes in a variety of training centres.

Other qualities include:

- Displaying a confident and competent level of personal sailing ability in single-handed, double-handed, symmetric, and asymmetric boats
- Demonstrating enthusiasm and an in-depth knowledge of the National and Youth Sailing Schemes (NSS and YSS), including fluency in the method ashore and afloat
- Demonstrating outstanding teaching and coaching across the spectrum of syllabi in the NSS and YSS
- Motivational and leadership skills
- Positive and enthusiastic approach based on effective communication skills, including the ability to be empathetic, approachable, and supportive for individuals and groups
- Clear ability and understanding of an effective coaching conversation, and skill in reviewing
- Displaying a high level of competence in the use of powerboats in a safety or coaching environment to a role-model standard

Application Process

Initial contact should be made with the relevant RYA Regional Development Officer, who can discuss the process and nominate potential candidates for consideration to the RYA Chief Instructor.

Senior Instructors based overseas need to contact the RYA Chief Instructor direct at RYA HQ.

It is a requirement to be an RYA member on application and for the duration of your appointment.

RYA Trainer: Selection Days

Following a successful application, candidates are invited to attend selection. The two-day selection comprises practical and theory sessions delivered to both the peer group and the RYA Training Team.

The aim of the selection is to enable the training team to form a view of the candidate's ability and experience and to assess their suitability for training Dinghy Instructors in the RYA schemes. To provide evidence of the qualities listed in the 'Eligibility' section, candidates will be asked to deliver a number of sessions to demonstrate the following:

- The ability to organise and deliver an effective, meaningful, and structured NSS or YSS session, including group control
- Knowledge and demonstration of the RYA teaching method
- The ability to organise and deliver an effective land-drill session
- The ability to review a Dinghy Instructor session as an SI using an RYA reviewing method
- The ability to drive a powerboat effectively in a teaching session. Demonstrate appropriate safety-boat and coach-boat skills
- Sail competently in a variety of boats including single/double handers
- Chair an effective discussion
- Show enthusiasm, motivation, leadership, and empathy

Assessment will be based on the candidate's performance over the duration of the selection and will be judged by the RYA Training Team. The outcome will be delivered and discussed with the candidate during the final debrief.

Successful candidates will be provided with development plans and invited to attend the RYA Trainer course.

RYA Trainer: Training Course

The training course is run over five days and looks into the delivery of each component of an Instructor course consolidating the skills, abilities, and knowledge required to train and assess RYA Dinghy Instructors, including:

- Reviewing skills
- Robust session delivery and group control
- Chairing and participation in discussions
- Personal sailing
- People skills, enthusiasm, motivation, leadership, and empathy
- Knowledge of RYA Training schemes and teaching models
- Powerboat/coach-boat driving to a high, role-model standard

Assessment is on a continual basis throughout the course, based on an overall impression of your abilities and participation, judged by the RYA Chief Instructor and coaching team.

Candidates who successfully complete the training course will normally be provided with development plans, which will vary between individuals.

On successful completion of the development plan, candidates will be appointed as an RYA Trainer by the RYA Chief Instructor. Those wishing to train Instructors in other boat disciplines, such as keelboat or multihull, should normally have suitable experience and/or the relevant Instructor endorsement.

Trainers wishing to become RYA Recognised Training Centre Inspectors should attend a one-day training course organised by the RYA.

RYA Trainer: Appointment Revalidation

Trainers are appointed annually by the RYA Chief Instructor, and attendance for revalidation is required on a five-yearly basis on a date organised by the RYA. The day includes a practical assessment of ability and current knowledge in the following areas to a role-model standard of delivery:

- Techniques for teaching and assessing Instructors to current RYA teaching methods
- Peer-to-peer reviewing
- Delivery of a practical on-water session
- Personal sailing ability to the minimum of Instructor pre-entry level
- Powerboat discipline and role-model delivery

To be considered for reappointment it is a requirement within this five-year period for the RYA Trainer to:

- Attend an RYA revalidation
- Attend at least one scheme-relevant RYA National Conference
- Run at least two full RYA Dinghy Instructor courses as Trainer
- Run National and Youth Sailing Scheme courses

At RYA National Conferences an update is delivered on changes to the schemes, and there is an opportunity to feed back to the RYA.

Who Teaches What?

	National Sailing Scheme in Dinghies	National Sailing Scheme in Keelboats	National Sailing Scheme in Multihulls	Youth Sailing Scheme
Assistant Instructor*	Levels 1, 2			Stages 1, 2, 3 in dinghies
Dinghy Instructor	Levels 1, 2, 3, Day Sailing, Seamanship Skills, Sailing with Spinnakers*			Stages 1, 2, 3, 4 in dinghies
Keelboat Instructor		Levels 1, 2, 3, Day Sailing, Seamanship Skills, Sailing with Spinnakers**		Stages 1, 2, 3, 4 in keelboats
Multihull Instructor			Levels 1, 2, 3, Day Sailing, Seamanship Skills, Sailing with Spinnakers*	Stages 1, 2, 3, 4 in multihulls
Advanced Instructor (discipline specific or with endorsement)	As Dinghy Instructor plus Sailing with Spinnakers, Performance Sailing	As Keelboat Instructor plus Sailing with Spinnakers, Performance Sailing	As Multihull Instructor plus Sailing with Spinnakers, Performance Sailing	As Dinghy Instructor plus Sailing with Spinnakers, Performance Sailing
Foiling Instructor	As Dinghy Instructor plus First Flights foiling course (or as experience dictates)			As Dinghy Instructor plus First Flights foiling course (or as experience dictates)
Senior Instructor	As Dinghy Instructor	As Keelboat Instructor	As Multihull Instructor	As Dinghy Instructor
RYA Trainer	All NSS and YSS courses plus Dinghy Instructor/SI courses and endorsements	All NSS and YSS courses plus Keelboat Instructor/SI courses and endorsements	All NSS and YSS courses plus Multihull Instructor/SI courses and endorsements	All NSS and YSS courses plus Dinghy Instructor/SI courses and endorsements

*An Instructor who is suitably experienced and approved by the Principal or Chief Instructor.

**A Dinghy Senior Instructor holding RYA Day Skipper Practical or above may teach and supervise the NSS in keelboats. N.B. All RYA tuition should be supervised by an RYA Senior Instructor.

***Assistant Instructors must never be allowed to work without direct supervision.

Racing: Who Teaches What?

	National Sailing Scheme in Dinghies	National Sailing Scheme in Keelboats	National Sailing Scheme in Multihulls	Youth Sailing Scheme
Race Coach Level 1	As Dinghy Instructor plus Start Racing, Club Racing*	As Keelboat Instructor plus Start Racing, Club Racing*	As Multihull Instructor plus Start Racing, Club Racing*	As Dinghy Instructor plus Start Racing, Club Racing*
Race Coach Level 2	Start Racing, Club Racing, Regional Racing	Start Racing, Club Racing, Regional Racing	Start Racing, Club Racing, Regional Racing	Start Racing, Club Racing, Regional Racing
Race Coach Level 3	Start Racing, Club Racing, Regional Racing, Championship Racing	Start Racing, Club Racing, Regional Racing, Championship Racing	Start Racing, Club Racing, Regional Racing, Championship Racing	Start Racing, Club Racing, Regional Racing, Championship Racing

Teaching Ratios

Type of Craft	Student: Instructor Ratio
Crewed dinghies and multihulls	3:1 for beginners with Instructor onboard. Maximum 9:1 but not more than six boats per Instructor (e.g. three Wayfarers with three students in each, or four Picos with two students in each).
Single-handed dinghies and multihulls	6:1 (applies only while the boats are used as single handers).
Keelboats	4:1 (Instructor on board). One Instructor must be responsible for no more than nine students (e.g. three boats with three students in each).

Ratios for Instructor Training Courses

Type of Course	Delivered By	Ratio	Moderated
Assistant Instructor	Senior Instructor	1:6	No
Instructor Training: Dinghy Keelboat Multihull	Trainer	1:6	Yes
Endorsements: Keelboat Multihull Advanced Foiling Racing	Trainer (with relevant endorsement)	1:6	No
Senior Instructor	Two Trainers	Minimum 2:6, maximum 2:12	No
Race Coach Level 2	Race Coach Tutor	1:6	No
Trainer	RYA Chief Instructor	RYA discretion	

TECHNIQUES FOR INSTRUCTING & COACHING

The main purpose of instructing or coaching is to help people learn. Therefore, any Instructor or Coach should have a clear understanding of how people learn, helping them make more effective decisions in creating a learning environment to support their students.

To be an effective Instructor and Coach we can use some helpful techniques to make the students trust us and want to learn from us. Our biggest influence is 'rapport'.

How you are perceived by others determines your credibility and therefore the influence you will have over them. First impressions are vital as it is estimated that up to 90 per cent of people's opinions of you are formed in the first 10 seconds of meeting you.

Therefore rapport = power in coaching terms.

How and Why People Learn

Understanding how and why people learn will assist our abilities and effectiveness as Instructors, helping us to understand the importance of adapting our sessions and delivery. The next section explains the different ways people absorb information and learn.

Absorbing Information

All of us see and experience the world in a variety of ways. We take in information through our senses:

- ✓ Visual – eyes
- ✓ Auditory – ears
- ✓ Reading – eyes and mental images
- ✓ Kinaesthetic – touch, feel, and movement

These senses are pathways to our brains. None of us use just one pathway exclusively – there is a significant overlap between them. You and your students are likely to have a preference:

Visual Learners

Visual preference students make up around 40–60 per cent of the population.

Students relate well to written information, pictures, and observation. Typically they will benefit from sessions where they can observe skills and possibly take notes. In some cases, information won't seem real unless they have seen it written down. They will respond well to demonstrations both ashore and afloat, and a range of visual aids.

Auditory Learners

Auditory preference students make up about 10–30 per cent of the population.

Students relate well to the spoken word. They like to hear clear, verbal explanations of skills both afloat and ashore. Often, written information will have little meaning until it has been heard, and it may help them if they read written information out loud. Auditory learners can be sophisticated speakers, and work in jobs which require this skill.

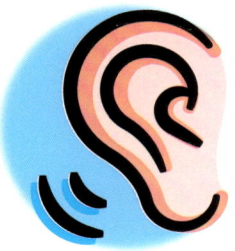

Kinaesthetic Learners

Kinaesthetic-preference learners make up around 10–30 per cent of the population.

These students learn well through touch, movement, and space, and learn skills through imitation and practise. During sessions they will like to have a go, touch, feel, and experience the skill.

Reading Learners

Will prefer to look at the relevant RYA publications. They will usually ask what topics will be covered on the next session so they can read up and investigate beforehand. Reading learners will read information to clarify and consolidate after each session. Always refer to the RYA publications to signpost where to get further information.

For further information on this area, take a look at the 'Communication Skills' section.

An Additional Learning Model

Academics Peter Honey and Alan Mumford describe learning styles in a slightly different way. However, it's important to remember there is no clear dividing line, as many people may conform to more than one style depending on what they are doing.

Active Learners – *'I'll try anything once'*

Active learners are enthusiastic and involve themselves fully in new experiences.

- They tend to act first and consider the consequences later
- They tackle problems by brainstorming and trying things out
- They become easily bored and will generally dislike activities which require them to take a passive role

Reflective Learners – *'I'd like time to think about this'*

Reflective learners like to ponder experiences and observe things from different perspectives before reaching conclusions.

- They listen to others before making their own point
- They may like to stand back and observe
- They learn by listening and sharing ideas with others
- They may prefer a slower pace and dislike taking action without having time to think

Theoretical Learners – *'How does this fit?'*

Theoretical learners make sense of skills by understanding the theory behind them and thinking through problems logically, step by step.

- They like analysis and detail
- They may ask lots of questions
- They learn best from activities which allow time to mix their observations with their theoretical knowledge
- They enjoy having books, models, and diagrams to study

Pragmatists – *'How can I apply this in practice?'*

Pragmatists think that if it works it's good.

- They are willing to try out new ideas to see if they work in practice
- They like to act quickly and confidently on ideas which attract them
- They enjoy good demonstrations
- They become impatient with long-winded explanations and discussions
- They learn best from practical sessions which allow them to test things for themselves

This information is based on the Honey & Mumford Learning Styles Questionnaire. A full version is available from www.talentlens.co.uk/product/learning-style-questionnaire.

Methods, Motivators, and Barriers to Learning

Adults and Children

Adults and children react to and learn from different styles. We need to know how to deal with both, and ensure we match styles, delivery, and also reasons for learning.

The Way Adults Learn	The Way Young People Learn
Typically more independent and self-directed	More random and Instructor/Coach led
Goal-orientated and structured approach to learning	Fun and experiential-orientated approach
Need to know why they are learning something. Want to know 'what', 'where', 'when' and 'why'. Usually need to do things for a reason.	Prefer a fun exercise or game rather than just practice
Accumulated life experience can be applied to the learning process for good and bad	May be experiencing the skill for the first time. Not biased by other experiences – free learners!
Often reluctant to get things wrong. Become frustrated when they do!	A more natural approach with fewer inhibitions. Happy to get things wrong!

Remember that everyone enjoys learning if it's fun. Make your sessions fun, inspiring, and stimulating for all.

Motivators to Learn

People are motivated by many reasons. Our awareness of this will help shape our teaching and delivery. Some examples of motivating factors are:

- Making or maintaining social relationships
- Learning to engage others – parents often learn with a view to involving the rest of their family
- A desire to achieve awards and qualifications
- Stimulation or escape from everyday life
- Interest in the subject
- Lifestyle aspiration
- Fear of failure

Barriers to Learning

If people are motivated to learn and we shape our teaching to support them, we should also be aware of the fear of failing. Some possible barriers we may encounter:

- Other responsibilities (families, careers, social commitments)
- Lack of time
- Environment – being wet and cold, or even too hot
- Feelings – looking or feeling silly
- Scheduling problems – when courses take place
- Insufficient confidence
- Inappropriate teaching methods
- Personality clashes – between student and instructor, or through lack of bonding in the group, friendships
- Being made to do the course by parent or spouse, and not interested or ready to do it

Fear

Fear is one of the main barriers a good Instructor can help students overcome. Adults and children have three principal fears when trying something for the first time:

1. **Fear of failure.** Be clear about students' progress throughout the course. Encourage them to try things out, even if it means making mistakes. If the course is being assessed, keep students informed of progress with details, and let students know the outcome as soon as possible.
2. **Fear of the unknown.** Keep students fully informed throughout each stage, and explain to them the reasons for the structure of the course.
3. **Fear of not being liked or fitting in.** Break the ice early and encourage groups to work together and get to know each other. Consider some games to help people relax.

Further Learning

A further barrier to people learning is the retention of false beliefs. For example, they believe that they can cram everything they need to learn into one short block, such as a two-day sailing course, expecting this to lead to a permanent change in high skill and knowledge level. It is important to reinforce how spacing their learning experiences out over time may allow them to remember and practise.

An individual's 'mindset' can be a factor, and can be a way of better understanding people's beliefs in relation to learning. People often hold beliefs that fit into one of two possible categories:

- Fixed-ability beliefs (Fixed mindset)
- Untapped-potential beliefs (Growth mindset)

Mindset is situational and dynamic. In some situations it might be more fixed than others – it can and does change.

- **Growth mindset:** Failure is an opportunity to grow. I can learn to do anything I want. Challenges help me grow. Feedback is constructive
- **Fixed mindset:** Failure is the limit of my abilities. I'm either good at it or I'm not. My abilities are unchanging. I can either do it or I can't. When I'm frustrated I give up

Ways to Break Down Barriers

- Ensure feedback reinforces the skill rather than being person orientated. For example: *'That tack worked really well because you were patient and waited for the boat to turn head to wind before you moved across the boat'*
- Create a positive atmosphere around getting it 'wrong' – 'Have another go so we can keep making progress'
- Reinforce that we learn by doing, which is better than being told
- Be passionate and excited about having a go at a new challenge
- Encourage the concept of testing, i.e. by setting them problems to solve

By using techniques like these you will be helping your learners to create more-helpful beliefs about their learning and move away from the less-helpful beliefs they might have arrived with.

The Stages of Learning

Instructing is the delivery of new practical and theoretical techniques, usually broken down into stages where the Instructor 'tells' the students what to do and how to do it, in a 'directed' style.

Coaching implies a shift towards helping students develop those techniques into skills. It might involve more observation, feedback, and questioning to check their understanding of the technique. However, while developing skills, people will often shift between being instructed and coached.

- INSTRUCTING (Directive behaviour): *Creating the building blocks, Instructor led*
- COACHING (Supportive behaviour): *Developing the sailor's techniques, watching, asking, supporting*

You can expect your students to follow stages when learning any new technique. The skills model below provides us with understanding of where students are in their learning cycle so we can shape our teaching and reviewing styles to match.

You will need to adapt to being both Instructor and Coach. The role chosen at any time will depend on a number of factors:

- The ability and experience of the Instructor
- The type of session (practical or theory)
- The subject (a new one or developing existing skills)
- The teaching method (discussion, demonstration, or student practice)
- The environment (ashore or afloat)
- The number of students
- Where they are in the RYA scheme

A typical session might follow this simple model which shows how your role evolves from Instructor to Coach as your students progress through their course. As students progress through the stages with one technique they may begin again at the first stage with new techniques. Therefore, even experienced sailors attending advanced courses will follow the same learning process and we need to match our instructional and reviewing styles to these stages.

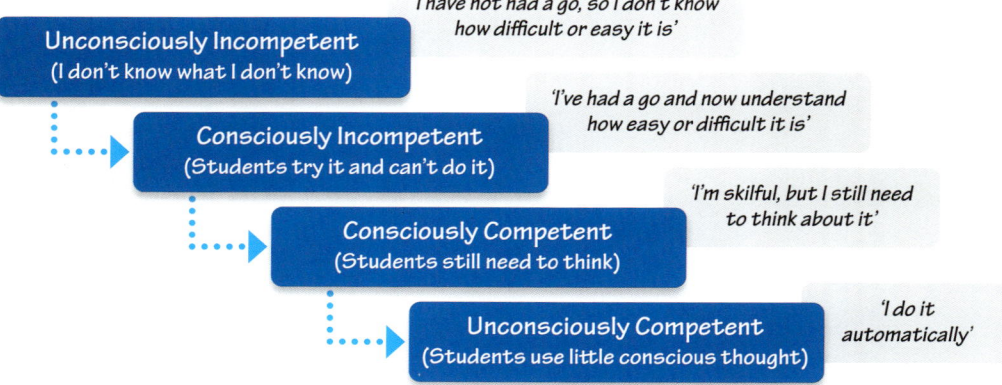

Exactly how you tackle these four stages can be determined by understanding how your students absorb information and learn new skills.

Communication Skills

As considered earlier in the 'How and Why People Learn' section, communication is more than just words. We are constantly communicating, even when we are saying nothing. Research has shown that 55 per cent of your communication is determined by your body language, posture, and eye contact, 38 per cent by your tone of voice, and only seven per cent by your actual words.

Therefore, to ensure you teach efficiently, concentrate on all these communication pathways.

Communication is a two-way process so remember you also have to listen effectively as well. The saying 'Two ears and one mouth' demonstrates the ideal ratio of an Instructor's use of words to their use of listening skills.

Effective communication can be achieved by the six 'Cs':

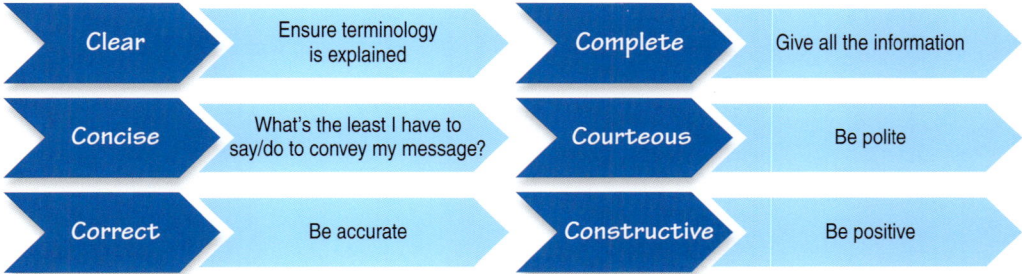

Communication while afloat is particularly important. Remember:

- Keep verbal communication to a minimum
- Project your voice towards your students and try to position yourself upwind
- Position your students where they can hear you best
- Signal students to come to you frequently for feedback and further instructions (single handers)
- Use pre-agreed visual signals and agree a signal to confirm understanding

Levels of Listening

- **Cosmetic:** It looks like I'm listening but I'm not really!
- **Conversational:** I'm engaged in the conversation, talking, thinking
- **Active:** I'm very focused on what you're saying

Where possible, we need to be actively listening to our students so we really understand what they say and mean, concentrating on both the verbal and non-verbal messages they are giving.

Whatever you say, your students will typically:

- **Filter:** Pick out more or less important bits for themselves
- **Distort:** Interpret things for themselves
- **Delete:** Remove any bits that they find unclear or too difficult

It is important to check understanding often. Never assume they understand. Open questioning gets the students to think and reply, rather than giving a yes or no response. **Often less is more** – keep your messages simple and free of jargon, and back them up with demonstrations and practical examples. We will look more closely at questioning in the 'Briefing and Debriefing' section (pages 48–52).

Remember: the most ineffective question in the world is 'Do you understand?'

Non-verbal Messages

People use a variety of behaviours, such as head-nods, smiles, frowns, and laughter, to maintain a smooth flow of communication. Your students' facial expressions provide you with some feedback on the session too. The posture of the group enables you to judge their general attitude and mood. Body language and effective communication is a huge subject, so try to be your natural self.

Communication Blocks

Communication difficulties between the Instructor and the student can sometimes occur for a number of reasons:

- The student's perception of something is not the same as the Instructor's
- The student may lack the understanding of what is being taught
- The student may lack some motivation
- The Instructor may have difficulty in expressing what they want to say
- The student or Instructor has other things on their mind

Remember that Instructors are communicating all the time. Their thoughts and emotions can often 'leak' out through our verbal and non-verbal communication. Instructors and Coaches should therefore:

- Develop their verbal and non-verbal communication skills
- Ensure they provide honest feedback
- Give all students equal or appropriate attention, building rapport with every individual
- Ensure that Instructors listen to their students. Listen more, talk less!

TOP TIP

Always consider:
- **Why** you need to communicate
- **Who** you are communicating with
- **Where** and **when** the message will best be delivered
- **What** you are explaining or demonstrating
- **How** you get the information across

Being an Effective Instructor/Coach

Effective instructing and coaching needs:

- A mutual respect between the Coach and the student, with a desire to coach and be coached
- Empathy towards your students
- To inspire students
- Good communication between Coach and student – a two-way process
- A focus on clear, achievable goals
- The ability to ensure or develop the most suitable learning environment
- Truthful fault diagnosis and empathetic correction

People Skills – 'What Your Students Think of You'

Tips for gaining your students' trust:

- **Communication:** Listen to your students and respect what they tell you, working through difficult questions or situations with them. Be honest.
- **Influence:** The more you listen, the more you can influence them, build confidence, and positively reinforce
- **Rapport:** Spend time with them, enabling a rapport to develop
- **Empathy:** Express concern for and empathise with students, establish support, and identify their needs and goals
- **Preparedness:** Always set up early and be ready for their arrival
- **Appearance:** Pay attention to your personal appearance – remember the all-important first impression

What You Need to Know About Your Students

Remember that your students are going to have differing ages, genders, backgrounds, skills, hopes, fears, expectations, and aspirations. It's a good idea to gather as much information as possible on these areas from your students prior to the course. Some of this can be done on the booking form or a simple questionnaire.

Questions you might want to ask beginners:

- Why do you want to learn this activity?
- Have you done any sailing or windsurfing before, when, where etc.?
- Do you take part in any other watersports?
- Do you think you will carry on after this course?

Being prepared with this information can help you to:

- Create the right environment
- Be warm, welcoming, and friendly
- Tell them a bit about yourself
- Get them talking about themselves
- Tell them what to expect (and what not to expect)
- Create the course together
- Break the ice, making them feel relaxed and part of the group

Helping Students to Learn

Our preferred learning style will affect our teaching style as Instructors or Coaches. Therefore, we adapt our teaching style to suit these preferences, as this will create a learning environment matching all learning styles. The RYA has adopted a model which will ensure we support students' learning.

Success depends on how well you manage students from various age ranges, backgrounds, and abilities.

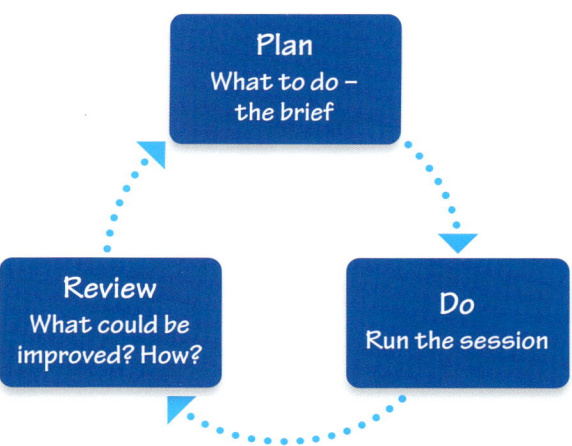

EDICTS

EDICTS is an RYA model used to ensure tuition matches all the learning styles.

E – **Explanation:** The Instructor gives a verbal description of the task to be taught

D – **Demonstration:** The Instructor demonstrates the skill to be taught (if needed)

I – **Imitation:** The students attempt to 'copy' the technique the Instructor has just shown them

C – **Correction/Coaching:** The Instructor provides corrective feedback to improve student performance

T – **Training/Try again:** The student can apply the feedback and repeat the technique

S – **Summary:** Before moving on to the next exercise, the Instructor summarises the skill with the student, the lessons learned, and confirms understanding

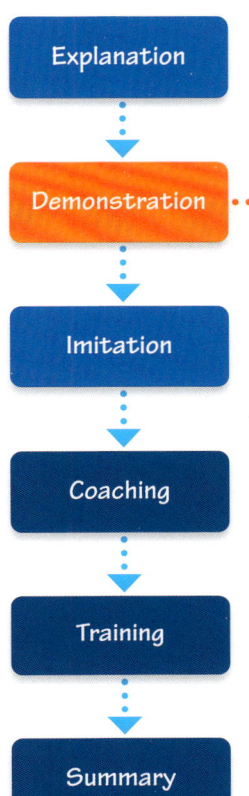

Land Drills – *'Making the "D" of EDICTS Effective!'*

Land drills introduce clarity and simplicity, and enable students to practise in a controlled environment. They are not necessarily used all the time, and can be used for students who need more development in the building of a new technique or if a technique is complicated. Land drills work particularly well before and after a demonstration afloat to convey or reinforce the 'actual technique'.

The delivery structure for any land drill is the **WHOLE – PART – WHOLE** teaching structure. This provides a demonstration breaking down sections of a skill through:

- **WHOLE** – Demonstration (possibly silent), allowing the student to concentrate on the actions and not what the Instructor is saying. This could be done as part of the 'Whole' demonstration
- **PART** – Identifying and breaking down a particular element you want the students to concentrate on, such as hand positioning or footwork. This would be an explanation of something to consider for the 'Part' delivery
- **WHOLE** – Bring the skill/technique back together, perhaps asking the students to tell the Instructor what to do, which confirms understanding for the Instructor

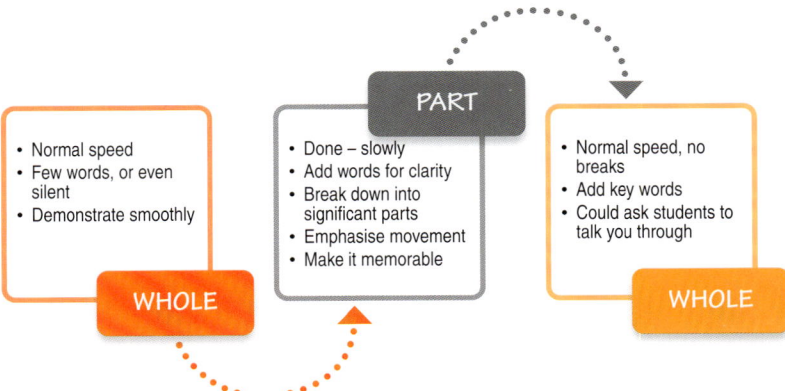

Involve your students where possible, e.g. moving the boom or balancing the boat. When teaching children, turn the drill into play through the use of songs etc. Land drills and simulators ashore are useful for a number of techniques where a complicated series of actions has to be co-ordinated (such as transitions like tacking or gybing), or more specific techniques (spinnaker work, anchoring, or reefing etc.) when sailing a dinghy. You can also adapt this model to deliver a skill in different sequences, such as 'Part-Part-Whole', depending on what you are trying to instruct, coach, or achieve.

Enhancing Our Instructing and Coaching: an Insight Into Emotional Intelligence

Being emotionally intelligent is important to us as Instructors. It allows us to create rapport or empathy with our students and also enhance our effectiveness within the team. Some researchers say emotional intelligence cannot be developed or learned as it is inborn, but let's take a look at how we can try to develop our emotional intelligence as Instructors and Coaches.

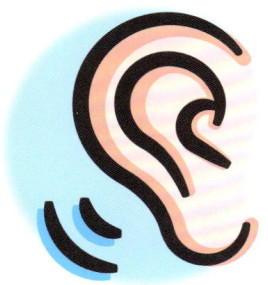

Listen

Take time to listen to what people are trying to tell you, with words (verbally), actions, and body language (non-verbally).

Body language can carry a great deal of meaning. When you sense how someone is feeling, consider the different factors that might be contributing to that emotion.

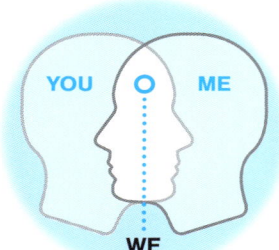

Empathise

Empathising is the ability to pick up on emotions and being able to understand another person's position. Practise empathising with other people by imagining how you would feel if you were them. Such activities can help build emotional understanding of a specific situation as well as developing stronger emotional skills in the long term.

Reflect

To reason with emotions, consider how your own influence your decisions and behaviours. When you are thinking about how other people respond, consider why they are feeling like this and how you may be able to help. Are there any unseen factors? How does your feeling differ from theirs? As you look at these questions you may find it becomes easier to understand the role emotions play in how people think and behave.

Presentation Skills

As an Instructor, we are effectively presenting all the time, but there are also times when we need to 'provide' a presentation on elements such as theory.

It is normal for people to be nervous about giving presentations. Some like public speaking; others shy from it. However, with experience and practice, the nerves will start to diminish.

Words

- Clear, concise language
- If you are using sailing terminology or new terms, ensure you explain
- Think before you speak
- Place emphasis on the important bits. Consider repetition to endorse/highlight an important word or sentence
- Summarise what you've said and ask questions often, especially at the end

Voice

- Vary your tone, pitch, and pace
- Speak in a conversational manner
- Build in pauses, especially at important parts
- Speak in a conversational way

Posture

Posture	Sit or stand. Try to be natural	Keep your head up. Try to breathe naturally
Hands	Uses your hands naturally if that's how you speak	Try to use your hands naturally as you speak
Movement	Moving around the group is okay as long as they can see you	Moving around the group will ensure you engage with everyone
Position	Ensure you are always in a position where all of the group can see you	
Use of notes and visual aids	Always face the audience. Stop talking while you look at your notes	It's best not to look at notes at all. Learn the presentation, and only use headings/key words in the notes
Eye contact	Ensure you make eye contact with every student often	

Good Presentations Depend on Several Elements:

The Content

WHAT – Consider context and audience. Initially, look at the syllabus from the logbooks.

- What is the aim of the session?
- What are the learning outcomes?
- What do I need to teach to what level?

WHERE – Consider where this would be delivered best. Would a classroom (using whiteboard, PowerPoint, models) or outside using actual equipment be the most effective place for delivery? Also consider where YOU are most comfortable – in a classroom environment, or using models or the real thing?

HOW – Once you have the **WHAT** and **WHERE**, you need to consider **HOW** you will structure your presentation. This depends on location. However, any presentation will have:

- ✓ The beginning
- ✓ The middle
- ✓ The end

The Beginning – Tell them what you're going to tell them

The opening few moments of a presentation are very important. You want the audience to feel and think 'This is going to be stimulating and important.' Prepare an **introduction** with a clear **aim** and **outcomes**:

- What are they going to learn and why
- Whether you will be giving a handout or they should make their own notes
- Explain your structure (give headings)
- How long you will take
- How you will deal with their questions (at the time or at the end)

Some possible ways of opening are:

- Ask a question that requires a show of hands
- Begin with a quotation or tell a story
- Ask the audience to do something

The Middle – Tell them

After you have attracted your audience's attention with your introduction, move to the bulk of your presentation, or 'the middle'. Remember, attention can wander and your audience will pay most attention at the beginning and end of sections.

- Have short sections with clear headings and summaries
- Check understanding at the end of each section by asking prepared questions

The End – Tell them what you told them
- Summarise your key points
- Ask for final questions
- Link back to your beginning by revisiting the aim. What has been learnt?
- Make it significant
- Ask final questions to check understanding
- Look forwards to next session

Some possible ways of ending are:

- Issuing a challenge
- Appealing for action
- Raising a laugh and telling a final anecdote (if you are a natural joke-teller)
- Pointing to the future
- Finishing with a quotation
- Asking questions about what you've said

Handling Questions

Set the Rules for Questions

Set rules for questions at the beginning (e.g. save questions for the end, or ask questions whenever you like). Remember: when planning your presentation, ensure you have sufficient time to cover everything by building in time for questions.

What to Say When You Don't Know the Answer

Honesty is the only policy when presenting to a group, and no one can know the answer to every question. It's how we deal with this situation which gives us confidence to accept there will be questions we don't know the answer to.

Compliment the Questioner

Always compliment the questioner in a sincere way. 'That's a very good question. I've never thought about it that way. Does anyone here have any ideas on that?' You might also combine this technique with 'I'll get back to you.'

The following strategies can help you field even the toughest questions with confidence.

Reflection

Repeat the question and ask your audience 'Does anyone here have any experience with that?' The audience can answer; they will love to be involved and share their knowledge.

Defer to the Expert

Sometimes a question is legitimately outside the area of expertise and there may be someone more experienced within the school or centre who you can pass it on to. You will need to decide who presents the answer – you or them. If you have used the tried and tested 'I don't know the answer but I can find out and come back to you', it is probably best for you to tell them.

Use of Visual Aids

Skillful use of visual aids can greatly enhance your presentation. Always remember that they are there to support you – they can take the attention off you periodically and allow you to think ahead. They should support what you are saying and add to the effect. Good visual aids support you, make an impact, and are memorable.

General Tips

- The best visual aid is a live example or 'real thing' of your subject matter. This enables your students to have a 'hands-on' experience, e.g. the actual equipment they will use – boat, board, sails, a buoyancy aid, a safety pack, etc.
- If the visual is comprehensive, consider giving it to your audience at the end of the lesson
- Whenever possible use pictures, diagrams, graphs, and colour
- Use visual aids to support learning, to add an impact, or to clarify a complex subject
- Models enable involvement and interaction
- Consider the use of video, white boards, and flip charts

Whichever Method You Use – Always:

Keep It Short and Simple.

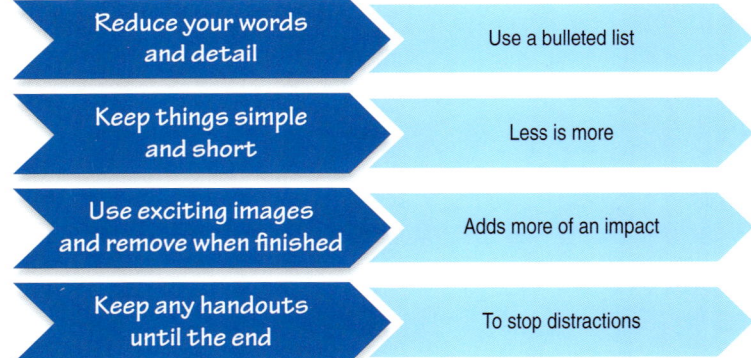

Discussions

A discussion is a way of getting everyone to have a say about a particular subject. It is very similar to a presentation in that it has a beginning, a middle, and an end, but a chairperson is needed to manage the flow and direction. Let's explore these in turn:

Beginning – Prepare an introduction with a clear aim and outcomes. This could include:

- What are we going to discuss and what the outcome is
- How long you will take
- Stressing that everyone is allowed a voice and is able to talk

Middle – The chairperson controls the discussion by:

- Getting the entire group to talk
- Managing the group
- Developing the conversations
- Keeping the discussion on track by stopping them wandering off course. Fuelling the discussion if needed
- Managing the time
- Taking notes and steering the conversation

End – Summarise the points they have discussed.

- Link back to your beginning, by revisiting the aim and outcome
- Summarise the key points in the discussion
- Thank everyone and end the session

Styles of Discussions

There are many ways of having a discussion. Let's look at some:

- **Formal** – The chairperson leads and the discussion can be round a committee table, using a flipchart or whiteboard
- **Buzz groups** – Set the aim and send them off into small groups. The chairperson checks each group is on track
- **Informal** – Like a structured conversation. Very informal, it could be with coffee, but thoughts are recorded and used going forward.

Briefing and Debriefing

Sailing Instructors teaching in double-handed boats can begin teaching their students as soon as they move to the dinghy. This will continue when they go afloat. However, a different approach will be required if teaching in single handers or as your students advance their skills, as input will need to have been provided before they go afloat.

Teaching and coaching becomes instantly easier with a good brief before the task. An effective debrief or feedback given afterwards makes for a successful session.

Creating Effective Conversations

Coaching conversations are more than simply asking questions or giving feedback. They help the learner make sense of what they just did.

If a student fails to perform a task successfully, Instructors and Coaches need to consider whether they would benefit from a coaching conversation or be better off just having another go. This may give them the opportunity to develop themselves – an equally powerful way of learning.

Conversely, if they attempt a skill but it regularly breaks down at the same point, a coaching conversation might help.

The Brief

There must be a brief *before every on-water session* and *before each new skill* is introduced. It is the most essential part to making the session effective. People should feel prepared and know what they are going to do.

A – **Aim** of session (What it is, why we do it)

B – **Briefing**, including how we do it (a demonstration may not be possible or appropriate), using visual aids/diagrams; where – sailing area etc.; when – timings, signals used, safety aspects

C – **Check understanding** of students (+ **coach** on the water, if possible)

D – **Debrief** – what happened, how can it be improved/developed?

The briefing should include:

A briefing is only good if the students understand it, so remember to check that they have. Don't fall into the trap of checking their understanding by asking the classic question 'Does everyone understand?' There will only ever be one answer: 'Yes.'

Ask questions that relate to the information that's just been given. For example:

- Where are we going to sail?
- What technique or task are we going to perform?
- How will you make it turn?
- Which way will we turn?
- What signal will I use to bring everyone back to the beach at the end? (single handers)

If the correct answers are given, then it's likely that an efficient brief has been given. A tell-tale sign of a poor briefing is when you move away to start the task, the students get into a huddle.

The Task

Allowing students the opportunity to make and correct their mistakes before you offer support can provide a good learning opportunity. It can also help to illustrate a point, but only if appropriate.

Reviewing and Debriefing

Good instructing and coaching allows students to learn in a variety of ways and is one important element of the Instructor's toolbox. Providing effective and constructive feedback during a debrief or review will help the student understand more and maximise that learning.

- A good debrief refers back to the aim of the training and contains areas for both group and individual learning.
- Each student should be told what they did well and what they need to do to improve. There could be some generic group learning for all.
- Once you have seen the session and have thoughts/notes on performance you need to structure them to provide the group and individuals with feedback using a debriefing/reviewing model. (Visit the RYA Training Support site "CPD section" for a webinar on Taking Notes.)
- **Feedback**, to be most effective, should happen as soon after the event as possible. This implies it should happen on the water as the student is performing the skill, or just afterwards. If this is possible, that's where it should happen.

However, it may take place on land once the group is safely ashore, the kit has been made safe, and the students are receptive. This may mean moving to a sheltered spot, getting warmed up/cooled down, having a hot/cold drink, and 'paying a visit'.

Plan — What to do – the brief

Do — Run the session

Review — What could be improved? How?

Ways to Provide Feedback

The RYA has chosen three feedback models as examples of review systems. These are known as the 'hairdryer', 'hamburger', and 'traffic light'. They are used in various situations to match outcome, students' needs, safety, and experience.

Rule of Threes

Providing feedback can help by reinforcing the bits of the skill that the learner performed as per the demonstration and providing a maximum of **three** key points they need to focus on again.

The critical point here is that **three** is plenty. Otherwise you run the risk of overloading the learner. However, before you give the feedback, ask yourself whether they need it, or do they just need another go?

The 'Tell' or 'Hairdryer'

There are times when we need to be clear and our instructions to be direct. Where safety is concerned, for example, we 'tell' – we are didactic in our delivery style. Another time we are direct is when students are new to the techniques and we have to tell them what to do to perform them.

What's positive about this model?

- It's quick
- The Instructor gets their point over
- Direct, specific, concentrated

What's negative about this model?

- It can feel harsh
- It can feel like a teacher at school
- It's a one-way process that omits input from the student
- Tell rather than sell

The 'Hamburger' – *Used when coaching to develop existing techniques*

When students have developed some skill in the technique and are starting to understand what they are doing or trying to do, we can shift our debrief style to being more inclusive, asking questions, and involving the student. They need a level of skill to be able to reflect on what 'good' looks like in order to reply with suitable responses to the questions about how to improve, etc.

What's positive about this model?

- It provides a framework
- It's simple to understand
- Everyone can grasp the concept at all levels
- It makes them focus on positive and negative areas

What's negative about this model?

- The Instructor may initially find it hard to create the questions until practised
- It can be weak in its directness
- Everyone is waiting for the 'But' scenario

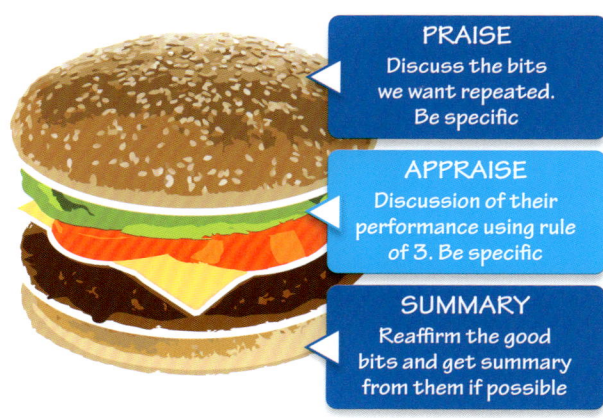

The 'Traffic Light' – *Used by experienced Instructors/Coaches to develop techniques*

This technique is question-based around performance. The traffic-light review opens up more opportunity for a flowing discussion. This works with experienced students; however, some may prefer a more direct approach and want to be told what's going wrong and how they put it right. This means it's back to the hairdryer! If a student invites this as a coaching solution there's no harm in accepting the invitation providing it's done with a degree of sensitivity.

However, asking questions and probing what the student thinks and feels will give you confidence that they know what they're learning and what they are trying to achieve.

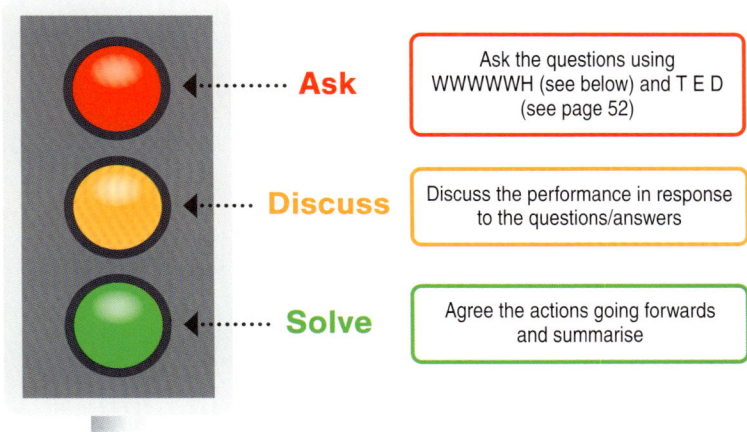

Ask the student about aspects of their performance.
- Start with open and general questions, then focus on specific areas of performance. Listen to their response
- Who, What, Where, When, Why, and How. Take care with 'why'

Discuss their performance, using the response to the questions given by the student
- What went well and what could be improved

Solve any problems, firstly by encouraging the student to seek the solution.
- If they can't, the Instructor will do this for them. However, the student should always be the one who identifies the problem and then provides the solution with guidance and help from the Instructor, agreeing on an action plan/route towards improvement

When Are the Various Feedback Models Most Effective?

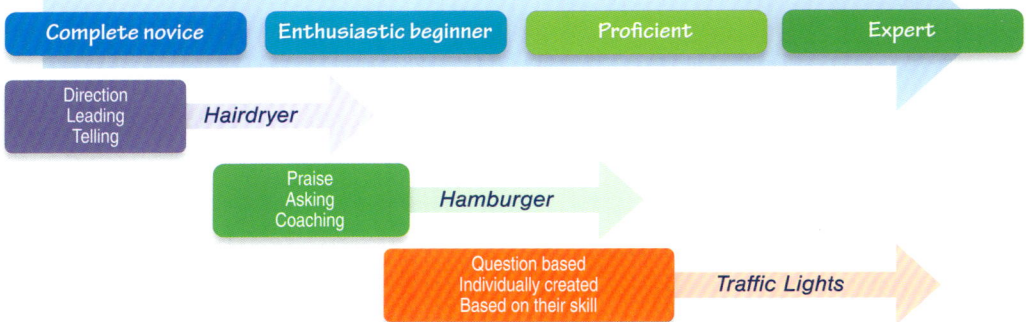

For inexperienced Instructors and Coaches, trying to create effective, question-style coaching conversations can be difficult, and many struggle to generate effective conversations even if they are proficient and have knowledge of the Who, What, Where, When, Why, and How (WWWWWH) question style.

To increase effectiveness and promote a simple, more natural questioning manner, a further technique to create an effective coaching conversation is **TED**:

- Tell • Explain • Describe

This technique will automatically force Instructors and Coaches into using one of the WWWWWH words when constructing our sentences. Starting a sentence with these three key words will make sure we lead into one of the WWWWW and H.

Here are a few example questions of **TED** being used:

TELL

- Tell me **w**hat happened
- Tell me **w**here you were looking during that move
- Tell me **w**hat order the hands and feet move in

EXPLAIN

- Explain **w**hat the customer said when they phoned
- Explain **h**ow you know when to tack to make that buoy
- Explain **h**ow the sail feels in a gust

DESCRIBE

- Describe **w**hat you could try next
- Describe **w**here you should be looking during the move
- Describe **w**hat your focus is this time

By allowing the student to start analysing their performance and seeking ways of improving, they will learn how to continue this process after they have left the environment of the structured session led by an Instructor.

In effect, the Instructor is preparing the student for when the Instructor is no longer there. After this training the student should be able to continue their own progress using the skills and learning process delivered by the Instructor.

Session Planning

Planning and preparation are essential in becoming an effective instructor. A well-organised and prepared session will go a long way to minimising unpredictable occurrences!

Once you have run a few similar courses or clinics, planning will become quicker.

By identifying the aims and objectives of the session, we can identify exercises, resources available, and activities that will form the structure of a session.

Session plans should be used regardless of session length; a one-hour taster, part of a course, or when planning the different sessions of a two-day course.

They also provide a record of what has been and needs to be covered. This is useful when handing a group over to another Instructor, or may be a requirement should a question be asked regarding the content of your course or clinic.

When planning your session, ensure that you also think about the group's progression during the course. It is important to find out if there is a specific end goal, such as the group or individual looking to gain a certificate, as this will dictate the content of your plans.

There are many ways to devise or lay out a session plan, but the general content should be the same:

- Group's age and gender
- Medical conditions
- Group's current ability and level of knowledge
- Course type/name and date
- Timing – estimated time for each exercise. This provides approximate overall timing
- Number in group
- Session duration
- Session aim and objectives
- Equipment – type and amount, including safety provision (powerboats/radios/mobiles etc.)
- Facilities available/required
- Weather forecast (including tide, if applicable)
- Sailing area – any hazards or other water users, taking into consideration their intended location (afloat and ashore)
- Exercises, including group dynamics (pairs, individual or whole); any resources or external tools required (buoys, powerboats, whistle etc.)

Example Session Plan

Course/Clinic:	Date:	Time:	Number in Class:
Training Centre:		Length of Session:	

Aim:	
Equipment Required:	
Safety Cover:	
Radio/Mobile:	
Ability:	
Planned Learning Outcomes:	
Weather Forecast Outlook:	

Exercise	Teaching Points (To inc. any specific learning outcomes)	Group Organisation (Individual, pair, small or whole group)	Timing

Comments	
Action	

Choosing the Right Session

Choosing the right session with the right content, exercises, and challenge level can be a difficult task, especially due to the changeable environment and conditions we work in. To ensure our students continue to learn and develop we need to challenge them, and this may require us to push them outside of their comfort zone.

To do this effectively we need to understand where their comfort zone is, and how far we can actually stretch our students. Knowing our students' aspirations can help with this.

Most of our students' longer-term (as well as some shorter-term) goals and aspirations are likely to sit outside their comfort zones. With this knowledge, as well as understanding their current abilities, we can develop our students through the use of 'stepping stone' sessions, which over time meet a longer-term objective.

If we view our students' 'comfort' levels in three different stages, it's the middle stage ('Development') which will aid our students' progression:

1. **Comfort zone**
2. **Development zone**
3. **Out of Reach zone**

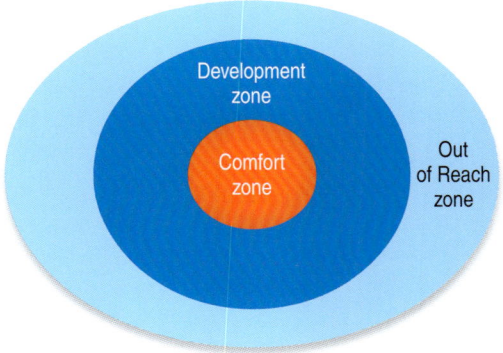

By considering the following three areas we can shape and question the effectiveness of our session:

- **Skill:**
    - The nature of the exercise
    - How difficult or complex the skill is
    - Do they have experience in the skill they are attempting, i.e. can they already do it?
- **Environment:**
    - Impact and consideration of the wind strength, water state, and temperature
    - Are they confident in these conditions, or are they new?
- **Equipment:**
    - Is their equipment familiar?
    - Is it equipment they normally use in the current conditions?
    - Does the equipment make their new challenge easier or harder?

A Few Examples

If our students are already able to do the skill and are comfortable in the conditions and the equipment they are using, then the exercise will be within their **comfort zone**.

If the student is new to the skill and conditions, and new or less comfortable on the equipment, then we may have gone past the '**development**' stage and therefore the optimal zone for challenge and development, perhaps into the '**out of reach**' stage.

A middle ground would be to introduce just one new element, a new highly challenging skill, but in comfortable conditions and on comfortable equipment.

We should usually only focus on one element at a time. For example, these could be footwork, hands, or weight, concentrating on just one of these elements at a time. This could be broken down further to include 'when to move' and 'how to move'. It's important to remember that often each of your students will be at different levels, so we may need to scale the challenge appropriately. Also, in the early stages of learning anything new, what's 'comfortable' may change very quickly, so you need to ensure we are maintaining a good level of challenge throughout a session.

TOP TIPS

- **KISS** – Keep it short and simple
- Is it a success? Instructors should test their students to see whether their session plan has translated into effective learning
- Time to learn – Instructors should make sure that their session is manageable. Don't try to cram too much into a session as students can only absorb a certain amount of information. Allow sufficient time in the session plan for the students to practise
- Learning styles – people learn in different ways, so remember it's essential to include different methods of putting something across. For further information on learning styles see pages 31–32
- Breaking down a skill into components will aid progression as it allows you to concentrate on a specific element as an example:
    - **Whole-Part-Whole** (work on the whole skill, then a specific part, before bringing the whole skill back together)
    - **Part-Part-Whole** (work on two specific but different parts of a skill and then bring it back together at the end of the exercise)

An example:

Part-Part-Whole: Improve Tack
1. **Part** – Run an exercise concentrating on the specific footwork
2. **Part** – Run an exercise concentrating specifically on vision when going through the tack
3. **Whole** – Perform the whole skill, combining the elements learnt by breaking the skill up, and see if there has been an improvement.

Group Control

Having good group control creates an effective learning environment for both students and Instructors. There are many influencing factors and, due to the teaching environment, some are easy to control while others are out of our immediate control.

What Factors Affect Our Control?

Different factors will affect different Recognised Training Centres depending on the location and courses they offer. Below are just a few of the main influences. The more experience an Instructor gains, the more likely they are to be able to adapt to or pre-empt situations, dealing with them as they occur.

The Environment

Wind, tide, and topography have an effect on how our sessions run. Strong or increasing wind often creates a more complex environment for teaching, as can a sudden decrease, especially in a tidal environment.

Stronger winds mean things happen faster. For some sessions it can be a valuable ingredient; for others it can create challenging conditions that students will find tiring.

The Task

Some skills are much easier to control than others. Exercises such as tacking and gybing can naturally keep a group close together. The addition of markers or aiming points will also help.

When students are learning skills, novices require a steady, light wind and we reef as a matter of course. As they progress they may require stronger winds and larger sailing areas, which are naturally harder to control.

The Student(s)

Ensure the task set is achievable in the prevailing conditions. If students start to struggle, don't hesitate in stopping the exercise, regrouping, and setting a new one that can be performed. Coming ashore between sessions or picking up a mooring where students can rest provides a place for feedback and/or further coaching.

Principles of Good Group Control

With experience and confidence, an Instructor is more likely to be able to keep control or 'predict' their group's chances of imploding! Below are a few considerations that will help:

Gain an Accurate Forecast

We are reliant on the conditions around us, such as wind, tide, and temperature. Gaining a forecast and outlook for the day of the course will ensure we can adjust our session accordingly. Although forecasting has advanced, it is still best to gain it on the actual day, rather than too far in advance.

Prepare a Session Plan

A well-organised and prepared session will go a long way to minimising unpredictable occurrences!

A Good, Clear Brief

See page 48.

- Aim
- Briefing
- Check understanding
- Debrief

Safety Signals: Three Basic Signals

1. Go in a certain direction – Point to direction (plus a given whistle signal)
2. Stop – Point and hold palm up to boat (plus a given whistle signal)
3. Home – Both hands over head like a house's roof (plus a given whistle signal)

Once proficient you can add:

4. Come to me – One hand on head (plus a given whistle signal)

GO   **STOP**   **HOME**
With whistle blasts

Whistle blasts are only used to attract attention. The hand signal gives the intention/command, apart from the 'Abandon' signal

Communication

In addition to a clear brief, 'good communication' in general is key from the moment you greet your students, through controlling the group during sessions afloat, to presenting the final debriefs at the end of the course. Most complaints occur due to a lack of communication, but communicating clearly also assists the understanding of expectations on all parts.

Sailing Area

Choosing a sailing area that is appropriate to the group's ability and the task ahead is crucial, but remember to discuss your plans with your Senior Instructor and other Instructors at the centre.

Should there be no choice in the sailing area, you may need to increase your students' challenges by adding buoys to sail around or within.

TOP TIPS

- Students' names: Try to learn names as early as possible, making the session personable and enabling specific attention to be gained
- If covering large distances, ensure there are places to aim for, stop, and regroup
- Wait until the group has reconvened before briefing a new session or changing a current one

Successful Learning

An earlier section established how we learn most effectively, and how, by trying to solve problems and 'doing', we can work out effective solutions.

This requires the Instructor or Coach to think carefully about the aims of their session and what exercises are set. Getting the right environment for the learner is fundamental, as is choosing the skill to be learnt/taught.

What is Successful Learning?

'Successful learning is not the process of repeating a solution; it's the ability to adapt solutions to different situations. Learning might therefore be more successful when people are challenged to repeat the process of finding a solution. One requires adapting to dynamic and changing situations, whereas the other is simply reproduction.' - Bob Muir, 2016.

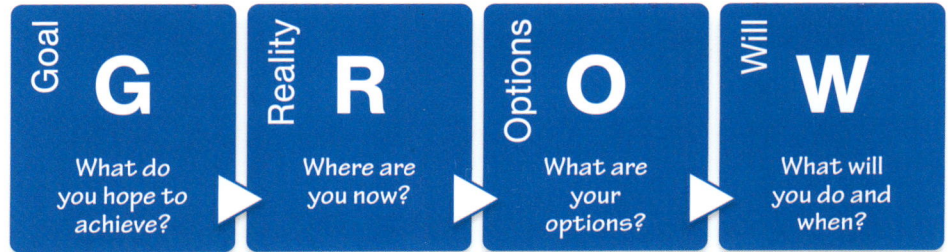

Adaptations to Teaching Techniques & Environments

Introduction

Through greater understanding and appreciation, there are many adaptations we can make in our training centres to create a better environment for everyone, ensuring inclusivity for those with learning conditions.

Some individuals who have been diagnosed with a learning condition may have a support network in place. By asking about and understanding an individual's likes and dislikes, as well as gaining an appreciation of the support network and strategies in place, an RYA Instructor and Recognised Training Centre will be able to provide a more effective learning environment. The centre can ensure that appropriate adaptations are in place and that all instructors are appropriately trained and briefed.

- Consider asking about learning conditions as part of the booking process to widen the understanding you have of the students on courses. This will enable you to prepare more effectively, and also appreciate any additional needs an individual may have
- An individual may also carry identification, such as 'Autism Cards', with them
- Remember, the extent to which the condition affects an individual determines the nature of the challenges faced, and the support and/or care required, as well as their ability to 'function' in terms of ability to learn, communication, social skills, and self-help strategies

Many individuals have a range of conditions. For example, an individual with autism may have difficulty with social interactions, understanding and showing emotion, communication, and a tendency to engage in obsessive and repetitive behaviour. The term 'autism' is an umbrella term, and therefore additionally understanding the term 'spectrum condition' helps us to appreciate the range of characteristics an individual may have, as well as the severity. Further information on this area can be found on the RYA Training Support site.

Not all individuals will have formal diagnoses of a specific type of learning condition. Others may not be completely aware, and for some there is a reluctance to seek one, perhaps due to fear; denial from the parents or the individuals themselves; concerns of labelling; stigma associated with special education, or simply the emotional impact of such a diagnosis.

The benefit of a diagnosis for both the individual and ourselves, if carried out correctly, is the help it provides with self-management strategies as well as accessing support, from both formal and informal sources. Knowing if an individual is diagnosed will assist us in the provision of tuition, understanding the effect the condition has on the individual's learning, and providing any adaptations to ensure an effective learning environment.

What Adaptations Can We Make?

It is important to remember that learning conditions come in many different forms. For some it's in their ability to read and write, while in others unfamiliar surroundings can cause anxiety due to uncertainty, which can lead to challenging behaviour or an individual becoming withdrawn and/or distressed. Therefore, the more we understand about an individual with a learning condition, the more we can adapt and in turn assist and enhance the experience we provide.

By adopting a *'Person-centred approach'*, where each individual is treated uniquely, we are able to consider how support can be provided, consider and incorporate the preferences and needs of an individual, and work with their strengths and abilities to enable them to achieve their full potential. Here is how we can achieve this 'Person-centred approach':

- **Communicate with the individual:** Ask them what their likes and dislikes are, what are their preferred communication styles, which situations might make them feel anxious or scared
- **Be empathetic:** Have an appreciation of the individual's needs and abilities in terms of social interaction and activities. Empower them to make their own decisions
- **Take an active interest in the person themselves:** This will enable you to learn about and work with them on their preferences
- **Create learning environments:** Structure and routine often assist many individuals through predictability and making the world feel like a safer, more accessible place. Therefore, knowledge of timings, as well as what is happening when, is important, as is sticking to those plans. Creating this environment will enable individuals to feel calmer while learning
- **Consider a 'Transitional Booklet':** This could be a great resource to introduce to your centre. It won't be required by everyone, but it will enable groups to talk and gain understanding about what they are going to do for those who will benefit. The booklet can talk about who they are going to meet, their names and what they look like, the centre, and what the centre looks like and the facilities (entrance, reception, changing rooms, toilets etc.). It can also describe what is involved in going afloat, the boats, safety boats, and the sailing area. A video version could also make a great resource for individuals or groups to watch prior to their visit, or recap afterwards
- **Enhance booking forms:** Consider adding a general statement for learning conditions, enabling the participant/parent(s) to provide information and complete if they wish
- **Break down activities and skills:** Use a 'step by step' approach. Repeating words or images will aid reinforcement and learning. Additionally, you could organise a number of days which slowly build on progression towards getting afloat:
    a. Invite the group/individual to take a look at the centre and walk round, feeling the wetsuits and touching the boats.
    b. Encourage them to climb into the boat when it is ashore or securely moored, try on a wetsuit up to their knees or wherever they feel comfortable etc.

Remember, *everyone* has a preferred learning style, generally a combination of a few, namely visual, auditory and/or kinaesthetic. It is therefore important to use a combination of visual, auditory, and kinaesthetic messaging to reinforce communication or instructions being given. These might include the written word, symbols and pictures, sign language, or electronic devices.

The need to wear specific clothing, or indeed the need for a change of clothing in a sailing environment, may be a consideration for some individuals. The ability to ease students into the environment in which they will be learning through short visits, the opportunity to walk around in advance of the course, or perhaps even visiting the venue for a picnic, will go a long way towards setting them up for a successful and enjoyable experience.

Other adaptations may include changing the scope of sessions. For example, keelboats, which are more stable and where wetsuits are not required, might be more suitable, whereas for others this may not be a problem.

Summary

To ensure inclusivity and increase the effective support we provide our students, we should aim to:

- Remember no two individuals are the same
- Create rapport, be empathetic, and develop our verbal and non-verbal communication
- Engage early with the support network and make specific, bespoke allowances, and ensure you understand their particular unique requirements/needs
- Consider bespoke sessions to create unique environments linked to their preferred learning styles, taking breaks from the programme
- Consider what pre-course guidance, specific resources, and assistance you may be able to provide
- Be conscious of any literal communication and language use
- Check out the many resources available to help, such as RYA Sailability; the National Autistic Society website, and other RYA Recognised Training Centres who may be able to provide guidance

Assessing Your Students' Abilities

All the RYA-certified schemes are based around a competence-based ability. Students are awarded the certificate based on their performance and practical knowledge. Therefore, the syllabi set out criteria for assessment to assist the Instructors. The types of student assessment are:

- **CAN** – They demonstrate the technique, albeit they may not be competent and skilful
- **UNDERSTANDS** – They affirm by question and answer that they know what they are expected to do, but again they may not be competent or skilful
- **KNOWLEDGE OF** – Students are not tested. Instructors deliver the session/theory topic etc. and there is no expectation or assessment of skill

As the course progresses the Instructor will be carefully monitoring students' progress to see if the pace is too fast, too slow, or just right to be challenging, informative, and achievable.

Finally, at the end of the course, the Instructor or Coach has to decide, with the help of the Chief Instructor or Senior Instructor, whether or not the objectives of the training have been achieved.

Ultimately, the question may be whether or not to award the certificate. Never forget that most people are doing this for fun, and recognising the progress that your students have made through the award of certificates is more likely to motivate them to continue than withholding the certificate because they cannot perform the task every time!

Certificates

RYA certificates provide a great incentive to continue training, giving a clear measure of an individual's progress. Certificates are signed by the Chief Instructor and/or Principal of the centre.

The Chief Instructor will advise on the importance of keeping students (and their parents, if children) informed of their progress through the course, and what students can realistically achieve by the end. It is important we manage their expectations as they progress. This could involve telling one of the students that they may not achieve the required standard laid down in the syllabus. The Instructor should highlight what can be achieved and agree with the student how to get the best-possible value from the course. The Instructor is typically supported by the Chief Instructor when dealing with parents of children.

A lack of communication between Instructor and student is one of the most common reasons for complaints about RYA courses.

THE RYA TEACHING METHOD

The RYA National Sailing Scheme (NSS) and the RYA Youth Sailing Scheme (YSS) can be taught in three boat disciplines (dinghy, multihull, and keelboat) with the RYA teaching methods providing a practical approach to the teaching techniques required for basic boat tuition.

When teaching in dinghies, there is a teaching method for single-handed and double-handed boats. For the delivery of tuition in keelboats and multihulls, the double-handed method is used. However, some elements of the National Sailing Scheme syllabus and teaching method may need omitting (such as capsize drill for keelboats) or adapting (such as man overboard for multihull).

The RYA teaching methods cover the basic and essential skills and techniques required to sail a small boat, using a step-by-step but progressive approach, with each technique broken down into easy stages to enhance learning.

The standardised approach enables Instructors to move from one centre to another and teach. Additionally, students can follow a course at a number of training centres, and Instructors will know exactly what has been covered and what needs to be taught next.

There are a variety of training boats available. Therefore, depending on what boats a centre has, adaptations to the method may be required, e.g. tacking/gybing. Where this is apparent, the variation is noted on the relevant session of the method.

Becoming an RYA Instructor

The Instructor course concentrates on the delivery of the 'method' while also embracing the overall philosophy and ethos of sessions being **SAFE-FUN-LEARNING**, and Instructors supporting our students to sail safely on their own as soon as possible. The Instructor always remains responsible for the full control of the boat during the learning period.

The following 'Teaching Method' section sets out the sessions within the double- and single-handed teaching method, as well as required adaptations. The following headings are used to aid explanation, understanding, and delivery of the session:

- **Aim**: An outline of what is going to be learnt and accomplished during the session, making it clear to participants what is to be covered and achieved
- **Session considerations**: The delivery of the session with any key outcomes or structure
- **Teaching sequence**: The order and method of the particular technique being taught, with any Key Teaching Points (KTPs) or points for reinforcement underlined

> ### Remember
> Very few students can absorb all the information in one go, so demonstrate using the 'Whole-Part-Whole' method. Further information can be found in the 'Teaching and Coaching' section.
> - **Whole**: Complete demonstration at normal speed
> - **Part**: Break down the technique with specific and clear focus on the particular relevant parts, such as hands/feet/tiller etc.
> - **Whole**: Complete the drill again with Key Teaching Points

The Five Essentials

Throughout a sailor's progress, whether beginner or experienced racer, the Five Essentials are used to sail a boat as efficiently as possible. To ensure our teaching is progressive and effective, an Instructor should refer to and reinforce these when delivering each of their sessions, regardless of level. It's a good idea to cover only one or two elements per session.

Balance

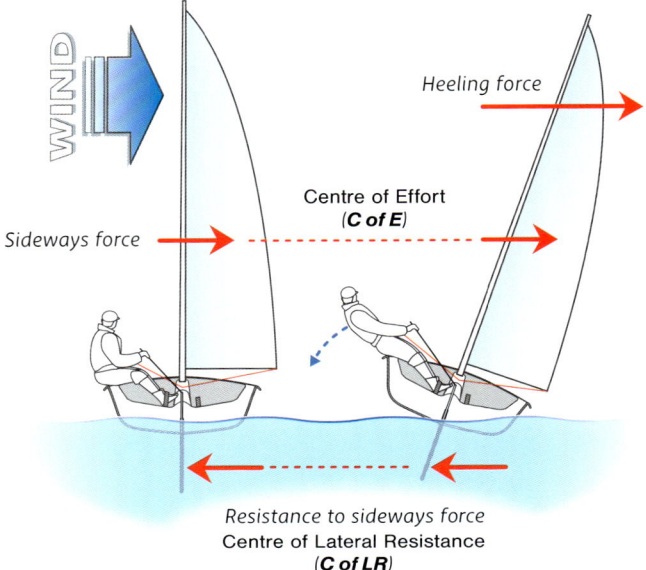

The 'side to side' or lateral aspect of the dinghy. The dinghy should be sailed as flat as possible and students must lean (hike) out or sit in to achieve this.

Trim

Trim is the bow-to-stern (front-to-back) balance of the dinghy, which affects boat speed. For example, if helm and crew sit towards the stern it will bury (dig in), causing drag (turbulence from the transom) which slows the boat. Helm and crew should adjust their position to reduce drag on each point of sail.

Sail Setting

The helm (and crew in a double-handed boat) work together to ensure the sails are working effectively on each point of sail. Both the jib and the mainsail should be trimmed together so they are just 'not flapping'. Always try to ease the sail to check.

Indicators such as sail tell-tales are used on the jib and mainsail to illustrate airflow. As students become familiar with this concept, they can progress on to using sail tell-tales.

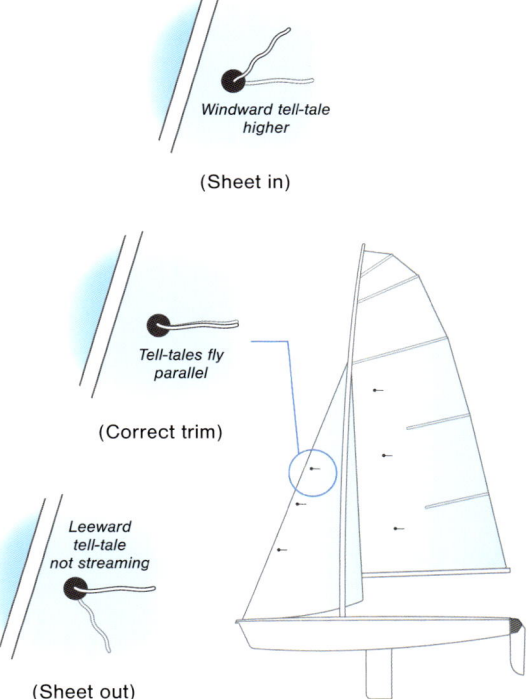

Centreboard (Daggerboard)

The forces of the wind on the sails are matched by the forces underwater, mainly created by the centreboard. This resistance is called the centre of lateral resistance (C of LR) and it is a combination of the centreboard and hull shape. Without C of LR the boat will slide sideways, especially sailing upwind. The crew must ensure that the centreboard is set correctly for each point of sail. As the dinghy turns towards the wind (luffs up) and the mainsail is sheeted in, the board goes down. As the dinghy turns away from the wind (bears away) and the mainsail is sheeted out, the board comes up.

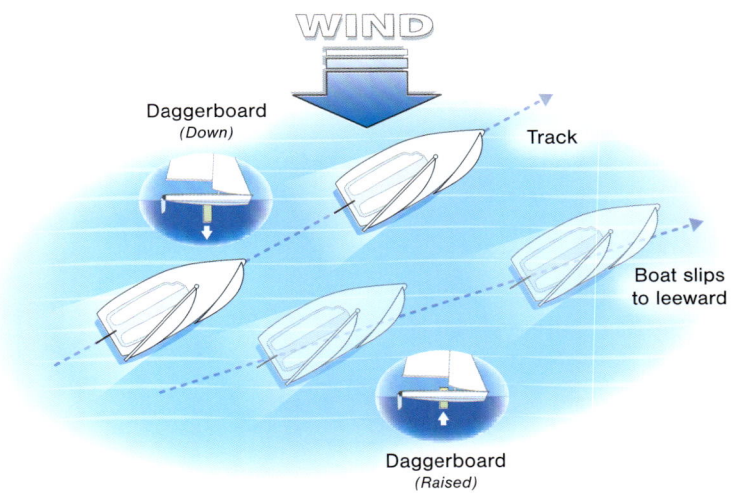

Course (Made Good)

The course sailed depends on a combination of the wind direction, tidal flow, other water users, hazards etc., and taking them all into consideration to sail the optimum course.

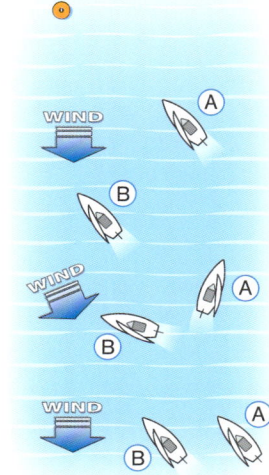

Teaching the Five Essentials in Keelboats

The double-handed teaching method and progression for learning to sail can be successfully taught in keelboats with a few simple modifications. Land drills are inappropriate. As an alternative, boat controls for sessions such as tacking and gybing can be demonstrated while secured to a mooring if required.

The main differences from teaching in a dinghy are:

- The Instructor will probably be teaching on board
- Students will take control if they are competent and the Instructor will sit to leeward and in front of students
- There are usually only **Four Essentials** (centreboard is excluded)
- Additional areas to be covered might include techniques for grounding recovery, use of engine and winches (if fitted), and adaptation to the man-overboard technique

With up to four students on board there is less helming time per person, although the crewing tasks are more involved, so regularly move everyone around.

Teaching the Five Essentials in Multihulls

When teaching in multihulls the Five Essentials become the **Four Essentials** (usually no centreboards/daggerboards), usually referred to as CAT, which stands for:

- C – Crew weight = **Balance** and **Trim**
    - This is where they sit
- A – Airflow = **Sail setting**
    - Setting the sails, using tell-tales etc.
- T – Technique = **Course made good**
    - This is tacking and gybing and different points of sailing (close reach to broad reach only)

This should be reflected when teaching the method in multihulls.

THE RYA DOUBLE-HANDED TEACHING METHOD

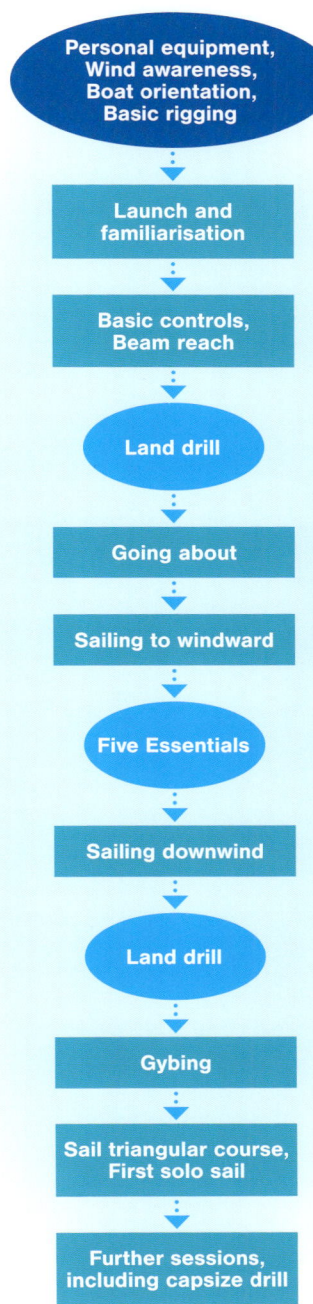

Session 1: Introduction to Personal Equipment, Boat Orientation, and Basic Rigging

Aim

Instructor to allocate appropriate clothing and provide a basic introduction to a dinghy and basic rigging.

Session Considerations

Introduction:

- Appropriate clothing for the prevailing conditions: wetsuit, waterproofs
- Appropriate footwear: wet boots, trainers
- Buoyancy aid: 50 Newton, correct size and securely fastened. The use of life jackets should be risk-assessed appropriately for each activity and student.
- Terms and parts of the dinghy
- Rigging (students to assist)
- Wind awareness

Rigging a double-handed dinghy (jib and mainsail)

Instructor-led and involving students fully in rigging the boat. Ask students to hoist sail, feed boltrope etc.

1. Rig boat quickly, head to wind (point out wind indicators ashore).
2. Briefly explain and introduce basic sailing terminology.
3. Furl or back the jib once rigged to reduce flogging.
4. Consider reefing mainsail and fit masthead float (safety consideration).

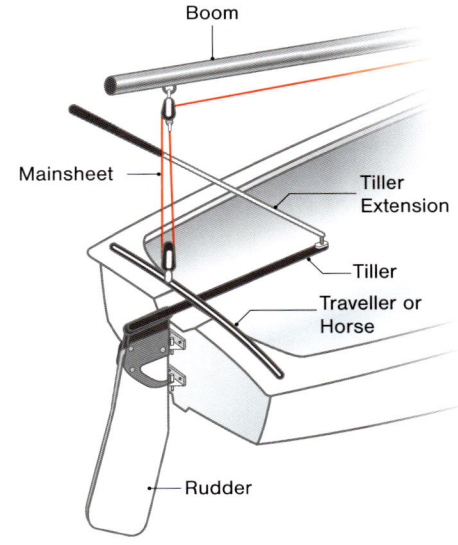

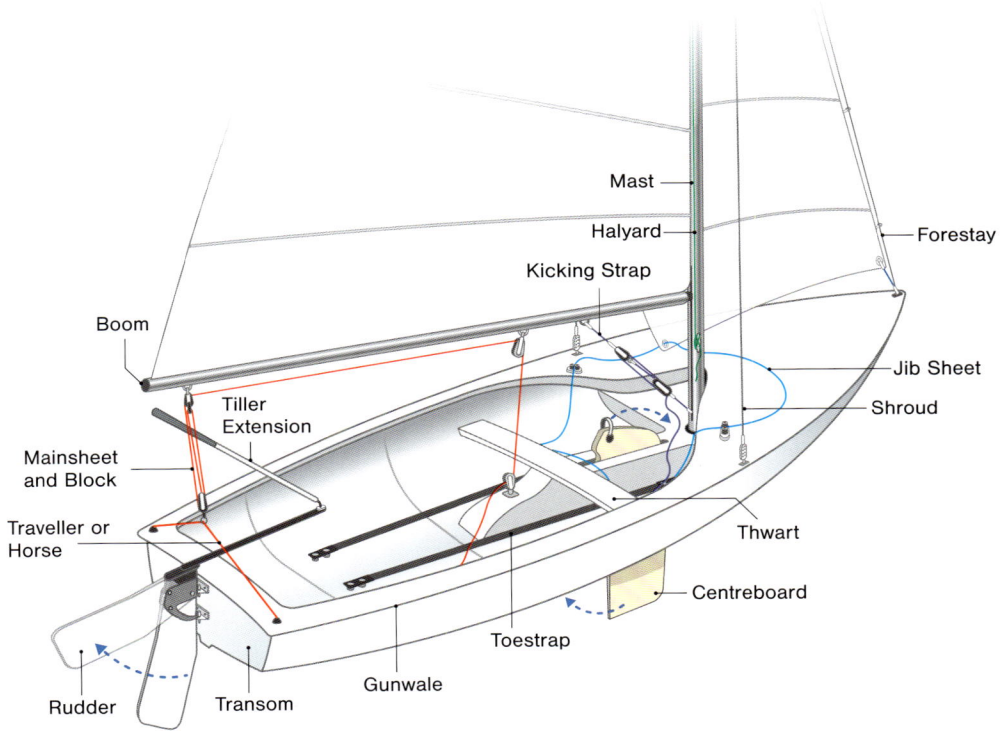

Rigging a Multihull and Keelboat

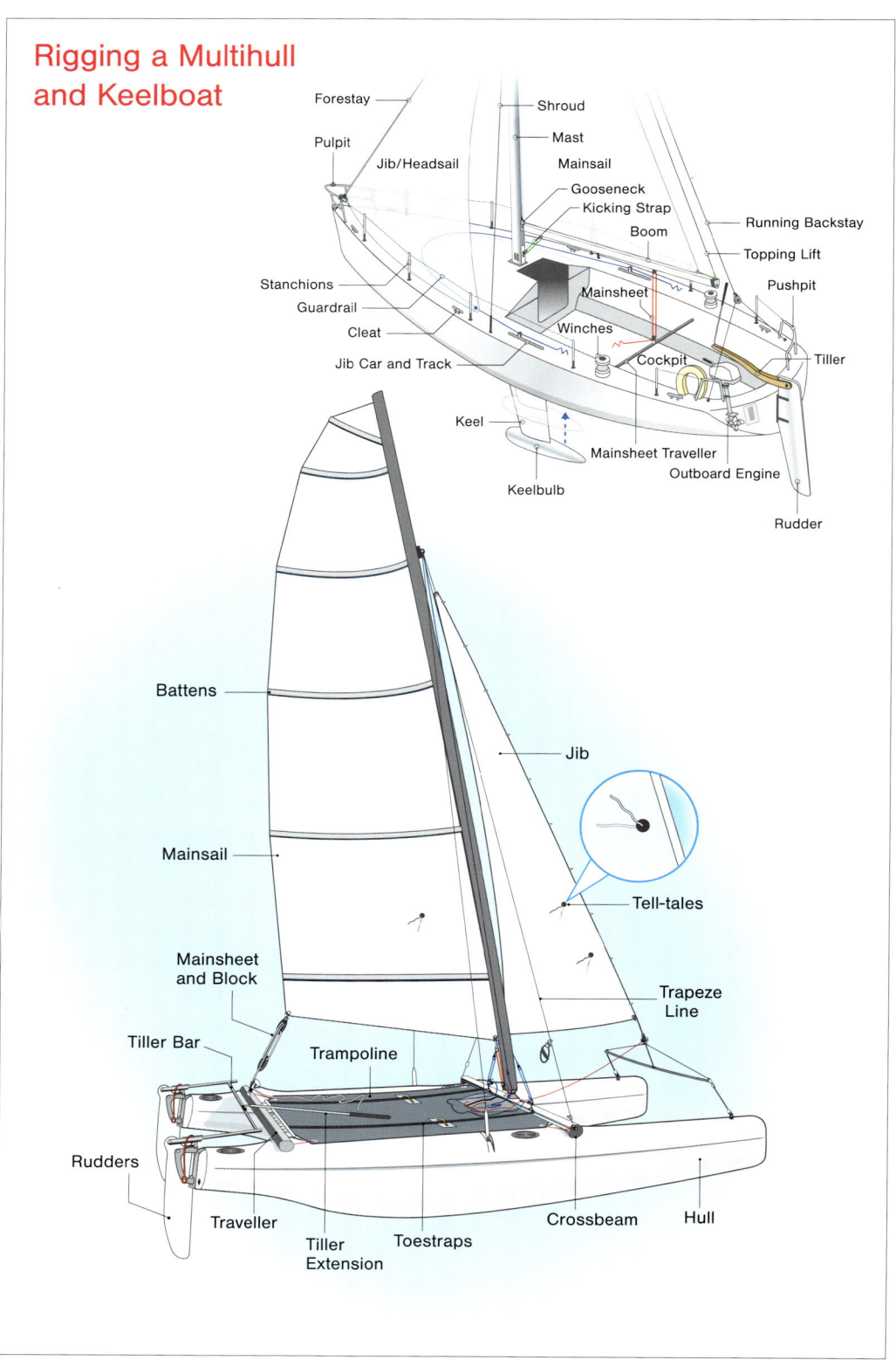

Session 2: Launching and Familiarisation

Aim

Basic introduction to launching, providing explanation (and consideration) of launching conditions, cross/on/offshore breeze, accounting for the prevailing conditions. Familiarisation allows the students to experience dinghy sailing, perhaps for the first time.

Session Considerations

When launching and under way:

- Instructor to ensure students are kept as dry as possible during launching and leaving the beach or pontoon
- This is the students' first time afloat, so Instructors should provide a pleasurable sailing experience

Note: Students will feel that the dinghy moves significantly, and may be cautious about the need to sit in what initially feels like a precarious position, as well as the need to change sides and balance the boat when the dinghy goes about.

Teaching Sequence

1. Rig boat ashore and then drop mainsail if there is an onshore breeze (lee shore). If the breeze is offshore (weather shore), the main can remain hoisted.
2. Roll dinghy down the slipway to the water (make sure the bungs are in!). Float dinghy off trolley.

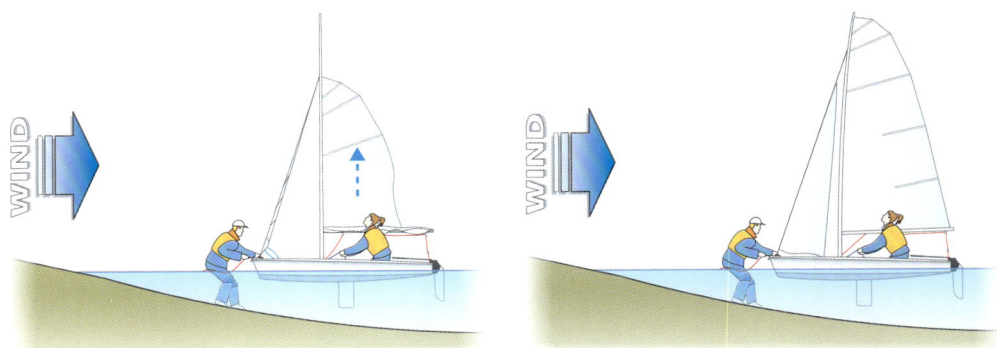

3. Instructor hoists main (if necessary) and fits remaining equipment, rudder etc.
4. Students join Instructor in dinghy. Instructor sails boat away from the shore.

Familiarisation:

- Short introductory session, sailing a figure-of-eight beam-reach course (<u>tacking at all times</u>)
- Instructor at helm
- <u>Students allocated tasks, including observations outside the dinghy</u>
- <u>Students to balance boat</u> and gain <u>awareness of wind</u> direction
- Instructor to point out landmarks, goal points, and wind direction

Multihull: Rigging and Launching

When teaching the rigging and familiarisation session in multihulls, the same approach and delivery should be considered for the areas listed below:

- Show students where to sit
- Demonstrate which items may be used as handholds
- Hoist mainsail first, head to wind to hook on halyard lock (if fitted)
- Tack downhaul must be left untensioned and mainsheet not attached
- Hoist jib and reeve jib sheets (unless fitted with a fully furling system). Back the jib to prevent flogging
- Attach rudders and lock them up
- Lift bows and slide trolley under
- Show students how to hold on to the boat, with one hand on the forestay bridle, the other holding the bow
- Trolley boat into water and float off
- Warn students of the danger of placing feet under hulls in shallow water
- Crew holds boat head to wind
- Helm attaches mainsheet
- Leave shore using one of the methods explained later in this section

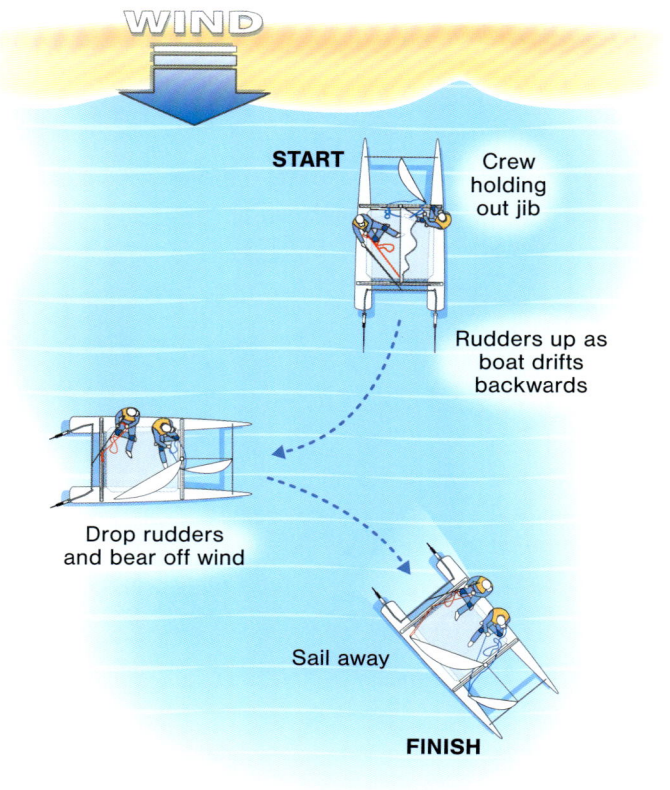

Keelboat: Rigging and Launching

When teaching the rigging and familiarisation session in keelboats, the same approach and delivery as the dinghy and multihull section above should be considered:

- Show students where to sit
- Demonstrate which items may be used as handholds
- Show where sails are stowed
- Boat must be head to wind to rig sails
- If on pontoon, crew will be kept dry
- If boat has a lifting keel, follow the dinghy method when launching. Make known any fixing mechanisms
- Hoist jib and fit sheets, and introduce winches if fitted
- Attach or lower rudder and keel (if lifting keel) and ensure that the keel is locked down once in deep-enough water
- Demonstrate engine starting, stopping, and raising/lowering
- Show students where all the safety equipment is fitted
- If on a pontoon in a marina, demonstrate use of engine to depart
- When clear, follow dinghy method:
    - Short introductory session sailing a figure-of-eight beam-reach course (tacking at all times)
    - Instructor at helm
    - Students allocated tasks, including observations outside the dinghy
    - Students gain awareness of wind direction and orientation
    - Instructor to point out landmarks, goal points, and wind direction

Safety: If winches are fitted it is important to ensure a safety briefing is provided which includes the correct techniques for loading, easing, and unloading. See G3 RYA Start Sailing for further advice on winch use.

TOP TIP

Try to keep students as dry as possible while you rig the boat.

Session 3: Basic Boat Controls

Aim

Introduce the four basic controls required to sail a dinghy, i.e. both sails (jib and main), centreboard, and rudder (using tiller and extension). Also introduce the lying-to and hove-to positions.

Session Considerations

Handing over the controls:

- Position the boat lying-to, sails depowered, flapping
- Students take the controls:
  - Sail on a beam-reach course, going about at each end (dinghy will need to be stopped and Instructor takes over to go about), point out goals to aim for
  - Use simple terms and instructions throughout ('Pull it towards/Push away' etc.)
  - From this session onwards, the Instructor should:
    - Sit to leeward and forward of the helm in the 'wet elbow position'
    - Keep hands off the tiller while student is helming, unless safety is compromised

Teaching Sequence

Demonstrate basic boat controls, from lying-to position:

1. Pull jib in to move dinghy forward and to turn away from wind
2. Student pulls mainsail in to move dinghy forward and to turn the boat towards wind
3. With students working as a team and communicating with each other, each student pulls in their sail, balancing the power in the sails to steer a straight course across the wind (beam reach). Students will be more successful if the main is reefed and the Instructor 'helps' by holding the tiller centrally

Under way:

1. Introduce the rudder/tiller/extension to the students to fine-tune steering (push to turn towards the wind, pull to turn away)
2. Demonstrate effect of raising the centreboard (look at wake to observe leeway)
3. Point out that sails depower (flap) as dinghy turns towards the wind, and fill again as the dinghy returns to sailing across the wind
4. Use goal points as aiming points or lay marks
5. Allow students time to practise. Discreetly moving Instructor weight may be necessary to guarantee success

TOP TIP

Demonstrate good boat control while sailing, balance the boat and sails, then take hand off the tiller momentarily to demonstrate that the boat continues sailing in a straight line if the power of the sails is balanced (start of Five Essentials).

Multihull: Orientation/Basic Boat Controls

When teaching the rigging and familiarisation session in multihulls, the same approach and delivery as the areas listed below should be considered.

Orientation is the same as dinghies. There are important differences in the basic boat controls session:

- Point out that multihulls have brakes (the rudders)
- The mainsail/jib controls used for monohull teaching are very different for multihulls, i.e. mainsheet is the 'kicker' and tightens the leech, and the traveller controls the angle of the mainsail to the wind
- Introduce two traveller positions: upwind/reaching (central) and downwind (two-thirds out)
- There are Four Essentials (no daggerboards)
- Remember CAT, which stands for:
    - **C**rew weight (balance and trim)
    - **A**irflow (sail setting)
    - **T**echnique (course made good)

TOP TIP

The combination of sessions one to three provides the perfect introductory taster sail. If time allows, you may wish to continue on to session four, tacking.

Heaving To

Heaving to is used whenever you wish to depower the boat and hold it at a constant angle to the wind while floating free. This is a more stable position than simply lying to with both sails flapping, due to the jib being aback.

- The easiest method to heave to is to tack, leaving the jib cleated on the old side
- Select a point with clear water downwind or downtide, whichever is the stronger
- Cleat the jib aback with the mainsheet fully eased
- Hold the tiller to leeward, and raise the centreboard halfway.
- Maintain a good lookout and be aware of leeway

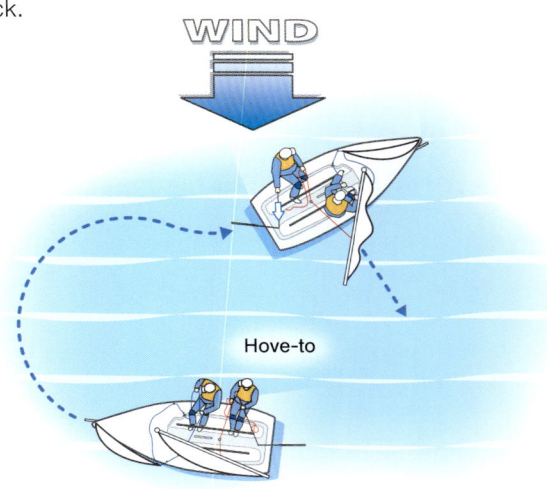

Hove-to

Session 4: Tacking/Going About

Aim

An introduction to basic tacking, turning 180 degrees through the wind (beam reach to beam reach, figure-of-eight course).

Session Considerations

- Delivered afloat and ashore as necessary
- A land drill is recommended to introduce and teach the skill. However, not all students will require a land drill
- Use of lying-to for students to change over
- Remember: very few students can absorb all the information in one go, so demonstrate using the 'Whole-Part-Whole' method for delivery
- Students should be provided with sufficient time to practise, sailing a figure-of-eight course, tacking at each end, and progressively reducing the amount of feedback from the Instructor

Teaching Sequence

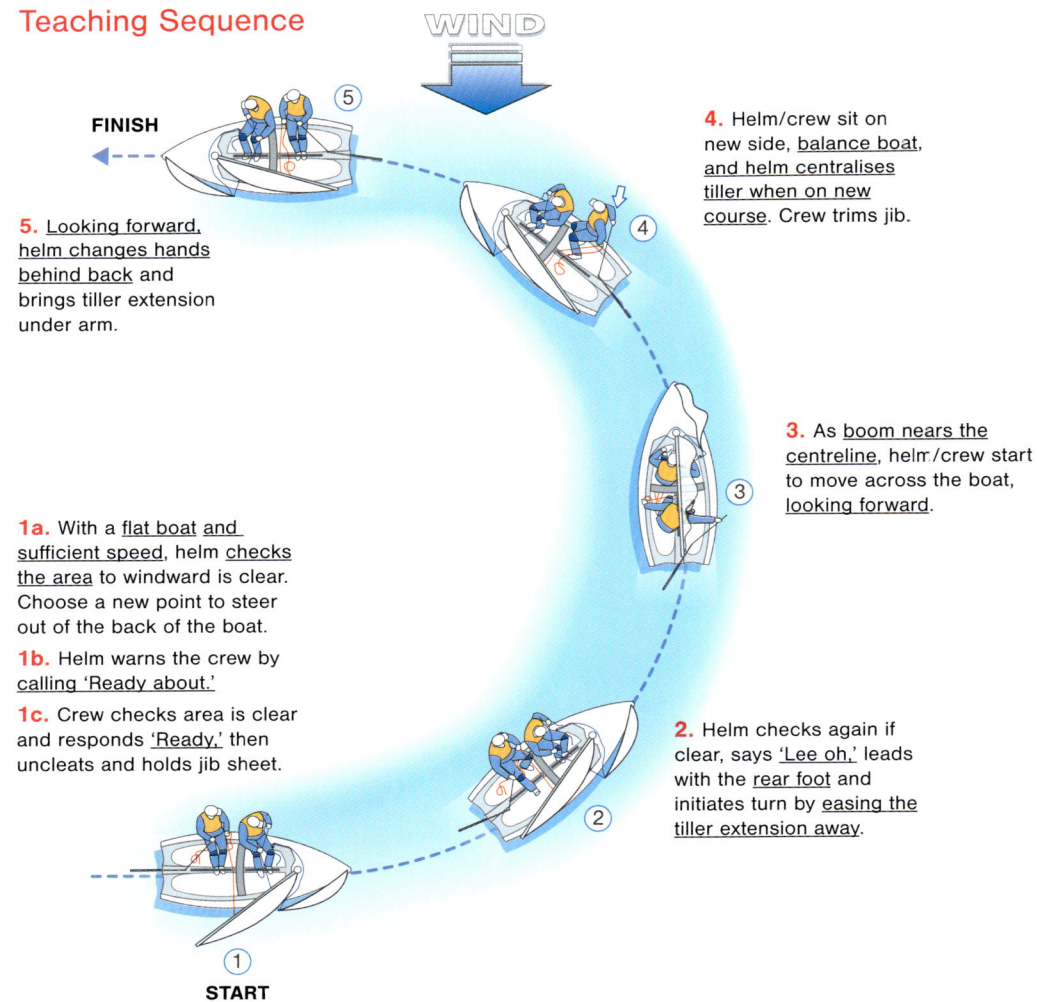

5. Looking forward, helm changes hands behind back and brings tiller extension under arm.

4. Helm/crew sit on new side, balance boat, and helm centralises tiller when on new course. Crew trims jib.

3. As boom nears the centreline, helm/crew start to move across the boat, looking forward.

1a. With a flat boat and sufficient speed, helm checks the area to windward is clear. Choose a new point to steer out of the back of the boat.

1b. Helm warns the crew by calling 'Ready about.'

1c. Crew checks area is clear and responds 'Ready,' then uncleats and holds jib sheet.

2. Helm checks again if clear, says 'Lee oh,' leads with the rear foot and initiates turn by easing the tiller extension away.

Helm and crew:

1a. With a flat boat and sufficient speed, helm checks area to windward is clear.
1b. Helm warns crew by calling 'Ready about.'
1c. Crew checks area is clear and, if ready, responds 'Ready,' uncleats, but holds jib sheet.
2. Helm checks again and, if still clear, calls 'Lee oh' and initiates the turn by leading with the rear foot and easing the tiller extension away, rotating the end of the extension forwards.
3. As boom nears the centreline, helm/crew start to move across the boat, looking forward.
4. Helm/crew sit on new side to balance the boat. Helm (sitting forward) centralises the tiller when on new course (use goal point, if necessary). Crew trims jib.
5. Looking forward, helm changes hands behind back (thumbs pointing together, thumb on 'old' sheet hand facing up the extension), bringing tiller extension under rear arm.

Crew (specifics) – take the following action as the boat is turned:

1. As the boom reaches the centerline, take up slack in new jib sheet and move across the boat.
2. As the mainsail fills, sheet in jib on the new side.

Adaptation for Longer Tiller Extension

Stages one to two are the same, then:

3. Helm slides hand down tiller extension as they cross boat and rotates the tiller extension around the back of the boat.
4. Helm/crew sit on the new side and balances the boat. Helm centralises when on new course, and crew trims jib.
5. Looking forward, helm changes hands behind back and brings the tiller extension over the rear shoulder.

Multihull: Tacking/Going About

1. With a flat boat and sufficient speed, helm checks area to windward is clear, with back leg tucked under front leg and tiller extension over the rear shculder.
2. Helm warns crew by calling 'Ready about.'
3. Crew checks area is clear and responds 'Ready,' uncleats, but holds jib sheet.
4. Helm checks again and, if still clear, calls 'Lee oh' and initiates the turn by easing the tiller extension away, moving rudders slightly (no more than 45 degrees), and crew allows jib to back.
5. Helm and crew remain on leeward hull as boat turns. Crew might allow jib to 'back' briefly, if the turn is slow.
6. When through the wind, helm/crew start to move across trampoline. Helm kneels, facing backwards, reaching around mainsheet falls, holds the mainsheet, and takes hold of the tiller extension behind falls in the 'old' mainsheet hand.
7. Helm/crew sit on new hull and, when on new course, helm centralises the tiller, takes mainsheet with front hand, and crew trims the jib.

WIND

FINISH

Duck to avoid sail

(7)

(5-6)

(3-4)

START

(1-2)

Session 5: Sailing to Windward (and Improving Tacking)

Aim

Going to windward and developing the skill of tacking through an increasingly narrow angle, until tacking close hauled to close hauled. This session provides the ideal opportunity to introduce the theory of the Five Essentials.

Session Considerations

- Introduce the theory of the 'no-go' zone:
    - Demonstrate that the sails flap as the boat turns towards the wind, so they must be trimmed accordingly
    - As students improve, highlight the 'no-go' zone. Use the luff of the jib as an indicator of the edge of the 'no-go' zone when sailing close hauled
- Deliver teaching sequence as an Instructor demo, or, if able, students could act on instructions given by the Instructor

Teaching Sequence

1. Helm steers towards the wind through a small angle:
    a. This will cause both sails to flap. Sheet both in until sails 'just stop flapping' (**sail trim**).
    b. This will also cause the dinghy to heel to leeward. Helm and crew 'hike' until the dinghy is flat (**balance**).
2. As the dinghy sails upwind, helm and crew should move their combined weight forward a little (**trim**).
3. To help with upwind performance, the centreboard should be lowered a little more (**centreboard**).
4. Repeat the above sequence until the sails are fully sheeted in and the centreboard is fully down (close hauled/beating to windward), and helm and crew are balancing and trimming the boat correctly.
5. By observing the sails, the students will be able to steer and see/feel the edge of the 'no-go' zone.
6. Having reached a desired mark or goal, tack through a reduced angle (close hauled to close hauled).
7. To make further progress to windward, repeat the process above.

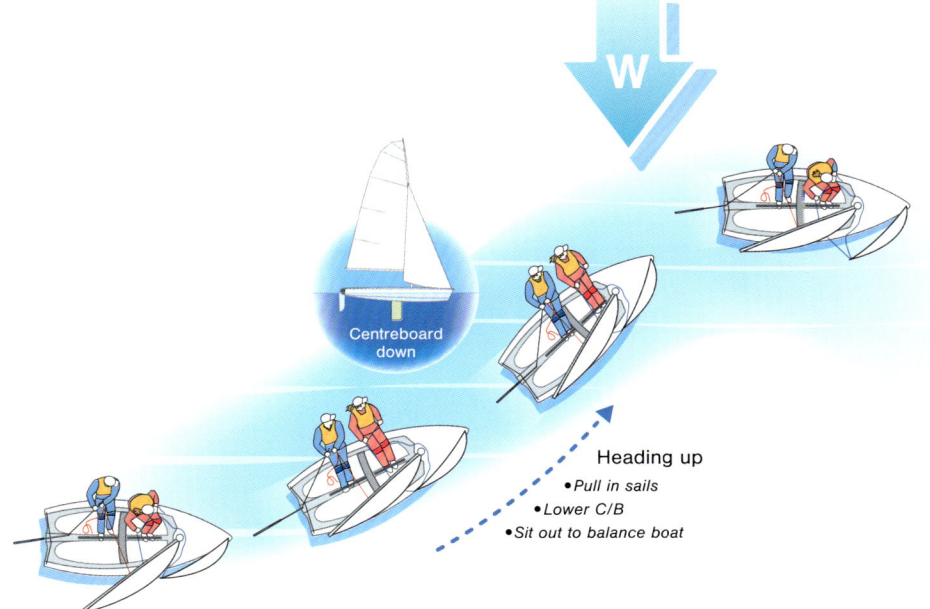

Session Development

During this session, tacking will eventually be through 90 degrees. The Key Teaching Points are:

- Ensure the <u>boat is flat with enough speed before initiating the tack</u>
- <u>Helm and crew cross together</u> as the boom changes sides
- Centralise the tiller, then sheet in the jib when the boat is sailing close hauled. This prevents oversteering

TOP TIP

When sailing to windward, sit well forward with the centreboard fully down and keep the boat flat.

Multihulls and Keelboats

The techniques and teaching sequence are the same. Gradually sail from beam reach to close hauled in small sections and demonstrate sail setting. With both multihull and keelboat, omit the centreboard.

Session 6: Sailing Downwind

Aim

The sailing-downwind session may be taught and lead on as progressing from Session 5, enabling the students to get back downwind. Alternatively, if better suited, they can be delivered as separate sessions. The aims are sailing downwind, consolidating the Five Essentials, and how to identify different points of sail and a training run using the jib. As in other elements, the Instructor may demonstrate or they may instruct the students to carry out the manoeuvres if they are competent learners.

Session Considerations

Sailing downwind (and the gybe):

- Consider reefing to reduce the power
- Choose an area with plenty of room
- Instructor should also teach or recap with the students how to 'bear away' effectively
- Avoid gybing during the <u>initial</u> downwind section
- Illustrate the change in the Five Essentials as the boat changes direction either away or towards the wind

Teaching Sequence: Downwind From an Upwind Course

1. From sailing an upwind course, to bear away the helm <u>eases the mainsheet</u> and gently pulls the tiller to windward. <u>Crew eases jib</u> and balances boat.
2. As the dinghy turns away from the wind, helm and crew heel the dinghy to windward (in reality, the boat remains flat). Apply the Five Essentials until on to a broad reach.
3. When ready, bear away further on to a <u>training run</u> where the mainsail is almost out to the shroud and the jib just begins to collapse. When it does, luff slightly to reinflate the jib.
4. <u>If a turn is required at this stage, use a 360-degree tack only</u>.
5. Students continue to practise bearing away from close hauled, through close, beam, and broad reach on to a training run, then progressively luffing back up to close hauled again, changing the Five Essentials for each point of sail.
6. End this session with a controlled demonstration of a gybe by the Instructor.

Session 7: Gybing

Aim

To progress the students on from sailing downwind and a training run to completing a gybe.

Session Considerations

The gybe:

- Introduction to gybing is best <u>delivered as a land drill</u>, but if the students' understanding is reasonable and conditions are favourable, it may be taught afloat
- Introduce gybing as the students develop confidence and are able to steer accurately on a given course
- Use the jib as an indicator of the training run
- Explain the difference between the tack and the gybe and stress the change in communication
- Reinforce smooth and deliberate actions
- Course sailed is a training run to training run
- Allow time to practise and reinforce <u>key points</u>: need for room, communication, main sheeted in so that the boom is clear of the shroud, minimal steering, positive movement to initiate the gybe

Teaching Sequence: Gybing

1. Sail on to a <u>training run</u> with the helm sitting forward, ensuring the boat is flat.
2a. <u>To gybe</u>, helm <u>checks</u> underneath the boom that the area to <u>leeward</u> is clear, and calls <u>'Stand by to gybe.'</u>
2b. Crew checks area is clear, responds <u>'Yes'</u> and uncleats but <u>holds</u> jib sheet. If needed, the helm sheets in the mainsail slightly to <u>bring the boom clear of the shroud</u>.
2c. Balancing the boat, <u>leading with the rear foot and facing forward, the helm moves into the middle of the boat, remaining on course</u>, and <u>rotating the tiller extension forwards while grabbing the mainsheet falls</u> in preparation.
3. Helm checks the area again and, if clear, calls <u>'Gybe oh'</u> and pushes the tiller a small amount (15 degrees) to where they had been sitting.
4. Helm guides the falls and, as the boom crosses the centreline, the helm swiftly <u>centralises the tiller</u> (so that <u>helm, boom, and tiller are all on the midline simultaneously</u>). Crew moves to sit in the middle/side, balancing the boat, and changing jib sheets.
5. Helm <u>sits on the new side</u> and <u>steers (behind back)</u> on <u>the new training-run course</u>. Crew trims new jib sheet.
6. Looking forward, the helm <u>changes hands behind their back</u>, bringing tiller extension under their rear arm (as per tacking).

Gybe Adaptation for Longer Tiller Extension

Stages one to five remain the same, then:

6. Remaining looking forward, the helm <u>changes hands behind back</u> and rotates the tiller extension forward over the rear shoulder.

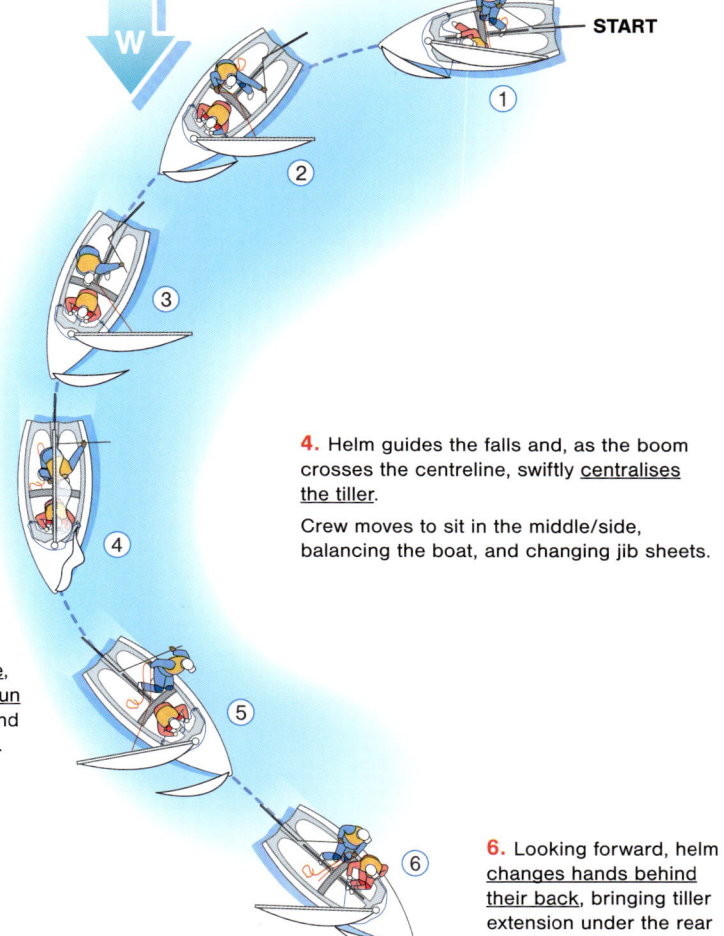

1. Helm checks area is clear and bears away onto a training run, ensuring the boat is kept flat.

2a. From the training run, helm checks area is clear and calls 'Stand by to gybe.'

2b. Crew checks area is clear, responds 'Yes,' and uncleats but holds jib sheet.

2c. Leading with the rear foot, facing forwards, helm moves to the middle of the boat, rotates the tiller extension forwards, and grabs the mainsheet falls.

3. Helm checks area again. If clear, helm calls 'Gybe oh' and pushes the tiller to where they had been sitting.

4. Helm guides the falls and, as the boom crosses the centreline, swiftly centralises the tiller.

Crew moves to sit in the middle/side, balancing the boat, and changing jib sheets.

5. Helm sits on new side, steers the new training-run course (behind back), and crew trims new jib sheet.

6. Looking forward, helm changes hands behind their back, bringing tiller extension under the rear arm (as per tacking).

FINISH

Multihull: Gybing

1. With <u>boat flat and with sufficient speed</u>, the helm <u>checks the area</u> to leeward is clear with their back leg tucked under their front leg, and tiller extension over the rear shoulder.
2. Warn the crew <u>by calling 'Stand by to gybe.' Ensure mainsheet traveller is eased to leeward</u>.
3. Crew checks area is clear and responds <u>'Yes,'</u> uncleats, but holds jib sheet.
4. Helm checks again and, if still clear, calls <u>'Gybe oh,'</u> then initiates the turn by <u>easing the tiller extension towards them</u> and moving rudders (no more than 45 degrees).
5. Once on a run, the helm moves to centre of trampoline while <u>facing backwards on their knees, reaches behind the mainsheet falls, and takes hold of the tiller extension with their mainsheet hand, still holding the mainsheet</u>.
6. <u>Helm changes hands</u>. The <u>old tiller hand grabs the mainsheet and</u>, with a positive movement, <u>guides the 'falls'</u> across the traveller. Helm keeps their <u>head clear of the blocks</u>, guiding the traveller to the leeward side as the mainsail gybes, and <u>centralises the tiller</u>.
7. Helm/crew sit on new hull, <u>check course</u>, and crew trims jib.

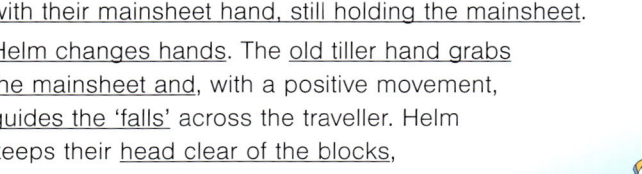

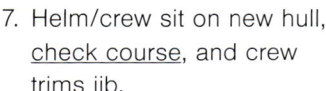
Duck to avoid sail

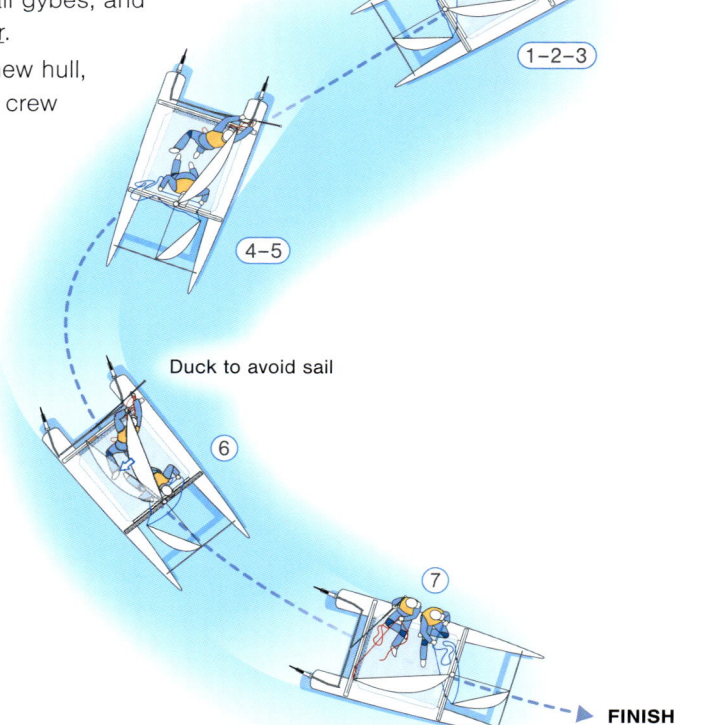

Session 8: Sail Triangular Course/First Solo Sail

Aim

Students sail the dinghy (without the Instructor on board) around a suitable triangular course on all points of sail.

Session Considerations

- Instructor should ensure that students can confidently and competently sail a triangular course
- Consider reefing
- Before leaving the students and moving into a safety boat, ensure that they know the following:
    - Simple rules for avoiding collisions, port/starboard, windward/leeward boat
    - In case of capsize, they should stay with the boat (The Instructor will return immediately to help right it)
    - If collision is inevitable, DO NOT fend off
- Provide support and instruction where necessary. Ask students to 'lie-to', and position the safety boat alongside the dinghy by the windward shroud to provide coaching
- Use a whistle and signals to control students; there is no need to shout over a distance from the safety boat
- Set a course, if necessary, which will enable sailing on all points of sail and which will require safe tacking and a single gybe at a mark, with achievable windward leg set for ability
- Ensure effective group control (whistle, signals, and sailing area)
- Masthead flotation should be fitted

Tacking and Gybing: Adaptations

Tacking: Aft Mainsheet

The helm faces aft during the manoeuvre and uses the 'frying pan' grip (palm up, thumb on top, tiller extension parallel to rear leg).

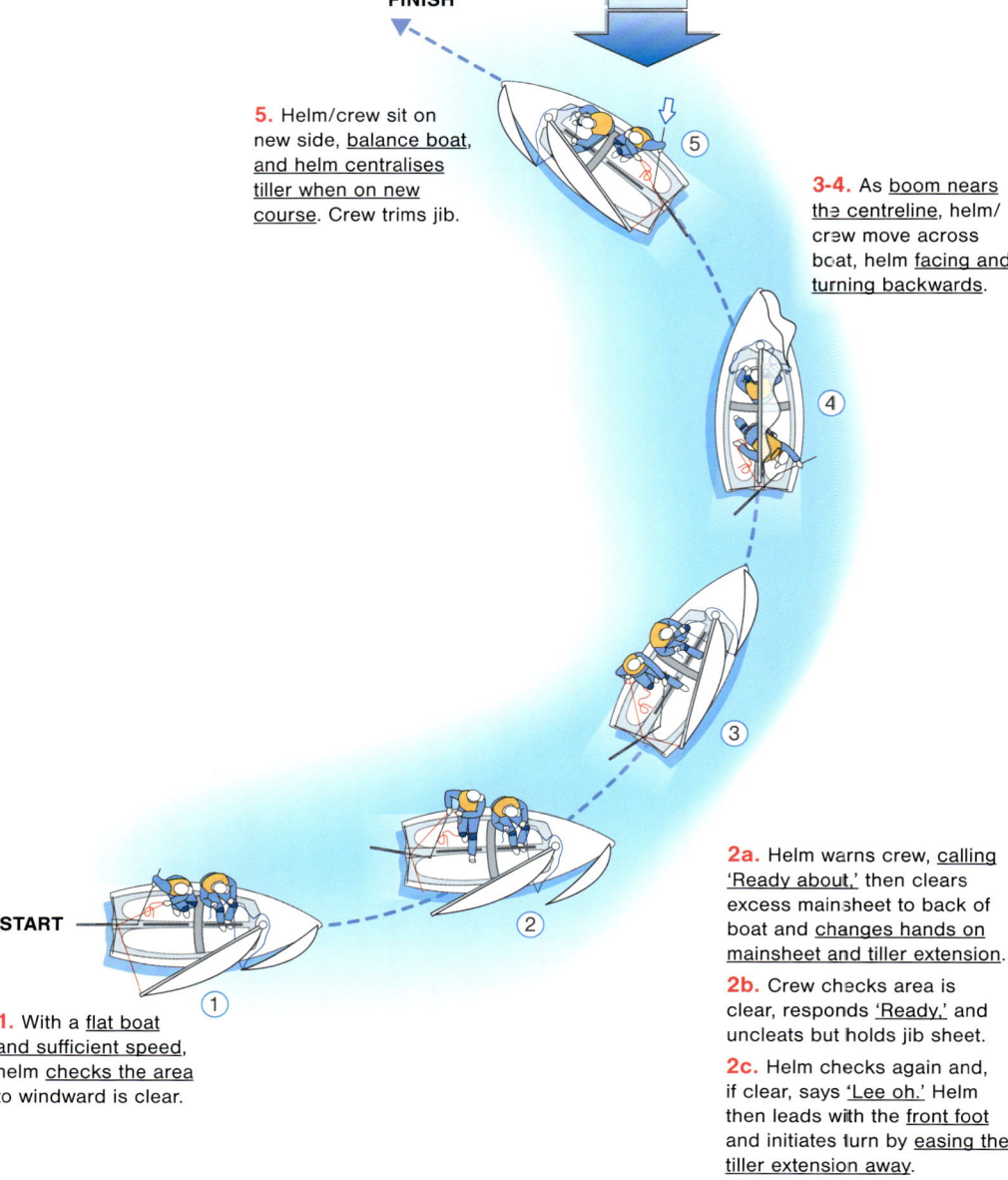

5. Helm/crew sit on new side, balance boat, and helm centralises tiller when on new course. Crew trims jib.

3-4. As boom nears the centreline, helm/crew move across boat, helm facing and turning backwards.

1. With a flat boat and sufficient speed, helm checks the area to windward is clear.

2a. Helm warns crew, calling 'Ready about,' then clears excess mainsheet to back of boat and changes hands on mainsheet and tiller extension.

2b. Crew checks area is clear, responds 'Ready,' and uncleats but holds jib sheet.

2c. Helm checks again and, if clear, says 'Lee oh.' Helm then leads with the front foot and initiates turn by easing the tiller extension away.

Tacking: Keelboat

During the tack, the helm may cross the cockpit facing in either direction, depending on the layout. It may be safer for the helm to cross the cockpit after the boat has passed 'head to wind'. Usually, keelboats are centre-mainsheet rigged, so techniques from pages 78–79 can be used. The mainsheet and traveller can be controlled by either the helm or a 'trimmer'.

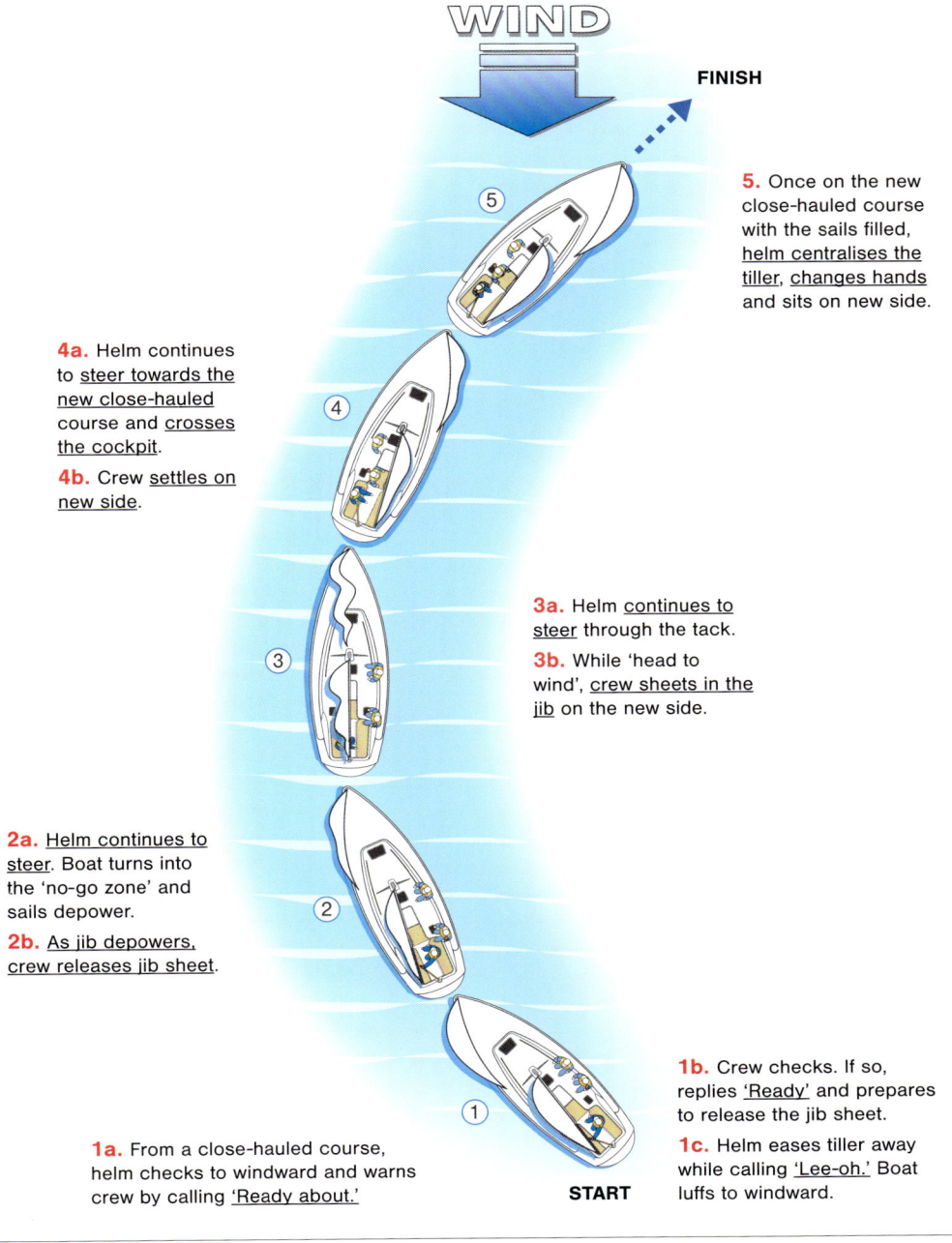

5. Once on the new close-hauled course with the sails filled, helm centralises the tiller, changes hands and sits on new side.

4a. Helm continues to steer towards the new close-hauled course and crosses the cockpit.

4b. Crew settles on new side.

3a. Helm continues to steer through the tack.

3b. While 'head to wind', crew sheets in the jib on the new side.

2a. Helm continues to steer. Boat turns into the 'no-go zone' and sails depower.

2b. As jib depowers, crew releases jib sheet.

1b. Crew checks. If so, replies 'Ready' and prepares to release the jib sheet.

1a. From a close-hauled course, helm checks to windward and warns crew by calling 'Ready about.'

1c. Helm eases tiller away while calling 'Lee-oh.' Boat luffs to windward.

Gybe Adaptation for Longer Tiller Extension
Gybing: Aft Mainsheet

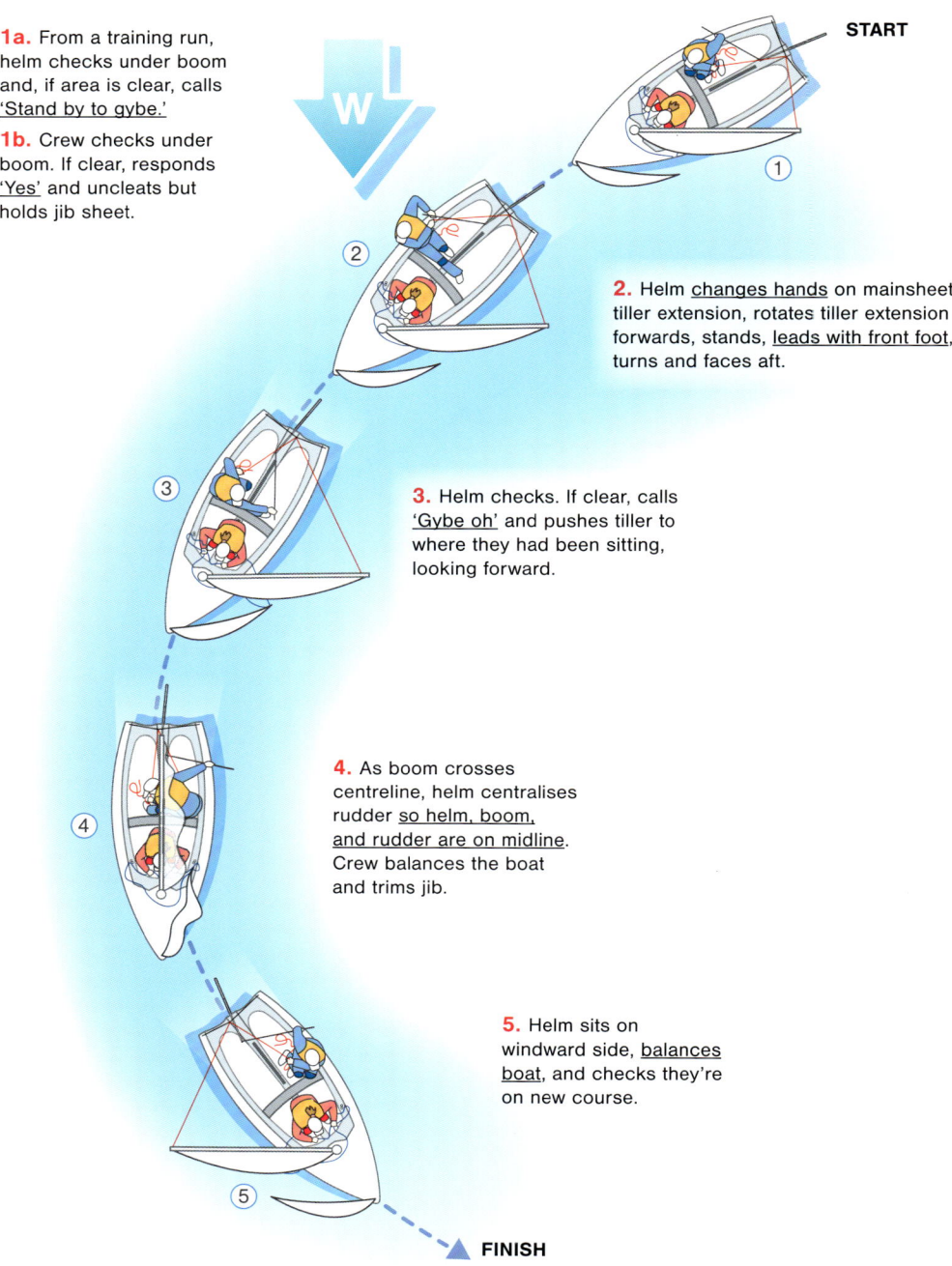

1a. From a training run, helm checks under boom and, if area is clear, calls 'Stand by to gybe.'

1b. Crew checks under boom. If clear, responds 'Yes' and uncleats but holds jib sheet.

2. Helm changes hands on mainsheet/ tiller extension, rotates tiller extension forwards, stands, leads with front foot, turns and faces aft.

3. Helm checks. If clear, calls 'Gybe oh' and pushes tiller to where they had been sitting, looking forward.

4. As boom crosses centreline, helm centralises rudder so helm, boom, and rudder are on midline. Crew balances the boat and trims jib.

5. Helm sits on windward side, balances boat, and checks they're on new course.

Gybing: Keelboat

During the gybe, the helm may cross the cockpit facing in either direction, depending on the layout. When crossing, helm & crew should avoid the mainsheet falls and traveller and never allow them to 'slam' over. It may be safer for the helm to cross the cockpit after the boom has gybed. Usually, keelboats are centre-mainsheet rigged, so the technique from page 85 can be used, particularly if smaller and lighter. Larger, heavier ones may use the method described below. The mainsheet can be controlled by either the helm or a 'trimmer'.

START

1a. Helm ensures that the boat is on a training run.

1b. Mainsail is out, traveller centralised, with the boom just clear of the shroud.

1c. Crew trims jib out.

2a. Helm checks that it is clear to leeward and calls 'Stand by to gybe.' If ready, crew replies 'Yes' and prepares to gybe the jib.

2b. Helm eases the tiller to windward while calling 'Gybe oh' and steers accurately to maintain a steady arc throughout the gybe (small rudder angle).

2c. On larger/heavier boats, as the helm steers, the mainsail is simultaneously sheeted in swiftly to encourage the mainsail to gybe. As the boom crosses, the main must be quickly sheeted out again to retain control.

3a. When on a run, helm may briefly centralise the tiller.

3b. On smaller boats, the mainsail is gybed using the 'falls'.

3c. Crew gybes the jib.

4a. Helm steers onto the new training run and crosses the cockpit.

4b. Mainsail is trimmed for the new training run. Crew sets the jib on new side.

5. Helm changes hands on the tiller, sits, and steers the new course. Crew settle and trim the sails accordingly.

FINISH

TOP TIP

If a traveller is used it is centralised prior to the gybe. Through the gybe, the helm controls the boom by sheeting in, gybing, and easing the mainsheet, which prevents the boom from slamming across.

THE RYA SINGLE-HANDED TEACHING METHOD

Introduction

The Instructor course familiarises candidates with a teaching method specifically designed for teaching single-handed when the Instructor may be on their own, with up to six students and dinghies.

Sessions should be short and the Instructor must always watch for signs of fatigue. Capsizes are more likely in a single hander than in the instructed larger dinghy, so suitable preparation must be made.

For sessions to be most effective, Instructors should:

- Keep them short
- Provide short clear briefings (essential) containing enough information to complete the task, and no more
- The aim of the session should 'just' challenge the students
- Regularly check the understanding of the students
- Debrief each session with effective feedback to the individual students
- Lay marks prior to each session so students can see the course before setting off
- Ensure boats are correctly set up before launching students, i.e. centreboard/rudder down, student sitting on the windward side, tiller and mainsheet in correct hands

The expectation is that most students will take around two full days or 16 hours of instruction to complete the RYA Level 1 course. However, in ideal conditions with keen students and good support, it may be possible to complete in a shorter period.

General Considerations

Advantages:

- Students are continuously at the helm
- They learn faster
- Boats tend to be light and durable
- Simple and exciting
- Particularly effective for teaching children
- Low skill level required to succeed in most boats
- Can be less expensive to run, with a more economical teaching ratio (6:1)

Disadvantages:

- Can be frustrating at first
- Students can tire easily
- Communication is harder
- Group control can be more difficult
- Students can become cold more quickly
- Students may quickly scatter over a large area

Teaching Equipment/Sailing Area

Instructors may have to adapt the equipment and select an appropriate sailing area to achieve the tasks set.

- Equipment: The right size of boat and sail area for the size of student
- Wind strength
- Wind direction
- Air and water temperature
- Sailing area
- Depth of water (can the foils be fully lowered?)
- Starting point (beach/pontoon/bank/slipway)
- Length of sessions (short)
- Any/other hazards
- Tide
- Instructor to check all boats before they go afloat

TOP TIP

Think 'What's the minimum I need to teach to get them to the next level?'

Group Control

- Consider setting a holding area for launch and recovery
- Frequent regrouping and briefings
- Recall signals (whistle and hand signals)
- Awareness of sailing area: use diagrams – set the course before students go afloat so they can see the boundaries
- Question students to check understanding before launching
- Consider using a 'buddy system' when launching/recovering
- Ensure that the whole group is in an area that is easy for the Instructor to observe and control
- Factor in the amount of space that you will need

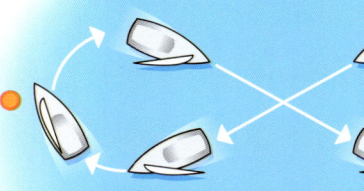

Course set.
Marks laid for course
- Holding area for launch/recovery
- Set sailing area for **group control**

Instructor positioned upwind
- On water first, off water last
- Good communication
- Vision – voice and whistle will carry downwind

LAUNCHING AND RECOVERY AREA

What If...?

Always consider:

- What is the worst thing that could happen and can it be managed?
- What changes can be made to cope with this?
- If there is any doubt: stop, reassess, and rebrief the session
- 'Count heads' regularly

Communication

- Well thought out and structured briefings (include problems that might occur)
- Size of sailing area
- Always use a combination of whistle and hand signals to ask students to stop for Instructor to go to them, or students to come to Instructor (when able to)

STOP **HOME** **COME TO ME**

- Be aware of the noise from an engine or a flapping sail
- Instructors may sail with the students providing they have ensured the required safety cover is available

Land Drills

Land drills introduce clarity and simplicity. They enable students to practise in a safe and controlled environment. They are not necessarily used all the time, but are fundamental to the single-handed teaching/learning process.

The delivery structure for any land drill should be via the 'Whole-Part-Whole' teaching structure. The 'Techniques for Instructing & Coaching' section (page 30) provides further information on how to deliver effective land drills.

Capsize

Because students are on their own and may not be very confident, point out:

- Righting a boat after capsize is easy, and a demonstration from the Instructor first will show this
- Wearing the right equipment means they will float in the water
- It can be fun

Remember:

- A land drill may help with understanding
- Be aware that even on a hot, sunny day students can get cold once wet
- Try to keep students as dry as possible (consider reefing)

Philosophy

The basic ethos of the RYA teaching method, as outlined earlier, applies just as much to single-handed teaching as to any other stage of, or way of teaching. At each stage Instructors should ask themselves:

- What do students already know?
- What are the priorities of our session?
- How do we ensure the most relevant elements are taught before moving on, ensuring our students are able to complete the next session successfully?

This should save unnecessary time ashore and prevent teaching irrelevant details.

The RYA Teaching Method: Single Handers

There is a progressive step-by-step approach to teaching each skill.

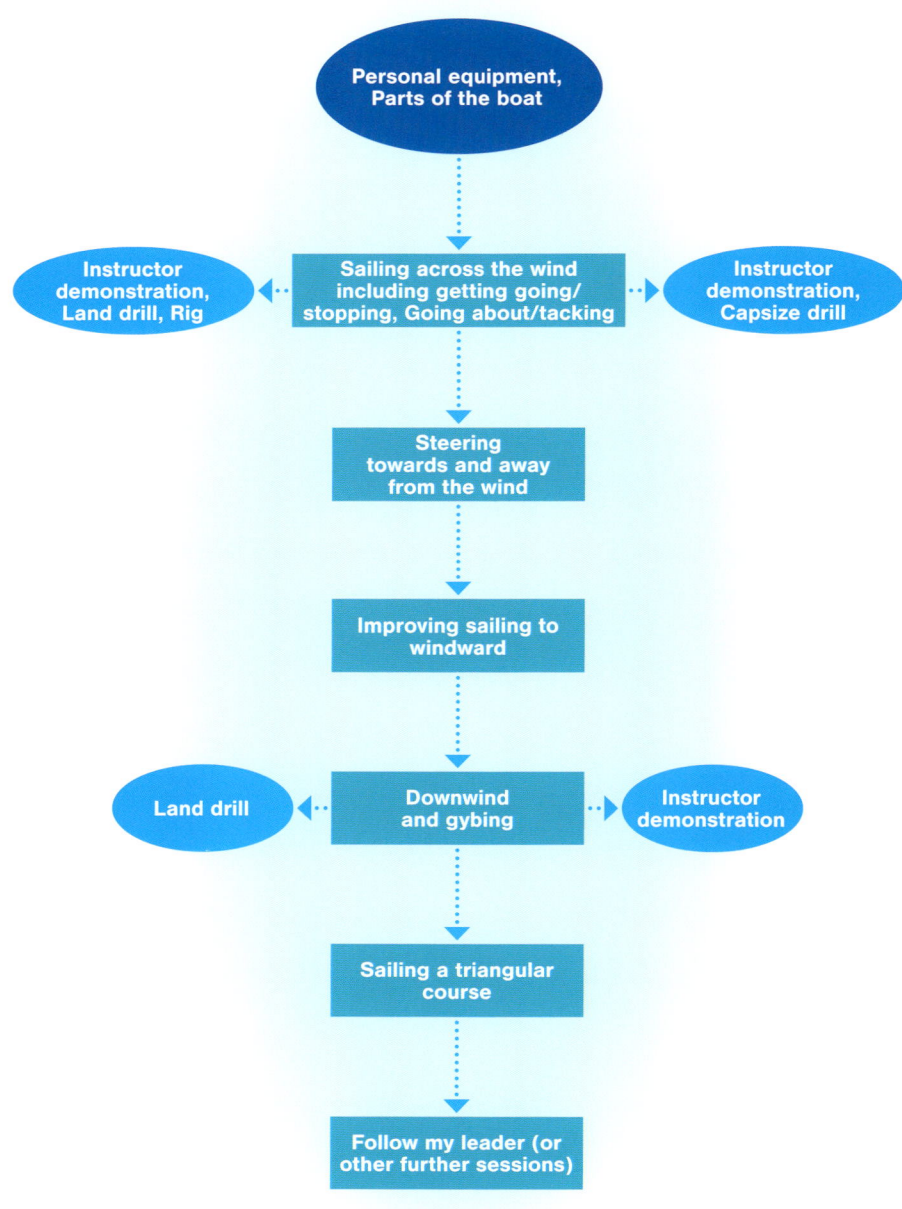

Single-handed Sessions

Session 1: Introduction to Personal Equipment and Boat Orientation

Aim

Instructor to allocate appropriate clothing and provide a basic boat introduction.

Session Considerations

Instructor to provide a basic introduction to personal clothing and boat orientation:

- Appropriate clothing for the prevailing conditions: wetsuit, waterproofs
- Footwear: wet boots, trainers
- Buoyancy aid: 50 Newtons, correct size, securely fastened. The use of life jackets should be risk-assessed appropriately for each activity and student
- Boat orientation: limited to simple terms and parts of the dinghy

TOP TIP

Instructor issues kit and clothing, but don't ask the students to get changed just yet.

Session 2: Rigging

Aim

Provide students with a basic introduction to rigging and an introduction to wind awareness.

Session Considerations

Once the boats are rigged, ensure sails are <u>furled</u> to reduce both sail noise and damage due to flogging.

Teaching Sequence

- Instructor led
- <u>Establish wind direction</u>
- Rig one boat a little at a time by way of demonstration
- Students then rig their own boats
- Provide brief explanations and <u>introduce basic sailing terminology</u>
- Instructor to check each boat before going afloat
- Reef as a matter of course and consider masthead flotation

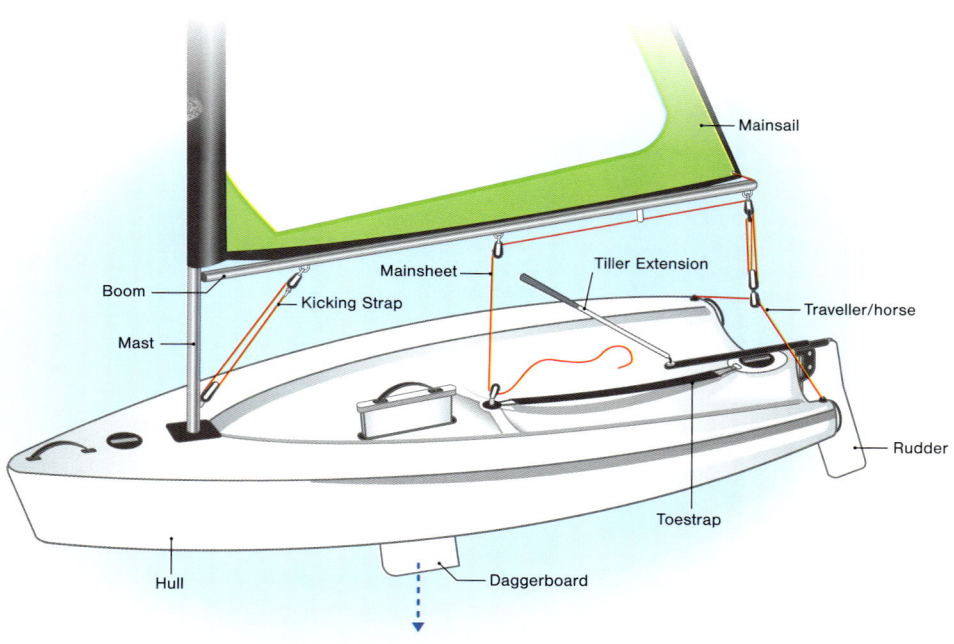

Session 3: Sailing Across the Wind

Aim

To introduce getting the dinghy going, sailing across the wind (beam reach), steering, going about, and stopping.

Session Considerations

Ashore:

- Instructor to demonstrate <u>ashore with a land drill</u> and then reinforce with a demonstration <u>afloat</u>:
    - Getting going (sheeting in)
    - Basic steering (towards and away from the wind)
    - Going about (from beam reach to beam reach)
    - Slowing down (sheeting out)
    - Stopping (lying-to)
    - Getting out of irons (push/push, pull/pull)
- Remember:
    - Very few students can absorb all the information in one go, so demonstrate using the 'Whole-Part-Whole' method for delivery
    - Actions are more effective than words
    - Each student should practise during the land drill

Afloat:

If environment and conditions are appropriate, a demonstration afloat may be all that is required.

- Instructor demonstration of <u>land-drill sequence</u>, including capsize recovery
- Sessions afloat should include Instructor in the water with a safety boat launched and ready nearby, upwind
- Launch and release <u>one</u> student at a time. Note: Student to tack near the mark as it is merely an aiming mark
- Provide on-water coaching and encouragement throughout
- Add boats to the course one at a time once it is clear students are sailing and tacking successfully
- If students are experiencing difficulty, consider rebriefing and limiting the number of boats on the water
- If there is to be more than one boat on the course, introduce a simple anti-collision rule
- As boats and students are added, the course may need to be lengthened

Teaching Sequence

1. With dinghy across the wind, climb in over windward side.
2. Lower foils and sheet in so sail is halfway in.
3. Head towards outer buoy.
4. When near the buoy, <u>check area</u> is clear to windward.
5. If clear, initiate the turn by <u>easing the tiller extension away</u>, rotating the end of the extension forward towards the front of the boat.
6. As <u>boom nears the centreline</u>, helm moves across boat, <u>looking forward</u>, <u>leading with the rear foot</u>.

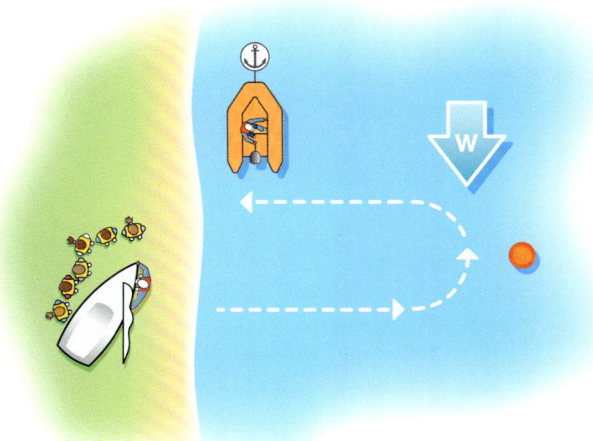

7. Helm sits on the new side, <u>balancing the boat (sitting forward), and centralises the tiller when on new course</u>.
8. <u>Looking forward, change hands behind back (thumbs pointing together, thumb of 'old' sheet hand facing up the extension)</u>.
9. Bring tiller extension <u>under 'new' rear arm</u>.
10. <u>To stop</u>:
    a. When closer to the shore, ease sail and raise the foils.
    b. Ease tiller away to stop the dinghy, lying-to.
11. Step out on the windward side.
12. To get out of irons:
    a. If stopped head to wind, <u>push</u> boom/<u>push</u> tiller extension to sail backwards.
    b. <u>Pull</u> mainsheet/<u>pull</u> tiller extension to sail away.
13. Capsize recovery:
    a. <u>Stay in contact with the boat</u>.
    b. <u>Go to the centreboard</u> and pull down on it.
    c. Once <u>boat rights, slide into dinghy over windward side</u>.
    d. Balance boat and <u>sort out mainsheet and rudder</u>.

Session Progression

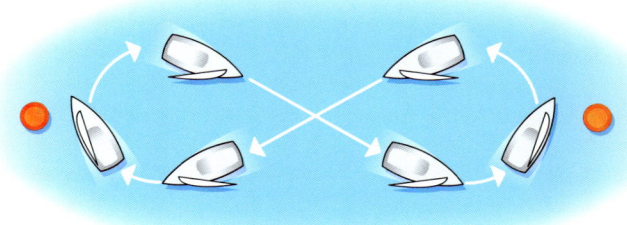

Tacking Sequence

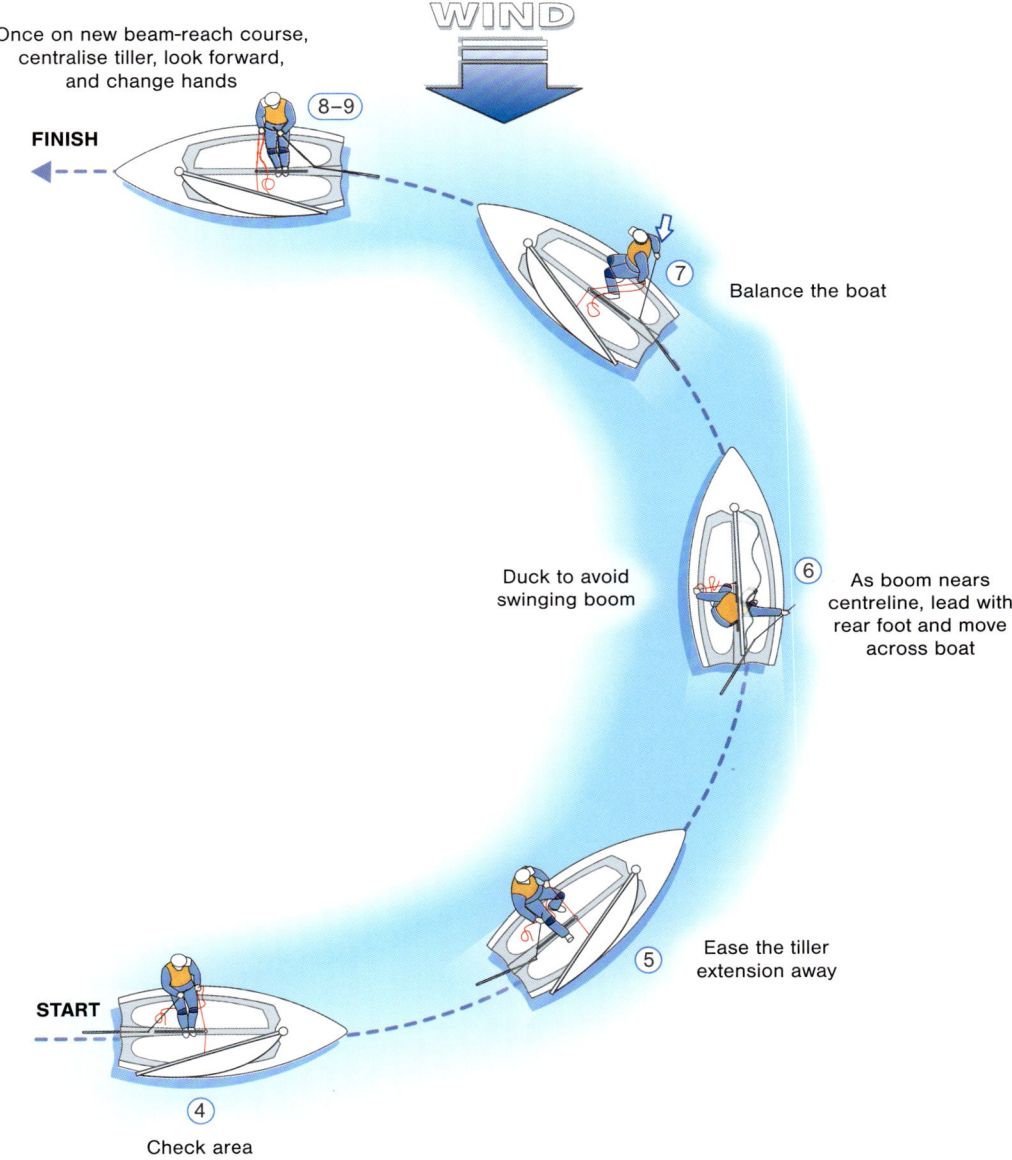

Adaptations

Tack adaptation for longer tiller extension – stages four to seven are the same, then:

1. <u>Looking forward, change hands behind back</u>, rotating the extension forward, over the rear shoulder.

Session 4: Improving Steering, Including an Introduction to Steering to Windward

Aim

The introduction of sailing to windward, and improved steering towards and away from the wind, using correct sail setting.

Session Considerations

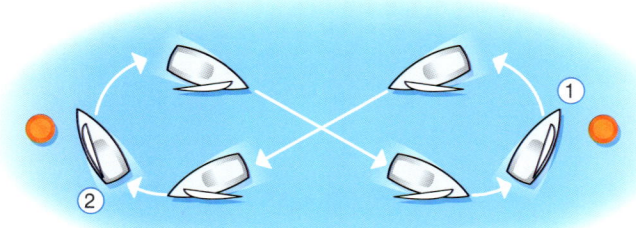

Diagram 1

- Instructor brief, using visual aids
- Show effects on sails, reinforcing wind awareness and sail setting at each step (Five Essentials introduction)
- Demonstrate ashore and/or afloat
- Lay a figure-of-eight beam-reach course

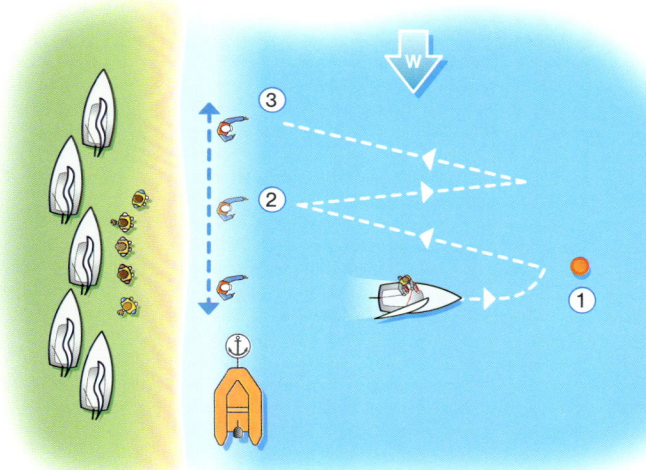

Diagram 2

- From a beam-reach course, progressively move the mark (or Instructor position) to windward using small increments.
- This gradual change will see the students sail to windward (offer coaching)

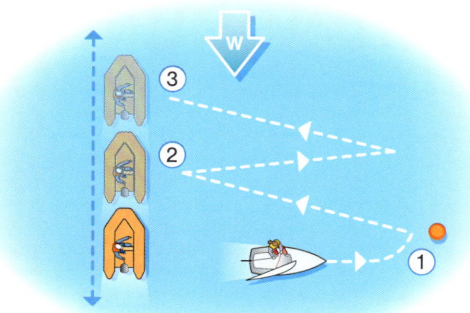

Diagram 3

- Use of the safety boat might be easier than moving a buoy
- Sailing upwind can often be introduced without the students realising, through the gradual moving of an aim point

102 RYA National Sailing Scheme Instructor Handbook

Teaching Sequence

1. From the original 'across wind' course, <u>identify the new course</u> slightly closer to the wind.
2. Steer by <u>easing the tiller away using small movements</u>, then hold this new course by <u>centralising the tiller</u>.
3. The change of course will cause the sail to flap. <u>Sheet in until sail 'just stops flapping'</u> (sail trim).
4. When you reach the aiming point, tack.
5. Steer away from the wind and steer to the original starting point, <u>easing out the mainsheet</u>, making <u>small tiller adjustments</u> as required.
6. Once aiming towards the original starting point, centralise the tiller and hold course, tacking at the original starting point. Then repeat the process to steer towards the next windward goal point.
7. <u>Further progression</u>: repeat the sequence above, gradually moving one mark/Instructor position towards the wind.
8. Once the students are able to sail on a close-reach course, the Instructor should progressively return downwind so the students resume sailing back on a beam-reach course before ending the session and coming ashore.

As students progress (Diagram 2), the aiming points at ② and ③ can be either a buoy or an instructor position.

TOP TIPS

- When launching and recovering, get students to work in pairs
- Carry a drop mark in the safety boat. If there is a problem you can drop the mark at position ② or ③

Session 5: Improving Sailing to Windward/Bearing Away

Aim

Development of steering and sailing skills to aid the student to sail upwind, refining and developing the tack through increasingly narrow angles, bearing away, and sailing downwind on a broad reach.

Session Considerations

- Lay a windward/leeward course, with an outer 'wing' mark
- Instructors must ensure that when students return downwind, they sail a course no deeper than a broad reach
- Instructor briefs session using visual aids to show the following:
    - Points of sail, including the no-go zone
    - Tacking through a narrower angle
    - Introducing the sailing terms 'luffing up', 'bearing away' and the Five Essentials
    - Action to avoid collisions
- Instructor provides an on-water demonstration of tacking through 90 degrees
- Instructor is now likely to use the safety boat as a teaching platform

Teaching Sequence

Sailing upwind:

1. Using smaller and more accurate tiller movements, steer on to a course closer to the wind.
2. Adjust sail setting appropriately, sheeting in as required **(sail setting)**.
3. Centralise the tiller and hold the course required.
4. Lower the **daggerboard** fully (centreboard).
5. Adjust body weight to maintain a flat boat. Hike if necessary **(balance)**.
6. Trim by moving weight forward, if necessary **(trim)**.

The tack:

1. Initiate the tack from a course closer to the wind, and exit closer to the wind.
2. Ensure the boat is flat and check all is clear to windward.
3. Use small rudder movements to make the turn.
4. On the new heading closer to the wind, centralise tiller and keep looking forward.
5. To make further progress upwind, repeat the above process.

TOP TIPS

Reinforce:
- The importance of body weight to balance and trim the boat when sailing upwind
- The importance of small and accurate rudder movements
- Centralising the tiller as soon as the mainsail fills will prevent 'oversteering' after the tack

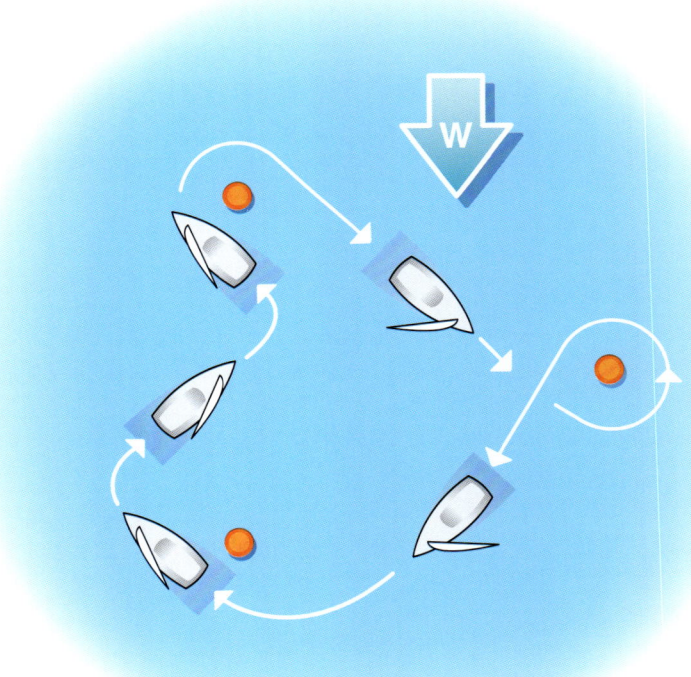

Session 6: Downwind and Gybing

Aim

To sail downwind and introduce gybing, while consolidating the Five Essentials.

Session Considerations

- Provide an Instructor demonstration of sailing on a broad reach and <u>controlled gybing</u> using a land drill ashore, then a demonstration afloat
    - Consider reefing
    - Utilise 'Whole-Part-Whole'
- Gybe should initially be from a <u>broad reach to a broad reach</u>
- Explain the centreboard position
- Importance of <u>helm, boom, and tiller being central during the gybe</u>
- Reinforce the Five Essentials
- Students should use the land drill to practise on both sides. Instructor provides corrective feedback
- Safety-boat positioning is important for effective coaching and communication. Place it by the gybe mark

Teaching Sequence

1. Raise daggerboard by one-third.
2. <u>Ease the mainsail</u> to bear away, steering until on a broad reach, and <u>hold this course</u>.
3. <u>To gybe</u>, check area to leeward is clear, and stay on that heading. Helm steers downwind by easing tiller towards them (small movement).
4. As the boom lifts slightly, helm moves quickly across the boat, facing forwards as you turn.
5. As boom crosses centreline, centralise tiller (<u>helm, boom, and rudder are on midline</u>).
6. <u>Sit on new side to balance the boat, steer (behind back)</u> on the new point of sail (broad reach). Change hands on tiller and mainsheet.
7. Steer to new goal point (or mark) on broad reach.

Adaptations

Gybe adaptation for longer tiller extension – stages one to four are the same, then:

5. <u>Sit on new side to balance the boat, steer (behind back)</u> on the new point of sail (broad reach). <u>Change hands behind back</u>, rotating the extension forward over the rear shoulder.

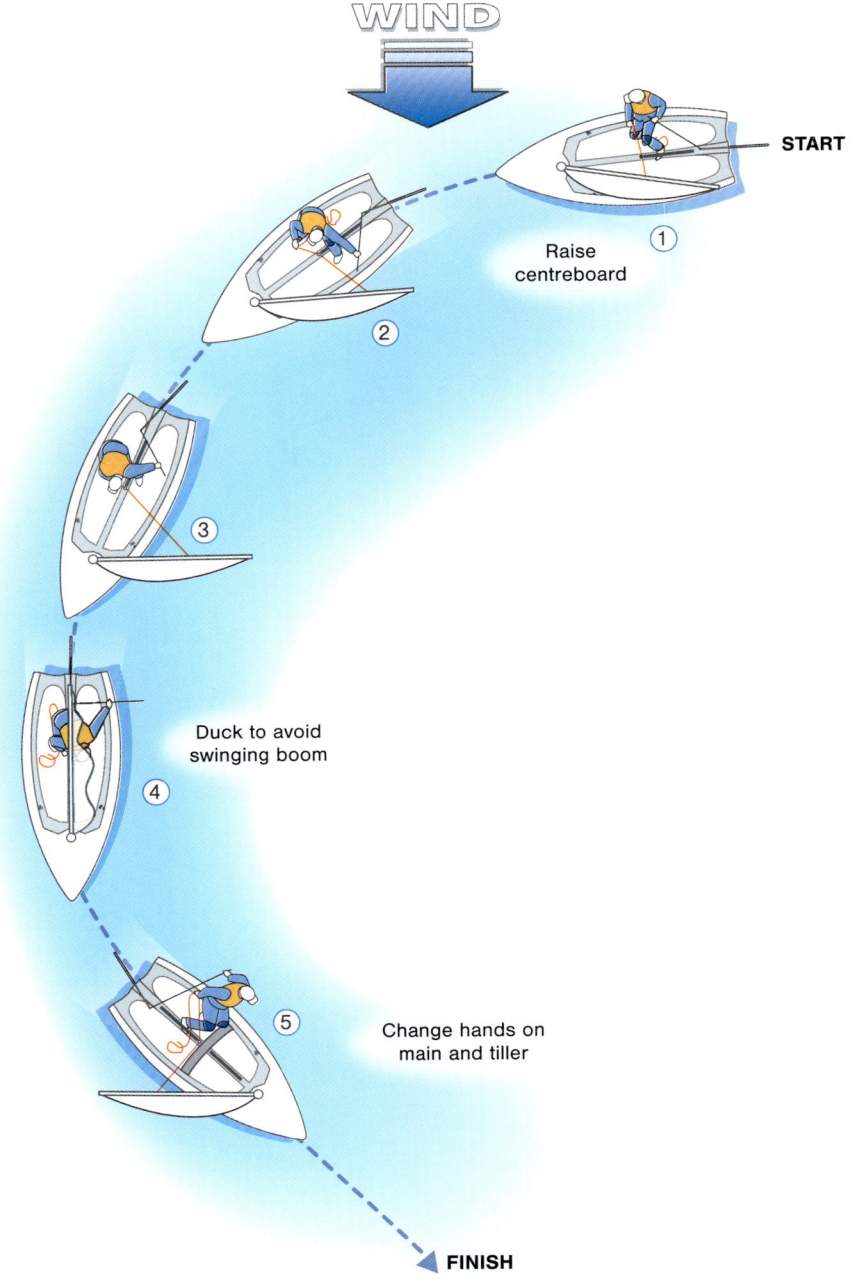

TOP TIP

On some types of dinghy, the gybe can be aided by a short 'pump' of the mainsheet. This encourages the boom to cross the boat and helps prevent the mainsheet getting caught on the transom.

Session 7: Sailing a Triangular Course Using All Points of Sail

Aim
To sail around a suitable course, developing all points of sail, particularly downwind.

Session Considerations
- Set a course for <u>all points of sail</u>, requiring both tacking and gybing, with <u>achievable downwind leg</u> set for ability (similar to that illustrated)
- At this stage, set for broad reach to <u>avoid</u> 'dead runs' and 'sailing by the lee'
- <u>Consider reefing</u>
- Provide briefing ashore and discuss actions to <u>avoid collisions</u>
- Application of the Five Essentials
- Wind awareness
- Provide support and instruction from safety boat as necessary
- Debrief ashore

Teaching Sequence
1. A course should be laid, enabling students to demonstrate their ability to <u>sail on all points of sail, tacking and gybing</u> when appropriate.
2. Ensure students can gybe in both directions. Run the course clockwise and anticlockwise.
3. Instructor should progressively move the gybe mark 'B' towards the windward leg as the students improve their downwind-sailing ability. Consider setting a 'dead run' when the students have the required skill.

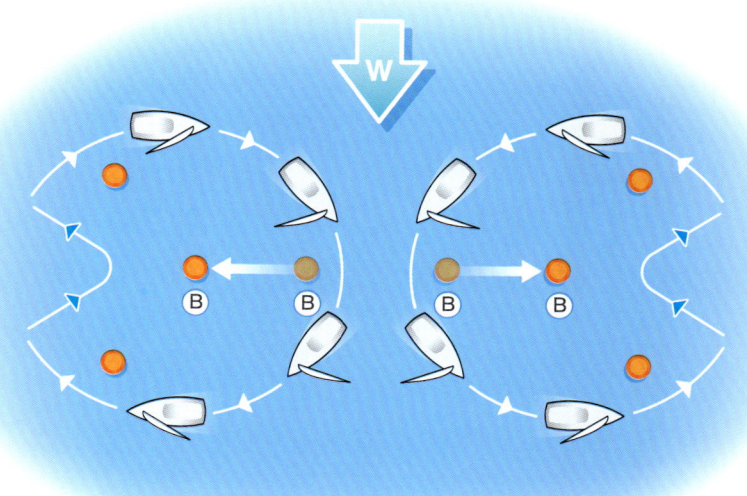

Session 8: Follow My Leader

Aim

This session should aim to develop speed control, Five Essentials, and improved steering ability. Students follow behind safety boat, or another dinghy helmed by a competent sailor.

Session Considerations

- Lead boat sails on a variety of courses and speeds
    - If using the safety boat, the Instructor should do the same
- Reinforce Five Essentials
- Following boats should tack/gybe <u>where lead boat turns</u>
- Two–three boat lengths apart. Students to maintain the gap by using accurate speed control, avoiding steering (luffing) if possible

TOP TIP

In the event of problems:

- Carry two drop marks in the safety boat
- Drop the marks on a beam reach and instruct the fleet to sail a 'sausage course' around them while the problem is dealt with

Teaching Sequence

Use the following manoeuvres and skills to consolidate learning:

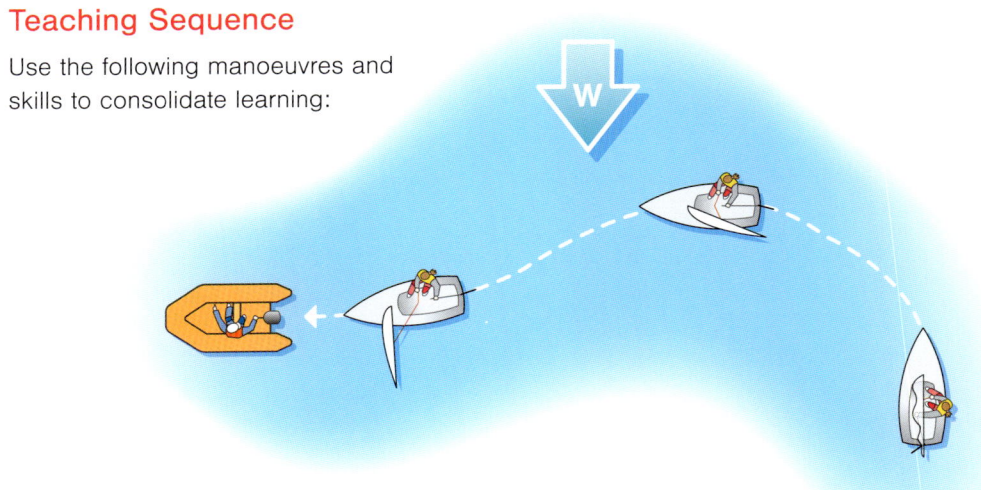

- Slowing down and accelerating while sailing upwind and downwind
- Tacking
- Gybing
- Consider 'negative' Five Essentials to slow down (trim aft to slow down, sheet in to slow down on a broad reach)

TOP TIP

Sail the fleet no higher than a 'close reach' and no deeper than a 'broad reach'.

THE RYA TEACHING METHOD: FURTHER SESSIONS

The purpose of the 'further sessions' section is to continue to develop the students' boat-handling skills through practice, in particular positioning and stopping, which will be useful when the students are returning to base, for example.

It is likely that the students will be able to sail on all points of sail without an Instructor and are comfortable tacking and gybing in moderate conditions. Therefore the Instructor should always be afloat in a safety boat and on hand to offer coaching input whenever necessary.

The Instructor will introduce a variety of techniques that will become progressively more challenging. The student will need the opportunity to practise these techniques in order to become more skilful.

1. The Instructor should use a variety of exercises (or sessions as outlined over the following pages) to help students practise and improve the techniques they have learned.
2. Instructors should utilise RYA resources and publications to accompany their teaching, especially G3 RYA Start Sailing and G12 RYA Advanced Sailing as they provide useful reference material.
3. It is important that students understand what is expected of them prior to any session, so an effective briefing is required beforehand, especially when the students are sailing on their own.
4. The use of exercises such as those contained in E-G100 RYA Race Training Exercises is really helpful.

The skills learnt can be brought together into a fun exercise or a seamanship game to aid consolidation.

Combining the techniques makes the practice enjoyable and execution more efficient, rather than feeling they are just drills.

Session Considerations

A more detailed explanation on creating an effective session can be found in the 'Techniques for Instructing & Coaching' section, page 48. In summary, the structure for an effective on-water session brief needs to include what, where, how, and safety, with confirmation (from students). The simple reminder 'A, B, C, D' is an easy way of remembering the structure of a briefing.

- **Aim (what):** Set the aim of the session. What is the outcome? What are we trying to achieve?
- Instructor briefing ashore:
    - Background information, why, and an explanation of how to execute the particular skill
    - Visual explanation and order of techniques, including the Key Teaching Points.
    - Consider a theory session
- **Sailing area (where):** Clearly identify the sailing boundaries. Use a diagram on a white board, use models, pebbles etc., or point them out if you are on the shore and can see the boundaries
- **How:**
    - Lay any marks prior to the brief so they are visible for briefing
    - Describe launching and how they will launch. Is there a holding area, or will you use follow my leader?
    - What happens on recovery/return to shore?
    - How long will the session last?
- **Safety:**
    - Explain that you will be in the safety boat and advise them what they should do if they have a problem
    - Explain use of whistle and what signals you will use. Remember to include a confirmation signal that they have understood
    - Confirm and include simple 'rules of the road' with 'port/starboard' and 'windward boat' as a minimum
    - It is important to include signals such as 'abandon, return to home/shore', 'you to me', and 'everyone to me', checking students understand their importance
- **Confirm** they understood the aim and structure of the session by asking specific questions

TOP TIP

Once the Instructor steps out of the boat, students may initially make a few mistakes. Provide them with time to settle and sort things out for themselves, as long as it is still safe to do so.

Instructing from a Teaching Boat (Power or Sail)

Initially, when teaching novices, the Instructor will be in the sailing dinghy, removing themselves whenever possible to allow the students to practise under supervision and with coaching tips when necessary.

Additional Practical Sessions

During the course, and as part of previous sessions, students will have departed and returned to base on numerous occasions and hopefully in various conditions (lee and weather shore).

They can now progress to learn the capsize drill, heaving to, reefing afloat, picking up a mooring etc. The Instructor should still be prepared to join students in their dinghy to demonstrate a particular skill if circumstances allow, while supporting and instructing from a safety boat. There may also be the need for a short theory session or land drill prior to launching.

In all of these sessions, demonstrations, and teaching points, we follow the same structure, PAME:

- **P**lan
- **A**pproach
- **M**anoeuvre
- **E**scape

There are generic skills for many of the techniques taught and approaches needed. Some are specific to dinghies, so if you are teaching in multihulls or keelboats then adapt these techniques to meet the specific boat type.

Upwind approach (example of skill: man overboard, PUM etc.):

- Position dinghy downwind
- Slow the boat in good time by easing the sails early
- Use 'spill and fill' (easing and/or sheeting in the mainsail) to help maintain steerage and passage through the water, providing small amounts of power from the sails when necessary
- Let the jib flap and use as a wind indicator
- On arrival at goal point, let the sail (or sails) out completely
- Release the kicker and raise the centreboard as soon as possible (which depowers the boat)
- Consider an 'escape' in the planning stage

Downwind approach (example of skill: lee-shore landing, PUM (tide)):

- Position dinghy upwind and stream main halyard overboard, which will reduce tangles
- Turn the boat head to wind, ease the kicker, free the cunningham, release the main halyard, and drop the mainsail (remove the halyard from the sail and secure). Crew can roll main
- Use the jib to bear away
- Raise centreboard and release/partially raise the rudder
- In the shallows, let the jib fly (or furl), then round up into wind. Crew get out on windward side and hold boat head to wind
- Consider an 'escape' in the planning stage

Fun Race

Assuming that you have covered the basic 'rules of the road', then the minimum extra knowledge needed by students to complete a short race is an explanation of the atypical port-hand triangular course and a basic starting procedure. You can even use '3-2-1-Go'; it's an informal fun way to end the course.

TOP TIP

Some people dislike competition. Consider their wishes and come up with fun alternatives, such as seamanship tasks etc. Points are awarded for good skill rather than who finishes first.

Seamanship Skills in Keelboats

When teaching Seamanship Skills in a keelboat, the following areas should be considered and covered during the course:

Grounding

- Lee-shore dangers
- Awareness of state of tide

If grounding on windward shore:

- Ease or drop main, back jib, heel

If grounding on lee shore:

- If quick, you may be able to sheet in the main and tack off. If not, drop the main quickly to avoid being blown on further
- If you have an engine, heel the boat and motor off
- With no engine, put out the kedge
- If the tide is falling and no help is available, protect the side of the boat as it dries

Emergency Steering

Keelboats can be steered rudderless by lashing the helm exactly amidships and using sail trim and (to some extent) balance as in a dinghy. Emergency steering can involve the use of an oar, a spinnaker pole or boathook, or even a bucket attached to each quarter.

Handling Under Power

- At Level 2, keep the power manoeuvres simply to coming alongside and picking up moorings
- Demonstrate prop-wash effect by engaging astern while secured alongside
- Practise turning the boat under power
- Prepare for coming alongside – observe the wind and tide, secure fenders and warps, position crew, communicate, ensure good boat control, and use springs

Session: Capsize Recovery

Aim

To right a capsized or inverted dinghy or multihull, with students completing a capsize recovery using the 'scoop method'.

Session Considerations

- Instructor briefing ashore:
    - Safety considerations
    - Background information (why and how)
- Consider a land drill/Instructor live demo or theory lesson before the actual drill
- Repeated capsizes may cause the buoyancy chambers to flood, making righting increasingly difficult
- Capsizing should be taught as soon as possible after completing the 'method' (unless there are favourable prevailing conditions and always at a time when students can get changed immediately afterwards)
- Consideration for weather and water temperature
- Instructor should be with the students and also enter the water, for both support and effective control
- Ensure sufficient safety cover is provided (use the Senior Instructor)
- Build confidence through a calm and smooth drill
- Ensure the dinghy is free floating in deep water and always use masthead flotation (unless teaching a practical inversion drill)
- When teaching capsize drill, a Dinghy Instructor must be in the dinghy with the students and enter the water when they do. The Dinghy Instructor will then supervise the drill while positioned at the bow of the dinghy

When covering inversion, in addition to the Instructor briefing above, safety considerations when inverting (entrapment) must be included, as well as:

- Demonstration by Instructor highlighting PAME (**P**lan, **A**pproach, **M**anoeuvre, **E**scape)
- Ensure helm and crew are dressed appropriately for the conditions
- Remove masthead flotation

Teaching Sequence

- Provide a shore briefing, explaining the 'scoop method' (or land drill with a boat on its side)
- Check students for contact lenses, glasses, watches, phones, and check personal and boat buoyancy
- Choose a suitable location away from hazards and ensure safety cover is present
- <u>Capsize by tacking</u>. Helm and the crew stay in their original positions prior to the tack, and <u>Instructor moves across to assist with the capsize</u>
- Instructor then <u>moves to the bow to control the drill</u>, and crew and helm swim to back of boat

1. <u>Helm checks rudder</u> and <u>crew passes mainsheet</u> to helm, who uses it as a safety line.

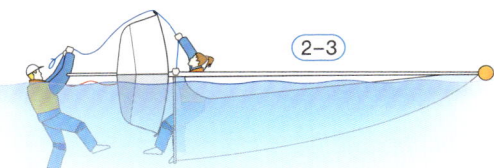

2. <u>Helm swims to centreboard</u> and holds it to prevent inversion, while crew watches them, then <u>swims inside the boat to the centreboard</u> case and checks centreboard is down (if the centreboard is not fully down, reinforce communication with crew before lowering it further).
3. <u>Crew passes jib sheet to helm (if no righting line is available)</u> and checks mainsheet is flowing freely. The helm confirms they have received it.

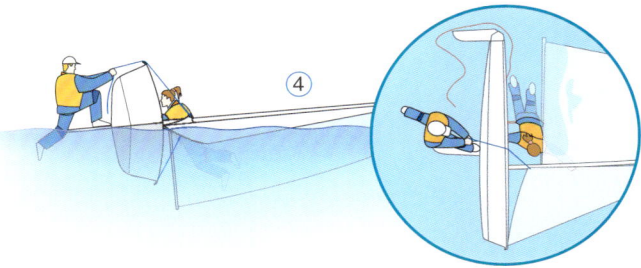

4. <u>Crew lies in water</u> and ensures they keep their weight off the boat (which can prevent righting).

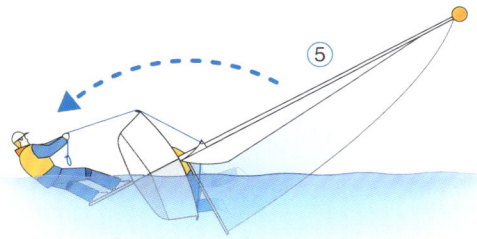

5. <u>Helm</u>, using their feet on gunwale or climbing onto the centreboard, uses the jib sheet or righting line and <u>rights the boat into the wind</u>.

6. As the boat rights, <u>with the jib backed the boat is 'hove-to'</u>, and the <u>crew balances the boat, assisting the helm over the windward side</u> or over the transom (if open transom).

Dinghy Inversion

Manoeuvre:

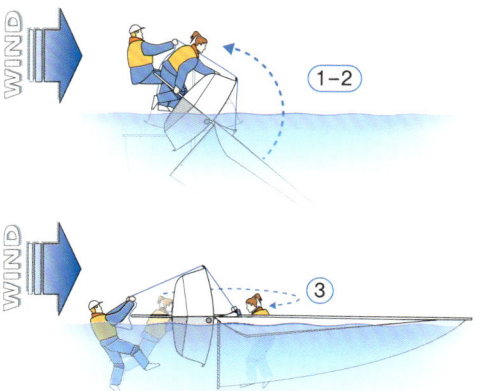

1. Both helm and crew move onto the hull, towards the windward back quarter to help break the seal of the air pocket.
2. Both lean back on the jib sheet or righting line to break the 'seal' and bring boat to a 90-degree position. The helm remains at the centreboard.
3. Crew swims inside boat.

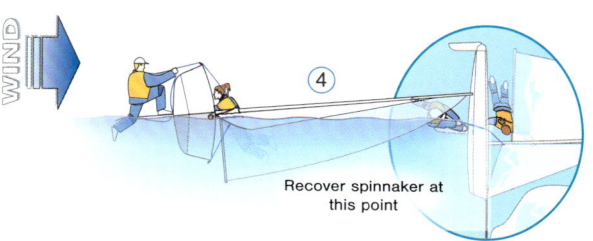

4. Crew checks centreboard and recovers spinnaker (if applicable).

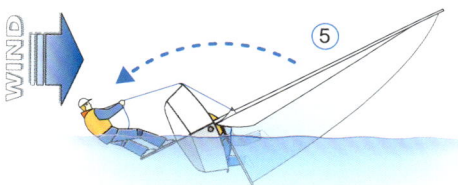

5. Helm applies pressure to the centreboard by leaning back, holding jib sheet/righting line. Crew prepares to be 'scooped' up.

6. As dinghy rights, crew balances it, and assists helm to board.

Escape: Ensure helm and crew keep clear if the boat is inverting, due to risk of entrapment.

Considerations

- If the boat has righting lines, the crew need not throw the jib sheet
- Stress the value of straight legs and back for maximum leverage
- Some helms find it difficult to get onto the centreboard, so any advice which you can provide is worth giving:
    - Larger helms will be able to right the dinghy by holding the centreboard
    - Lighter/smaller helms should be advised to climb on the centreboard, keep as close to the hull as possible, and weight their back foot on the centreboard to provide the necessary righting moment
- Helm to be brought aboard by windward shroud, or transom
- Discuss the option of rolling the boat to windward if you have a lightweight crew and a larger helm
- Helm entering over stern can bear boat away, so a speedy entry is necessary
- Modern boats have buoyancy built into the floor and sides of the hull, increasing speed of inversion more readily after capsizing, so always consider masthead flotation

Development Method of Capsize Recovery: Teaching Sequence

1. At the point of capsize, the crew <u>nearest the highest point</u> of the hull steps over the gunwale and onto the centreboard as the mainsail reaches the water.
    - Their priority is to keep the mast level on the surface of the water, which prevents the boat from inverting
2. <u>Check the other crew member is present</u> and ask them to release the mainsheet and kicker to depower the rig.
    - If they <u>can't detect the other crew's</u> presence, their priority is to start bringing the boat upright using their weight and leaning back against a jib, spinnaker sheet, or righting line
3. If the crew <u>is present</u>, they can also check the rudder is still attached to the boat, and they are ready for the righting process to begin.
4. The boat is then righted by the crew member on the centreboard leaning back and holding <u>on to the sheets</u> to assist.
5. As the boat passes through the point of pivot, the <u>crew on the centreboard can step over</u> the gunwale and back into the boat as the other crew is scooped up by the lower gunwale.
6. If the rig is pointing into the wind, the boat needs to be <u>righted slowly</u>. This can be achieved by good communication and the crew on the centreboard warning whomever is in the water to lie along the length of the gunwale so the boat is brought up. That crew's weight will act as a 'damper' and will stop the boat from capsizing again.
7. Helm must take great care to avoid the boom as it sweeps across the boat from windward to leeward.

Multihull: Capsize Recovery

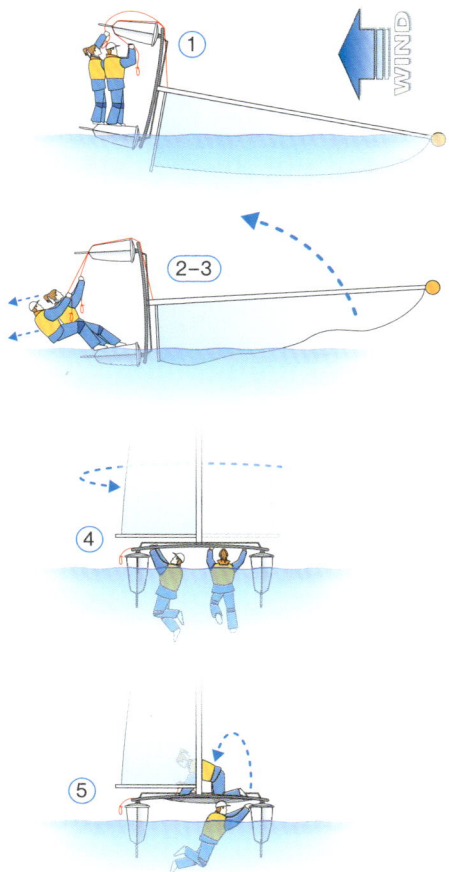

Manoeuvre:

1. The helm and crew climb onto the <u>lower hull</u> (①). Helm <u>releases traveller and mainsheet</u>, crew releases jib. Crew finds <u>righting line</u> (usually in a pocket at the base of the mast) and <u>throws it over</u> the top hull.

   Using the righting line for stability, helm and crew move carefully <u>forwards towards the bow</u>. This will cause the bow to 'dig-in', which will allow the multihull to <u>pivot head to wind</u>.

2. Helm and crew now <u>move back to midships</u> and <u>lean back</u> on the righting line, causing the multihull to begin righting (②-③). Wind blowing against the underside of the mainsail will help.

3. As the mainsail is released from the water, righting will '<u>speed up</u>'.

4. As the multihull rights, helm and crew <u>MUST avoid</u> the top hull coming down. They do this by <u>moving quickly to the forward crossbeam</u> and holding it tightly. Applying their weight here prevents any possibility of a recapsize.

5. Helm and crew then assist each other in <u>boarding over the crossbeam</u>. Both tidy up lines and begin sailing again.

Escape: Ensure helm and crew keep clear if boat is inverting, due to risk of entrapment. Remain in contact with the boat. Meet at the stern.

Multihull Inversion

Manoeuvre:

1. The helm releases the mainsheet and traveller. The crew releases the righting line and puts it over the windward hull.

2. Both the helm and crew move to the stern of the leeward hull, which will sink the stern, screwing the bows upwards.

3. Both helm and crew use the righting line to pull the masthead to the surface.

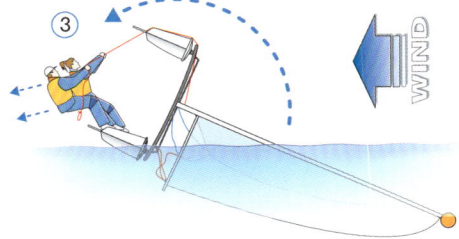

Once the multihull is partially righted so that the rig is flat to the water, continue the righting process as described in 'Multihull: Capsize Recovery' on page 118.

Session: Reefing Afloat (Dinghy, Keelboat, and Multihull)

Aim
To reef the mainsail afloat.

Session Considerations
Instructor briefing ashore:

- Why reef, when and what types (slab or roll)
- Where to reef: away from hazards, starboard tack if possible (explain), consider drifting space
- How: order of events, co-ordination, and communication between helm and crew
- How much: appearance of reefed sail, i.e. efficient shape, boom level, no wrinkles, kicking strap still effective

Instructor shore drill with active student participation:

- Set a suitable sailing area for the exercise

Teaching Sequence
Plan:

1. Prepare reefing system (slab or roller reefing).
2. Identify and consider a suitable location with sufficient drift space.

Approach:

3. Heave to: jib backed, rudder over, starboard tack (if possible), centreboard half raised.
4. Consider picking up a mooring to reef afloat.

Manoeuvre:

5. Stream halyard overboard, ease kicker tension, drop mainsail by one-third, or down to the reefing cringle on the luff (remove kicker altogether if roll reefing).
6. Consider remaining seated, helm and crew balance dinghy, dinghy on starboard tack.
7. Place reef in mainsail using system fitted on dinghy, multihull, or keelboat, ensuring no slack is left at the reefing tack and clew.
8. Rehoist mainsail, tension kicker, raise centreboard slightly if necessary. Neatly coil and secure excess halyard.
9. Tension kicker and other sail controls, centreboard raised slightly if necessary.
10. Stow excess main halyard and sail away.

Escape:

1. If sailing into a dangerous area, rehoist main and sail clear of hazard.
2. If there is a snag in the halyard, rehoist main to clear, then complete drill (streaming the halyard overboard before dropping the mainsail helps).

TOP TIP

This session can be progressed by:

- Sailing around a course once reefed
- Timed reefing/shaking out
- Reef on the whistle

Session Considerations

To 'roll reef':

Manoeuvre:

1. Sail onto starboard tack, release main halyard, remove kicker and drop mainsail one-third. Resecuring the halyard makes the next part easier.
2. Remove boom from the gooseneck.
3. Helm puts a 'tuck' into the leech while keeping the new 'foot' tight.
4. Using a sail bag or thick (perhaps knotted) rope as a kicking strap fixing point, the helm and crew 'roll' the excess sail neatly around the boom.
5. Reattach the boom to the gooseneck, reattach the kicker to the 'new' fixing point, and tension kicker.
6. Sheet in the mainsail and sail away.

Session: Leaving and Returning to the Shore

Aim
Provide the knowledge and understanding to depart and land on a lee or weather shore.

Session Considerations
- Instructor briefing ashore – consider a theory session
- Consider dangers of <u>both lee- and weather-shore</u> departure and recovery
- Use a buddy system when launching and recovering single-handed dinghies

Lee Shore Departure (Upwind Approach)

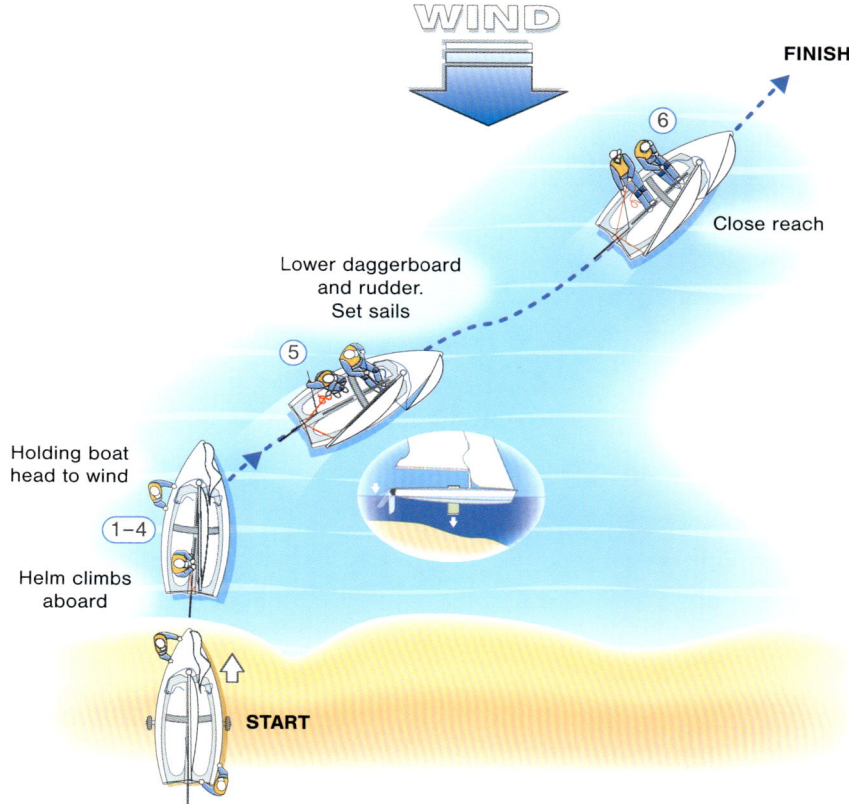

1. <u>Hoist sails ashore, head to wind</u> (fully battened sails are best rigged ashore).
2. <u>Launch boat, head to wind</u>, crew holds painter, or <u>windward hull on multihull</u>.
3. Helm hoists main (if needed), fits mainsheet block (multihull), <u>partially lowers centreboard (if fitted), and rudder (windward rudder on multihull), but does not secure it yet</u>.
4. Helm identifies <u>favoured tack</u> (which would allow the dinghy to sail more directly away from the shore), and crew <u>pushes bow in that direction</u>.
5. Crew swiftly gets in on windward side and lowers the <u>centreboard fully when possible</u>, as <u>helm sails on close haul</u>.
6. Once clear of shore, helm can put <u>rudder(s) fully down</u>.

Lee Shore Landing (Downwind Approach)

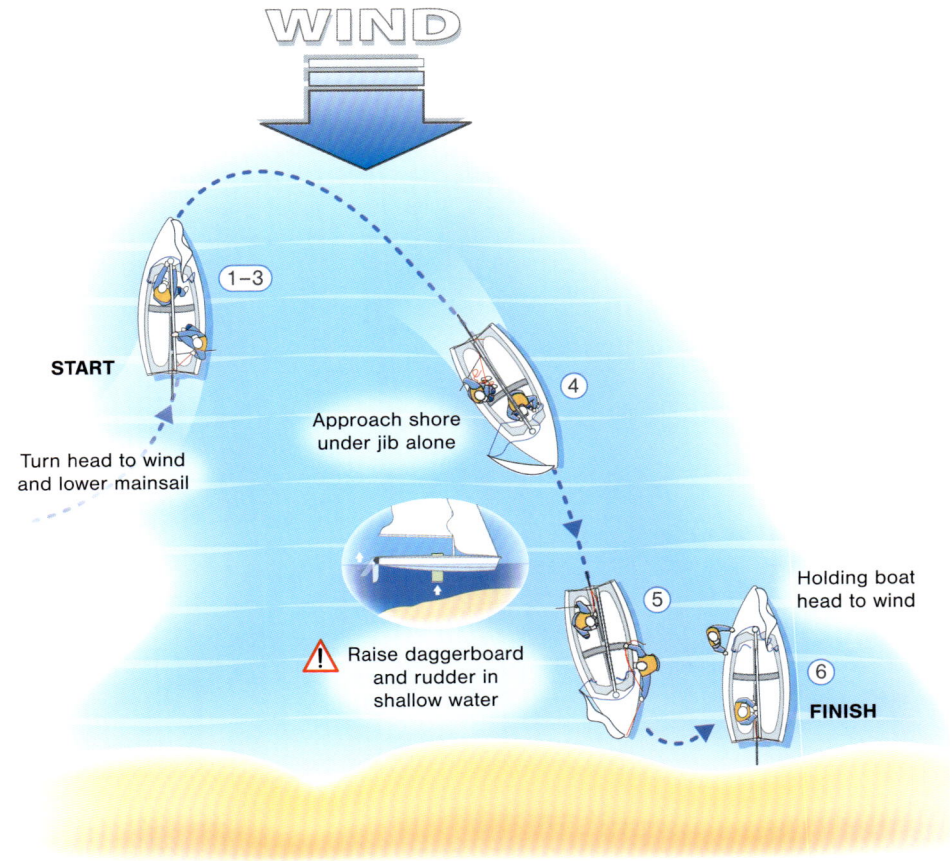

1. Crew streams main halyard (if fitted).
2. Helm stops upwind/uptide of landing site.
3. Lower mainsail, remove/secure halyard. Crew raises centreboard, helm releases and partially raises rudder.
4. Helm steers to shore and crew uses jib to control speed.
5. When close to shore, crew raises/removes centreboard, helm raises/unlocks rudder(s).
6. In shallows, crew exits on windward side and holds painter (or windward hull). Boat will lie head to wind.

For multihull:

1. In a safe area away from the shore, sail multihull head to wind. Helm removes mainsheet from the mainsail and secures it.
2. Helm raises both rudders.
3. Both crew sit on the hulls, forward of the main beam, and 'steer' the boat by lowering the appropriate crew's legs into the water. Backing the jib on one side or the other can also assist.

Windward Shore Landing

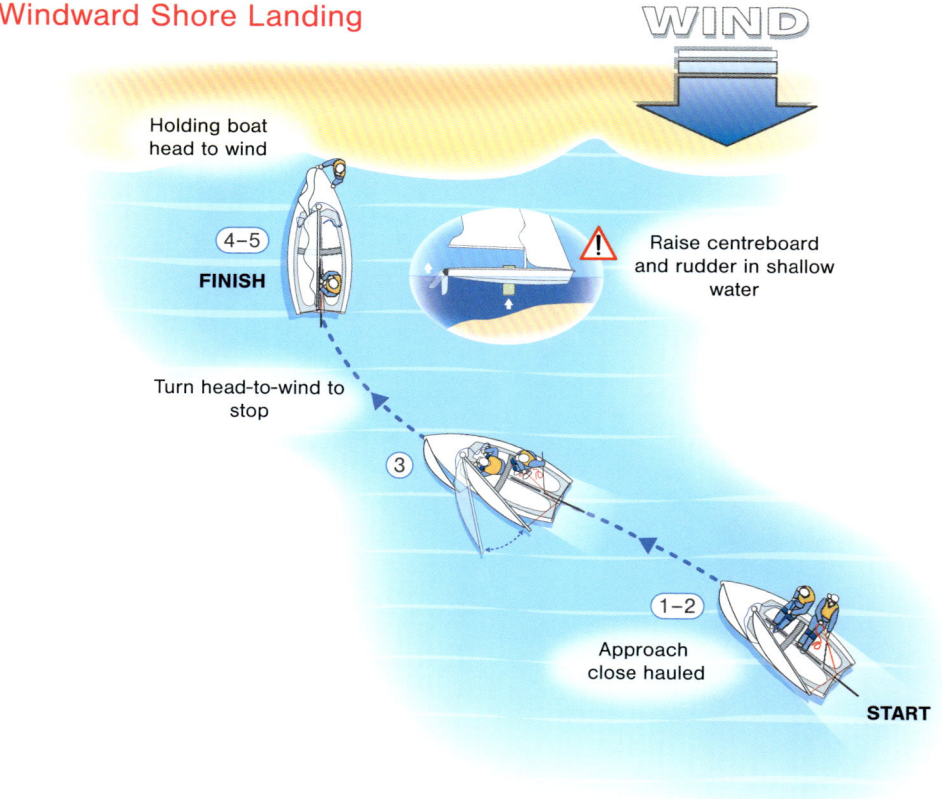

1. Helm <u>releases rudder downhaul</u> and then steers towards the shore (multihulls: raise rudders slightly).
2. <u>Approach on a close-hauled</u> course.
3. When near to shore, crew <u>prepares to raise centreboard</u> and helm prepares to raise rudder (multihull helm eases mainsheet and plays traveller).
4. In the shallows, <u>helm luffs up head to wind</u>, and crew enters water when it's waist deep, and holds painter or hull.
5. Helm <u>lowers sails, raises centreboard, and removes rudder</u>.

TOP TIP

When coming ashore on sandy beaches with an onshore wind and large waves, the technique is different, and the multihull is the only boat it applies to:

- Depower the mainsail
- Pick the right area. Both helm and crew sit aft to keep the bows up
- At the right moment the helm trips the rudders and keeps going straight for the shore
- Take care when alighting from the boat and turning it head to wind
- For a multihull windward-shore departure, see page 74

Session: Pick Up A Mooring (PUM)

Aim
Pick up and secure to a mooring and leave under control.

Session Considerations
- Instructor briefing ashore:
    - Background information, why and how to execute the skill
    - Visual explanation and order of technique, including Key Teaching Points
    - Link to previous learning, i.e. speed control
- Demonstration by Instructor (if required), highlighting PAME (Plan, Approach, Manoeuvre, Escape)
    - Allow students to have a number of attempts as helm and crew
- Instructor to ensure all dinghies have appropriate and secure painters, or that all moorings have secure lines attached and the dinghies have fairleads
- Before attempting the task, students should consider stopping near the mooring to check the wind, tide, and rate of drift. This will enable them to assess the necessary approach angle and/or direction

Teaching Sequence
Plan:
1. Having assessed the conditions, helm positions dinghy for the required approach.
2. Crew prepares the painter on the windward side, clear of the jib sheets.
3. Mooring is to be picked up on the windward side, just forward of the shroud.
4. Helm and crew agree on an escape plan. If the approach is too fast, or the buoy is not going to be reached, bear away in good time, reassess, reposition and make another attempt.

Approach:
5. Using the plan from above, helm begins the approach from downwind/tide of the buoy (upwind approach).
6. Helm controls the speed of approach by sheeting the mainsail in and out ('fill and spill') and through direction (close reach).
7. Helm takes into account the 'drift' encountered when depowering.
8. Crew prepares to pick up the mooring.
9. Helm and crew communicate throughout.
10. At two-three boat lengths from the buoy, crew releases the jib completely (flapping jib provides a wind indicator).

Manoeuvre:

11. Helm continues the approach, controlling the speed.
12. At <u>one boat length</u> from the buoy, helm <u>luffs</u> to slow dinghy to a standstill.
13. Helm <u>stops</u> the dinghy with the buoy <u>beside the windward shroud</u>, in the <u>'lie-to'</u> position. <u>Crew picks up buoy</u> (forward of the shroud) and secures to it (round turn & two half hitches). <u>Centreboard is raised</u>.
14. Sails are dropped and stowed, rudder is raised/removed and stowed.
15. To depart:
    a. Helm and crew <u>raise the sails</u>. Helm refits/lowers the rudder (but not the centreboard). Crew prepares to release the painter.
    b. After communicating with the helm, crew <u>releases</u> the painter and secures it inboard. Crew <u>backs the jib</u>.
    c. The bow will 'slide' off to leeward.
    d. When on a <u>close/beam reach</u>, crew <u>lowers the centreboard</u>. Helm and crew <u>sheet in</u> and sail away.

Wind against tide:

1. Crew prepares the painter (as above).
2. Helm positions the dinghy <u>directly upwind</u> of the buoy, allowing plenty of room. Crew streams the main halyard overboard.
3. Helm lies-to. Helm and crew <u>drop the mainsail</u> and stow it. Centreboard is raised two-thirds.
4. Using the <u>jib for power</u>, helm <u>bears away</u> and <u>sails downwind</u> towards the buoy. Crew <u>controls</u> the speed by <u>trimming</u> the jib accordingly.
5. At <u>two–three boat lengths</u> from the buoy, crew <u>slows</u> the dinghy by <u>easing</u> or <u>furling</u> the jib. Helm can assist by <u>trimming</u> their weight <u>aft</u>.
6. With the <u>buoy</u> at the <u>windward shroud</u>, crew <u>releases/furls jib</u> completely, picks up the buoy and secures to it (see above). Centreboard is raised.
7. Crew drops jib (if no furler). Helm raises/removes rudder.
8. Escape: If the buoy is missed, sail to a safe location, raise both sails, reposition and make another approach.
9. To depart:
    a. Crew <u>hoists the jib</u> (if no furler) and prepares to release the painter.
    b. Helm refits/lowers the rudder. Helm and crew prepare the mainsail.
    c. After communicating with the helm, crew <u>releases</u> the painter.
    d. The tide will carry the dinghy backwards. <u>Once clear</u>, crew <u>lowers</u> the <u>centreboard</u> and <u>sheets in the jib</u>.
    e. The dinghy is sailed to a <u>safe area</u>. Helm and crew <u>raise the mainsail</u> and sail away.

Session: Coming Alongside (CAS)

Aim
Come alongside a moored or anchored powerboat.

Session Considerations
- Instructor briefing ashore:
    - Background information, why, and how to execute the skill
    - Visual explanation and order of technique, including Key Teaching Points
    - Consider a theory session
- Briefing given by Instructor highlighting PAME (Plan, Approach, Manoeuvre, Escape)
    - Allow students to have several attempts as both helm and crew

Teaching Sequence

Plan:
1. Select the correct side to approach alongside:
    a. Boom outside RIB.
2. Plan an escape route.

Approach (upwind):

3. Approach under control on a close reach ('spill and fill'), allowing for tide (upwind approach.
4. Select the correct side to approach – boom outside RIB.
5. Understand how to depower dinghy once alongside.

Manoeuvre – wind with tide (wind and tide flowing in same direction):

6. Approach from downwind on a <u>close reach ('spill and fill' zone)</u>.
7. Jib flaps and shows wind direction.
8. Stop with the <u>boom outside the moored boat/pontoon</u>.
    a. Multihull bringing mooring between hulls.
9. Once alongside, raise centreboard and ease kicker.
10. To depart:
    a. To depart (centreboard fully raised), back jib on side nearest to the moored vessel. When on a close reach, swap jib to leeward side, lower centreboard, sheet in the main, and sail away.

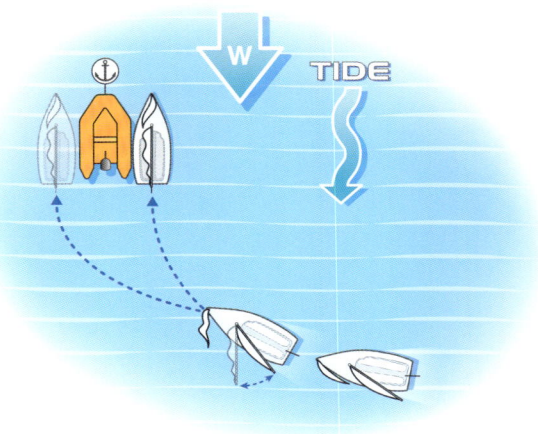

Manoeuvre – wind against tide (when tide is stronger than wind):

1. Position dinghy well upwind of the moored vessel.
2. Go 'head to wind' and drop the mainsail.
3. Using jib only, bear away onto a run and sail back towards moored vessel.
4. Control approach speed by releasing/sheeting in jib or, furling jib in/out. If still too fast, trim crew weight aft.
5. On arrival, completely release and drop or furl jib, raise centreboard fully, and make fast alongside.
6. To leave in a safe, controlled manner, use jib only. Once clear, raise the mainsail and sail away.

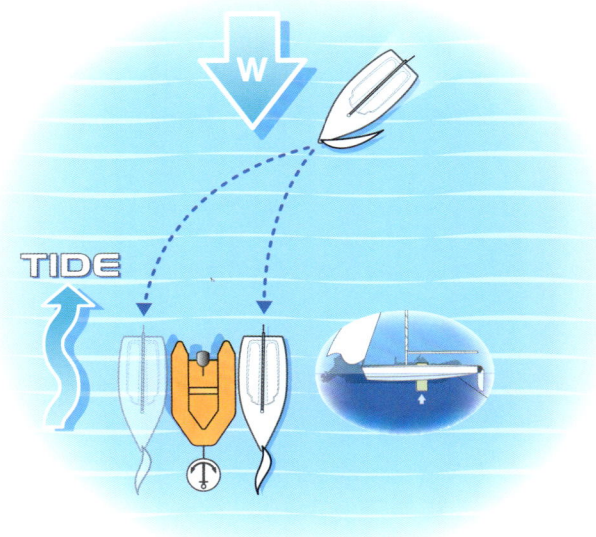

Escape – consider a suitable escape route:

1. If too fast on approach, sail away and retry exercise on opposite tack.
2. If too slow, head to wind, sail away and approach on close reach.

Manoeuvre – alongside a pontoon.

Position A: If the approach fails, with the dinghy 'head to wind' the tide will take it away from the pontoon.

1. Prepare fenders (if available, and if on a keelboat).
2. Approach on a beam reach. When within five boat lengths, release jib.
3. Continue approach on close reach using 'fill and spill'.
4. When within one–two boat lengths, luff up to 'head to wind' and alongside. Raise centreboard.
5. Quickly, make fast. Drop sails.
6. To leave, hoist sails.
7. One option is to release the mooring lines and back jib on the pontoon side. When dinghy is on a close reach, swap jib over, lower centreboard, sheet in mainsail, and sail away.
8. The other option is to hoist sails, release mooring lines, and lower centreboard. The tide will draw the dinghy away from the pontoon. When in space, 'push, push, pull, pull', and sail away.

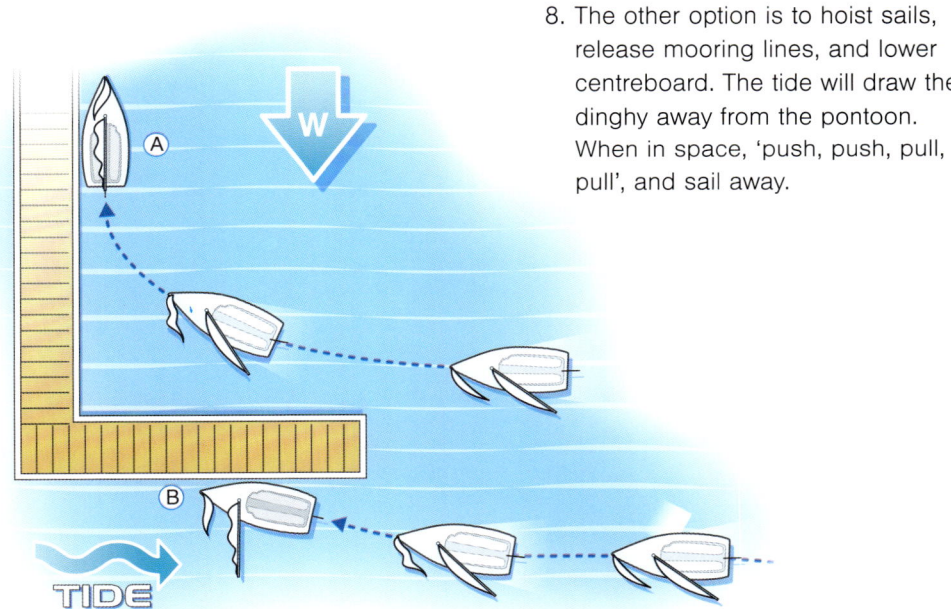

Position B: If the approach fails, bear away so that the bow crosses the tidal stream (to port in the illustration), sheet in, and sail away for another attempt.

1. Approach downwind of the pontoon, but on a beam reach. Prepare fenders.
2. When five boat lengths away from the pontoon, luff up onto a close reach.
3. Release jib and continue on a close reach.
4. 'Fill and spill' mainsail to control speed.
5. Balance speed with strength of tide and dinghy will 'ferry glide' towards the pontoon.
6. On arrival, fully sheet out mainsail, raise centreboard, and make fast. Drop sails.
7. To leave, raise sails, cast off, and back jib towards pontoon.
8. Once bow has crossed over the tidal stream, swap jib over, lower centreboard, sheet in sails, and sail away.

Keelboats making fast alongside a jetty:

1. Remember to fit fenders.
2. Bow and stern line.
    a. Figure-of-eight turns.

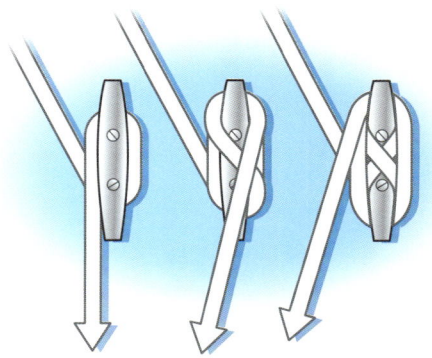

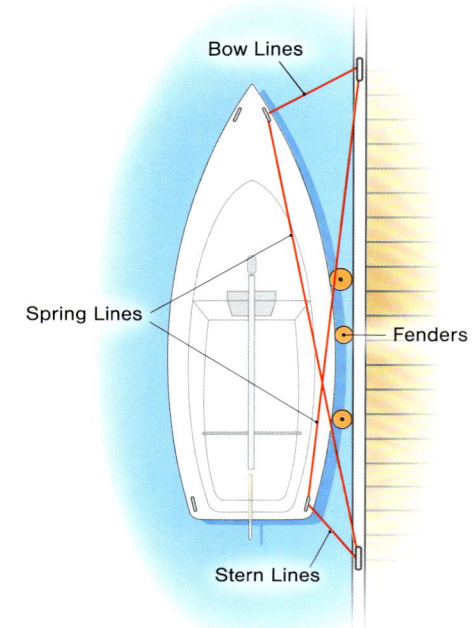

3. Fore and aft spring lines.
- Round turn & two half hitches for securing to mooring-buoy ring.

Session: Man Overboard Recovery (MOB): Dinghy, Keelboat, and Multihull

Aim

The safe approach and recovery of an MOB (upwind approach).

Session Considerations

- Instructor briefing ashore:
    - Background information, why, and how to execute skill
    - Visual explanation and order of technique, including Key Teaching Points
    - Consider a theory session
- Use a suitable dummy (never use a real person)
- Once your students have mastered the basic principles, encourage further practice by introducing the helm who 'falls overboard'. Therefore, when the dummy is dropped over the side, the helm should let go of the tiller and mainsheet, and move out of the way, resulting in the crew having to regain full control of the dinghy
- Outline the aftercare needed for a real casualty

Note: Should an MOB happen for real, the MOB should shout or whistle to gain attention. They should 'float' in the water, remaining as still as possible to reduce rapid loss of body heat.

Teaching Sequence (Dinghy and Keelboat)

Plan:

1. Once dummy has been placed overboard, the crew releases the jib sheet, sits in the middle of the dinghy, and does not assist in any way, as if they had actually gone overboard.
2. Helm regains control, <u>sails away on beam reach</u> for a suitable distance (approximately <u>10–15 boat lengths</u>), and then ensuring they keep watch of the MOB.

Approach:

3. <u>Tack and then immediately bear away</u>, sailing over wake into a downwind position.
4. Remain on a broad reach until it is clear that a return to the MOB on a close reach is possible (boom will point at MOB and/or use flapping jib as a wind indicator).
5. Approach the MOB on a close reach, using 'fill and spill' to control speed. Using the falls will allow this to be done more quickly. When slowing, check for unwanted drift.
6. Slow and <u>stop the dinghy in the lying-to position with the MOB on the windward shroud</u>.
7. Helm then leaves the controls and moves forwards to the windward shroud to recover the MOB.

Flicking the tiller to windward prior to moving will prevent the boat tacking.

Escape: If the approach is unsuccessful, sail away on a beach reach and repeat on the other tack.

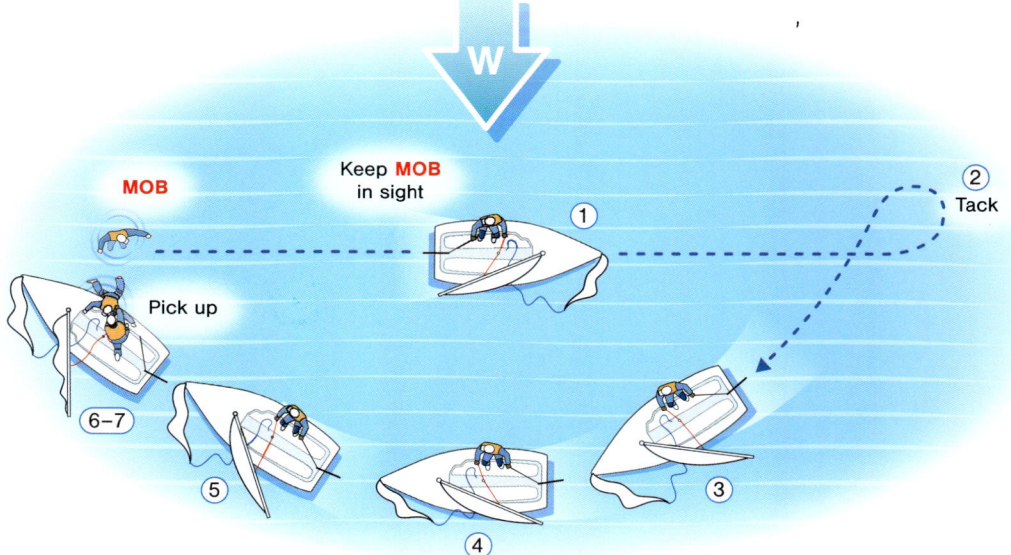

TOP TIP

- After you have tacked and sailed downwind, point the bow towards the MOB to assess when to turn on to a close-reach course ('poke and hope')
- Outline aftercare needed for a real casualty, including for cold-water shock

Man Overboard: Keelboats

Small keelboats should use the dinghy method of recovering an MOB. However, if fitted with an engine it should be ready for use if necessary. However, the keelboat will then become a powerboat, so the appropriate protocol for powerboat MOB should be observed.

Man Overboard: Multihull

Note the use of a gybe instead of a tack.

Plan:

1. The remaining member of crew regains control, releases the jib, then <u>sails away on a beam reach</u> for a suitable distance (approximately <u>15 boat lengths</u>). Ensure that the MOB is kept in view.

Approach:

2. Gybe the boat.
3. Remain on a broad reach until it is clear that a return to the MOB on a close reach is possible.
4. Approach on a <u>close-reach</u> course.
5. When one–two boat lengths from the MOB, helm luffs hard into wind, with the MOB between the hulls. The combination of the windage on the multihull and the braking effect from the rudders fully over will stop the multihull quickly.
6. Helm moves forward, ready to bring the MOB aboard over the forward crossbeam.

Escape: If unsuccessful, sail away on a beach reach and repeat on the other tack.

TOP TIP

Sailing head to wind, placing the rudders fully over will stop the boat quickly.

Session: Anchoring (Dinghy, Keelboat, or Multihull)

Aim
To rig, set, and recover an anchor.

Session Considerations
Instructor briefing providing background information and on-water drill explanation.

Instructor demonstration and briefing ashore (using PAME):

- Type of anchor and selection of suitable anchorage
- Nature of seabed
- Shelter
- Depth (changes with tide)
- Length of warp
- Swinging area

Teaching Sequence
Plan:

1. Rig and ensure that the bitter end is attached to the dinghy and stowed securely.
2. Ensure warp is fed through a bow fairlead (crew).

Approach:

3. Approach on close reach or against tidal stream.

Manoeuvre:

4. Prepare anchor and line.
- Drop jib (wind and tide together)
- As dinghy stops, carefully lower the anchor. Do not throw.
- Pay out warp as boat drifts backwards, assess the length/depth.
- 'Snub' the anchor by making a quick 'pull' on the warp and secure warp round a strongpoint
- Check anchor is holding by using transits
- When holding, stow sails, remove rudder, and lift centreboard

5. Recover anchor:

- Prepare dinghy by hoisting the mainsail and refitting rudder, but leave centreboard raised
- Crew recovers anchor and stows it securely
- Crew hoists jib, helm sheets in mainsail, and dinghy sails away

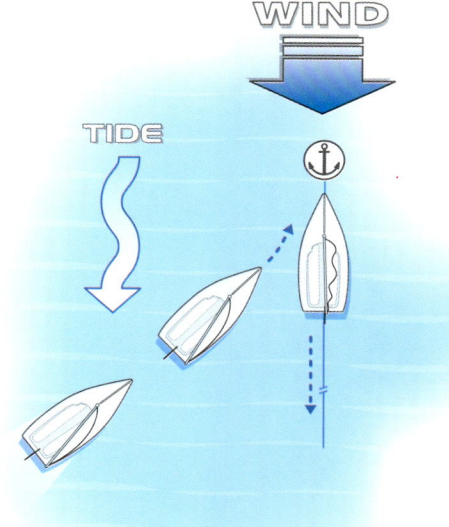

Escape:
- If anchor is dragging, hoist sails, recover anchor, sail away, return and retry process

Wind against tide (drop mainsail):
- If confident of being able to sail against the tide with jib only, sail upwind into a safe area, prepare the anchor and line, and then drop the mainsail (1)
- Using jib only, sail downwind and uptide towards the anchoring spot
- Sail 'beyond' the desired anchoring site, then stop the dinghy
- Lower the anchor carefully, allowing the dinghy to drift back with the tide
- When over the chosen site, 'snub' the anchor. Check that it is holding by using transits
- If holding, drop sails and raise centreboard. If not, recover anchor, sheet in the jib and reposition.
- To leave, hoist jib, partially lower the centreboard, and recover the anchor
- Sail under jib to a safe spot. Raise the mainsail, and sail away

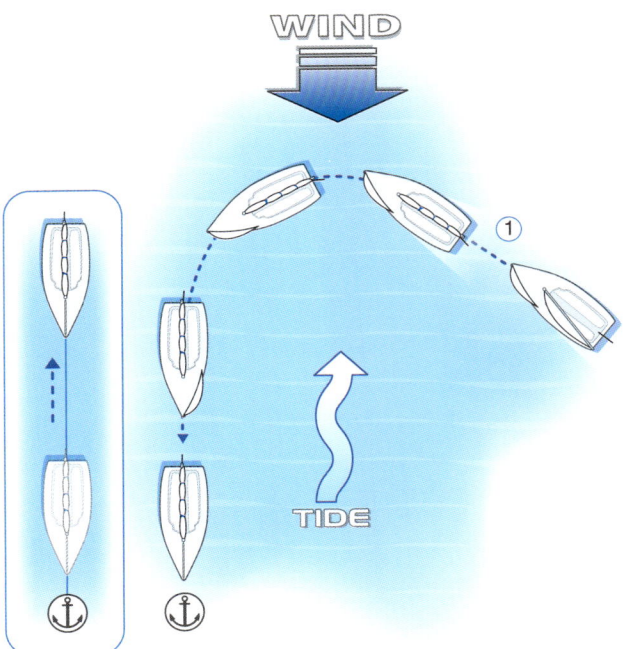

Session: Sailing Without a Centreboard (Dinghy Only)

Aim

To provide the skills and understanding to enable a shallow triangle to be sailed without a centreboard.

Session Considerations

- Instructor briefing ashore
    - A theory session covering background knowledge and understanding, including the Five Essentials (effects of the centreboard)
    - Visual explanation
- Consider laying a shallow triangular course or similar
- Lay a shallow, attainable triangular course for the students

Upwind

From lying to/hove to:

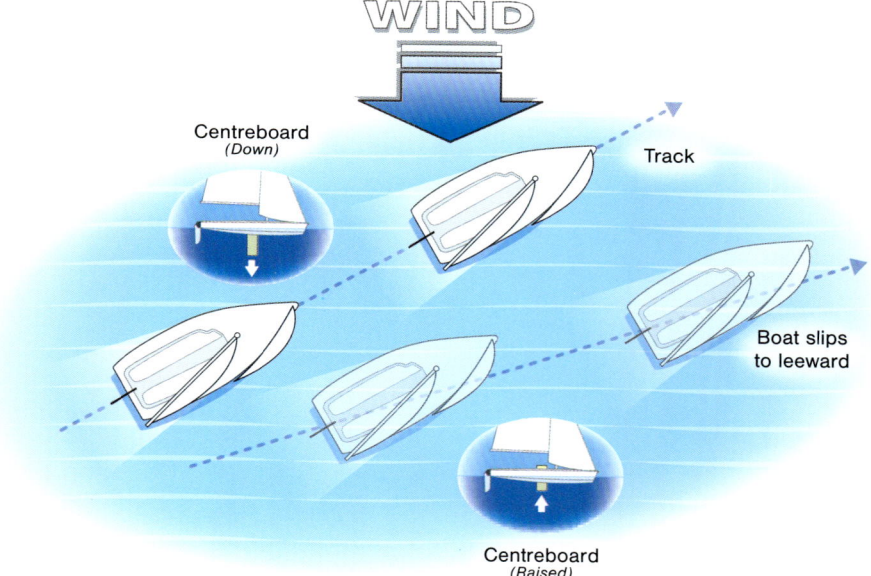

1. Raise centreboard.
2. Helm steers on to close-hauled course.
3. Helm and crew balance the boat and set sails for close hauled.
4. Move helm and crew weight forward to dig in bow. Look at leeway at stern – boat's wake.

Downwind

From the close-hauled course:

1. Helm and crew <u>bear away</u>.
2. Note the remaining Four Essentials.
3. Helm and crew <u>balance the boat</u> and <u>set sails for a broad reach</u>.

Tacking and Gybing

Tacking
Tack as normal – boat will slip sideways and may stop head to wind in no-go zone.

Gybing
Gybe as normal – there will be no significant difference to the gybe.

Session: Sailing Backwards

Aim

To provide the knowledge and understanding to sail backwards. This session can be adapted for both single- and double-handed dinghies.

Session Considerations

- Instructor briefing ashore:
    - Background information (why and how)
    - Visual explanation and order of drill and technique
- Consider laying marks to aid aiming and stopping
- Ensure the chosen sailing area allows sufficient space between boats
- Consider alternate exercises or holding areas if required

Teaching Sequence

1. Sail the dinghy 'head to wind'. Release jib. Helm pulls through the spare mainsheet, providing 'slack'.
2. Crew raises centreboard halfway and sits forward.
3. When completely stationary, crew 'pulls' boom fully towards them (to the shroud).
4. Helm also sits forward towards the bow, beside the thwart (lifting the transom).
5. Helm briefly steers tiller away from the boom (small angle only).
6. As dinghy gathers sternway, causing flow around the rudder, helm steers (with small amounts only) directly downwind.
7. Helm and crew continue communicating, especially regarding pressure on the mainsail.
8. To stop, helm deliberately points the tiller towards the boom (45 degrees only).
9. This will cause the dinghy to turn across the wind. Crew releases the boom, which remains outside the dinghy.
10. Helm and crew sheet in and sail away.

TOP TIPS

- Boat must be stopped head to wind
- Small rudder movements
- Crew sits forward to trim bow down, increasing directional stability
- Consider coming alongside safety boat. Instructor can help them to start sailing backwards (it also brings in and consolidates 'coming alongside')
- Consider reefing, reminding both crew to remain seated. Remind crew that if the pressure on the mainsail is too much to warn the helm before releasing the boom

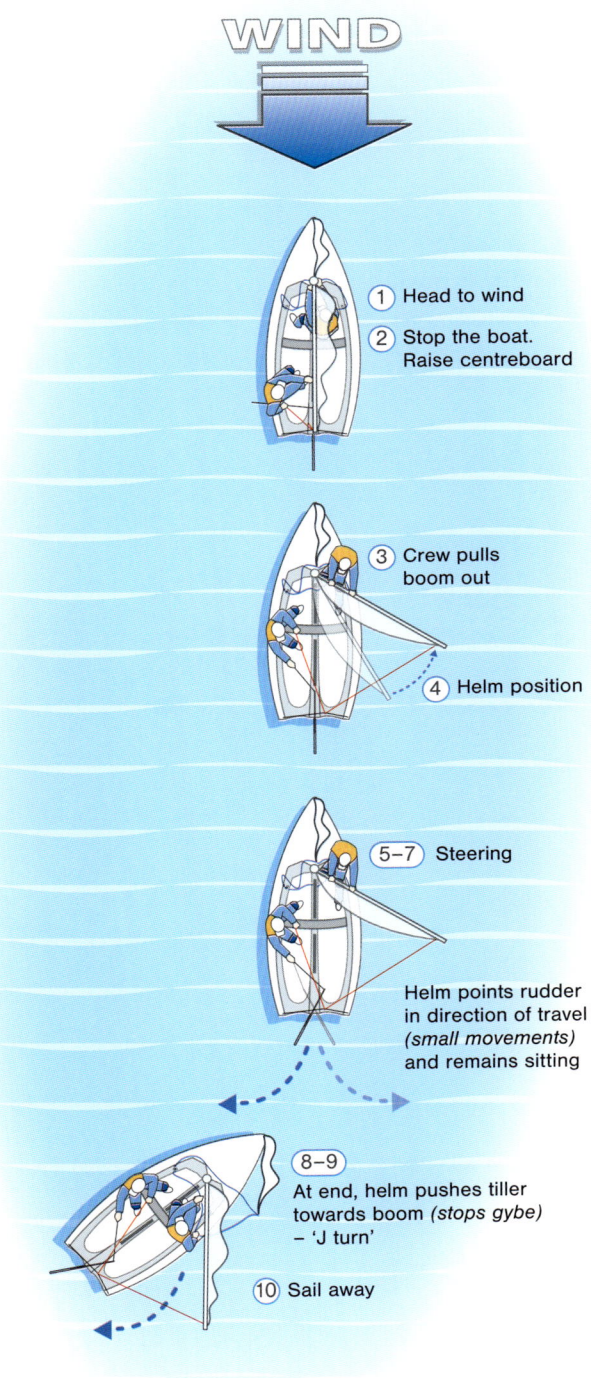

Session: Sailing Rudderless

Aim

To provide the skills, knowledge, and understanding to sail a triangular course rudderless using the Five Essentials and all the boat's equipment.

Session Considerations

- Instructor briefing ashore. Provide a theory session to ensure knowledge and understanding, and focus on each of the Five Essentials
- Demonstration by Instructor, if necessary
- Consider using bungee to hold the rudder in centreline
- Consider size of course required and ensure that avoiding collisions is covered
- Initially reef mainsail and reduce the number of 'falls' in the mainsheet
- It is suggested to have only one dinghy in the fleet sailing rudderless at a time, or set separate courses
- Set a different task for the remaining dinghies – perhaps centreboardless

Reaching

From lying to, sails flapping:

1. Raise the centreboard halfway.
2. Set crew weight, sheet in, and set jib. Boat will start to sail.
3. Helm sets weight and plays main, i.e. with the jib set, sheeting in the main more will cause the dinghy to 'luff', and easing the main will cause it to 'bear-away'.

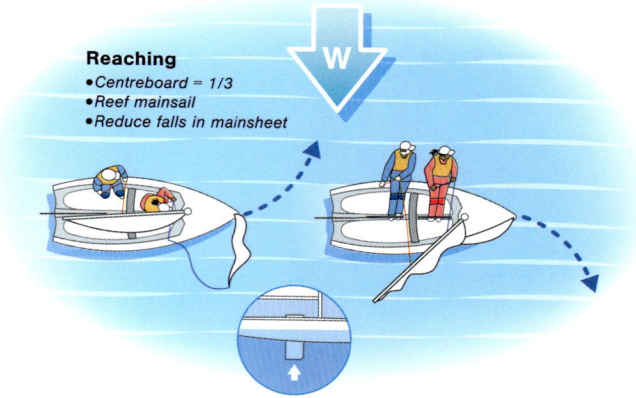

Reaching
- Centreboard = 1/3
- Reef mainsail
- Reduce falls in mainsheet

Steering: Luffing Up

1. From a reach (as above), crew balances dinghy and only moves if requested to by the helm.
2. Helm briefly leans in to leeward to encourage a leeward heel, and smoothly sheets in the mainsail.
3. As dinghy luffs, and just before arriving on the correct course, helm sits out to flatten the dinghy, causing it to steer a straight course.
4. Helm fine-tunes course by trimming the main appropriately (see above).

Steering: Bearing Away

1. From a reach, helm eases the main and leans to windward.
2. Crew can move to windward to assist bear away, and keeps jib cleated.
3. Helm continues to lean out.
4. As boat turns downwind, the helm and crew balance the boat.
5. Main and jib are fully eased and now dinghy can be steered by using helm's weight, i.e. weight to windward, dinghy bears away; weight to leeward, dinghy luffs up.

Tacking

Sailing on a close-hauled course:

1. Ensure effective communication between helm and crew.
2. Helm checks to windward and usual tacking communication is exchanged.
3. Helm leans in to leeward while fully sheeting in mainsail
4. As dinghy turns towards the wind, crew fully sheets in the jib.
5. As dinghy passes though 'head to wind', the crew briefly 'backs' the jib to ensure the dinghy completes the tack.
6. At the same time, the helm eases the mainsheet to allow the dinghy to bear away.
7. Helm and crew retrim sails for the required point of sail, and sail away.

Gybing

Sailing downwind on a training run:

1. Ensure effective communication between helm and crew.
2. From a training run, helm checks to leeward and usual gybing communication is exchanged.
3. With weight forward (near thwart) to assist the turn, helm bears away by heeling boat to windward.
4. As dinghy passes a dead run, helm swiftly gybes the mainsail using the falls. Crew sheets jib to the other side.
5. As the boom passes the centreline, helm swiftly moves to the 'new' windward position to prevent the dinghy from luffing up.
6. Helm and crew set sails for the new training run and sail away.
7. Development – as skill levels improve, helm/crew can shake out the reefed mainsail and raise/lower the centreboard by one-third/two thirds.

Teaching Day Sailing

Session: Day Sailing

Aim

To plan, organise, and execute a short day sail.

Taking students on a day sail (dinghy, multihull, or keelboat) can be a really enjoyable and fun way to consolidate the skills and techniques they have learnt. A day sail provides an exercise which takes them away from the sailing area they have been used to, making students think about other considerations and hazards, and also how they are utilising the skills they have learnt to go somewhere fun and exciting!

One day of a Day Sailing course should be spent undertaking a day passage, ensuring all students are involved in the pilotage. The Senior Instructor, or Instructor, is responsible for the safety of the whole group and should not hesitate to change or abandon the plan if weather or other circumstances dictate.

> **TOP TIP**
>
> G12 RYA Advanced Sailing provides a comprehensive guide to delivering the Day Sailing course. If a student wants some additional learning, they can do the RYA Essential Navigation & Seamanship course.

Planning and Pilotage

Pilotage is usually a visual exercise rather than sailing for long distances on a compass bearing. From a known position, with the aid of a chart and compass it should be possible to identify where to go next.

- Use laminated charts and a chinagraph pencil
- Create a passage plan on a separate sheet or RYA Wet Notes (easier to look at than a chart)
- Create an expedition sheet, including number of participants and other relevant information. Give a copy of the sheet to a contact ashore
- Consider informing the coastguard and/or harbour master
- Confirm position or alter course through known positions, e.g. buoys

Teaching Sequence

1. Pre-planning:
    a. Safety: VHF, flares (coastal), mobile phone (other, depending on area).
    b. Equipment.
    c. Tidal information (if coastal), including high/low water, BST correction, springs and neaps.
    d. Weather information. This will dictate the route (non-coastal passage).
2. Essential information/equipment:
    a. Obtain once you have chosen a direction (by tide or weather).
    b. Equipment:
        i. Almanac, charts (up to date), etc.
        ii. Tidal information, detailed weather forecast.
        iii. Safety plan: safe havens along the route and safety network, VHF, local telephone numbers, and hazards.
3. Pilotage plan:
    a. Predict weather and tidal conditions.
    b. Predict length of passage including any tidal factors.
    c. Predict any tidal gates or hazards along the passage.
    d. Have a plan B, including alternatives to get ashore and plan for safe havens.
    e. Create passage plan – pilotage, use pictures, compass bearings, and transits.
    f. Check all details and double check Speed Over Ground (SOG) and Course Over Ground (COG), and leeway – finalise passage plan.
4. Equipment for the passage:
    a. Ensure all safety equipment is loaded and easy to access.
    b. Ensure all other items are waterproofed and fixed into the boat.
    c. Leave passage plan with someone ashore and agree an emergency plan.
    d. Remember food, drink, and spare clothing.
5. Actual passage:
    a. Follow the plan and if you make changes ensure you let the person ashore know.
    b. Transits for navigation are effective for course to steer.
    c. Remember the sea state may change and you should always keep an eye on the weather.
    d. Ensure you reef early in strong winds or sail to a safe haven promptly.
6. Emergency considerations:
    a. If there are problems, abort and sail to safe havens, and inform the person ashore.
    b. In an emergency situation, use VHF to call emergency services.

Teaching Performance Sailing

Session: Asymmetrical Spinnaker

Aim

Provide the knowledge and understanding to rig an asymmetric spinnaker; hoist, drop, set, and gybe in various wind conditions, and additional actions required to recover from a capsize.

Session Considerations

- Instructor briefing ashore.
    - Provide a theory session, including rigging and the zones for hoist, power, and drop
    - Instructor to provide an explanation and land drill
- Course Made Good (CMG) v. Velocity Made Good (VMG)
- Consider land drills ashore
- Consider size and shape of course required for effective spinnaker sessions (windward/leeward)
- Introduce the RYA 'Power' diagram to assist student understanding. (Refer to G12 for spinnaker work and the Power Zone)

Asymmetric Spinnaker Hoisting

Hoist

1. <u>Helm bears away into hoist/drop zone</u>, stays on windward side, and concentrates on keeping the boat flat and on course. Calls 'Hoist spinnaker.'
2. <u>Crew sets jib and passes spinnaker sheet to helm, moves into middle of the boat, hoists spinnaker</u> and bowsprit facing forward (some boats have separate systems. If so, deploy bowsprit first).
3. <u>Helm sets spinnaker when hoisted</u>.
4. Crew sits on windward side, <u>takes back spinnaker sheet. Helm luffs to create 'power'</u>.

Power Control

To deal with the additional power that the spinnaker generates in the 'Power Zone', the helm should take the following actions:

- If power increases, and causes heeling to leeward, without helm and crew sheeting out any of the sails, the helm should bear away swiftly to flatten the dinghy. It should be a positive and committed action
- If power decreases and causes heeling to windward, the helm should luff up to keep the boat flat

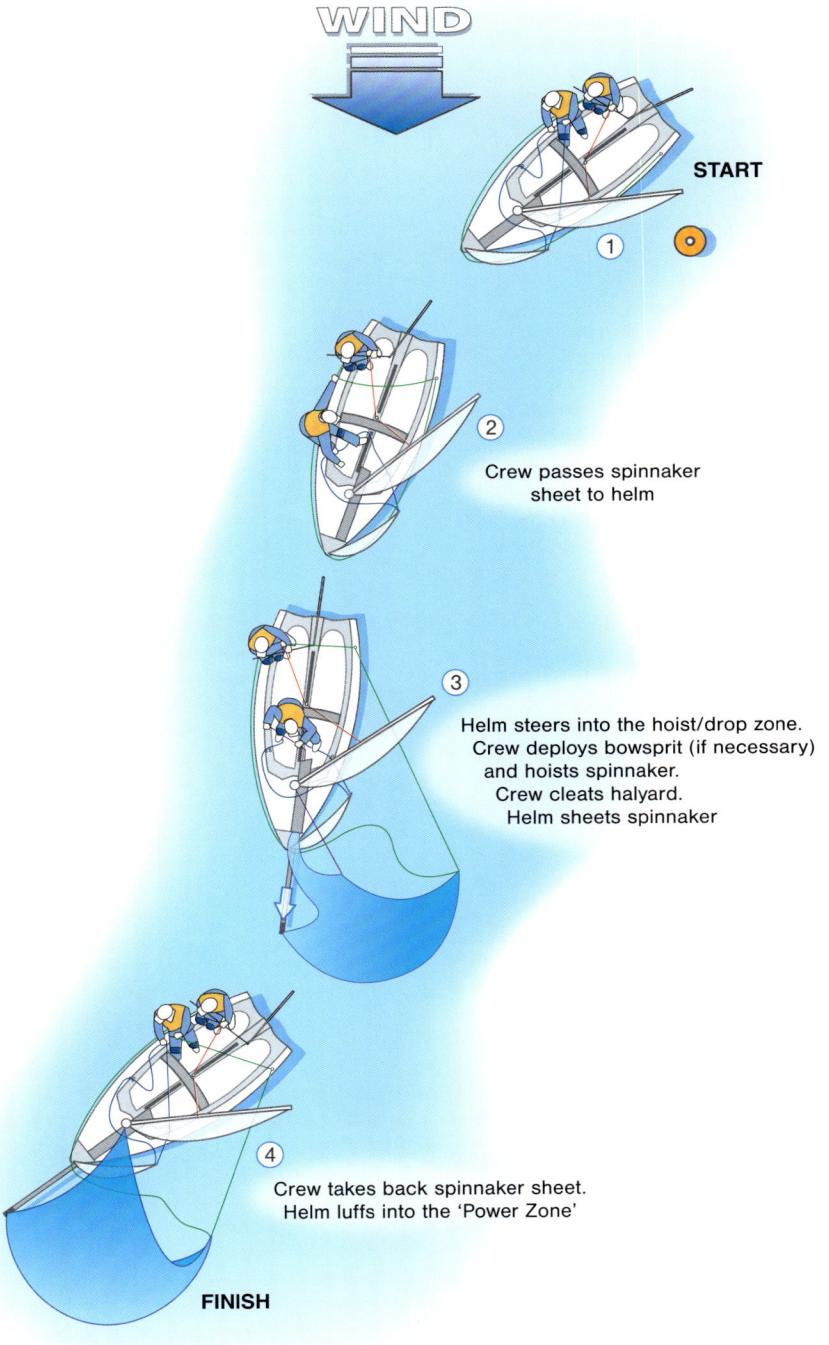

Asymmetric Spinnaker Drop

Teaching Sequence

1. Helm bears away in the hoist/drop zone (training run) and takes spinnaker sheet from crew, and continues to trim it.
2. Crew moves into the boat and takes slack out of retrieval line (depowers spinnaker).
3. Helm calls 'Drop spinnaker.' Crew uncleats halyard (if there is a separate pole system, uncleat this too) and drops spinnaker as helm steers to keep the hull under the mast.
4. Helm steers new course, crew balances boat and sets jib.

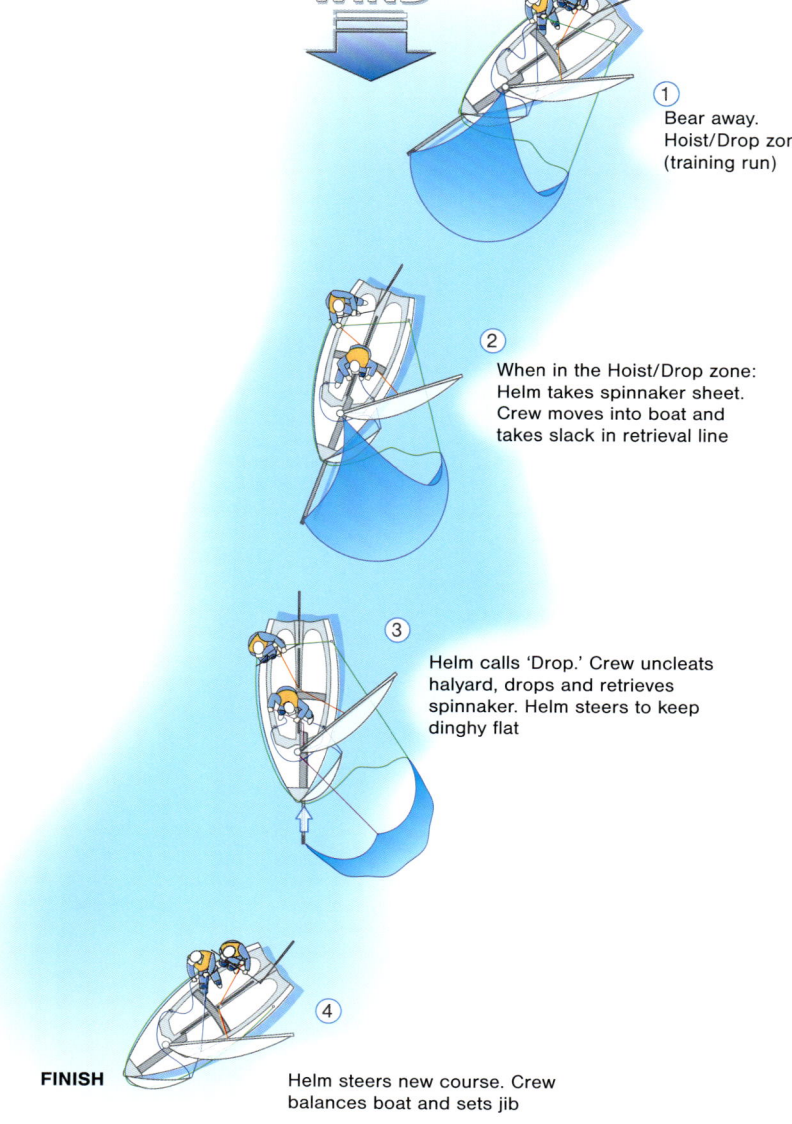

Asymmetric Spinnaker Gybing
Teaching Sequence
1. Helm bears away into the hoist/drop zone, calls 'Stand-by to gybe,' and continues to concentrate on steering accurately. Crew takes up slack in new spinnaker and jib sheet.
2. <u>Crew eases weight inboard</u> and keeps spinnaker set.
3. <u>Helm calls 'Gybe oh' and gybes</u>. Crew crosses the boat, pulls on old spinnaker sheet to flatten spinnaker across jib.
4. <u>Crew</u> moves, <u>pulls in on new sheet, releases old sheet</u>. As spinnaker fills, crew <u>eases then sets spinnaker, balances the boat</u>, then sets jib.

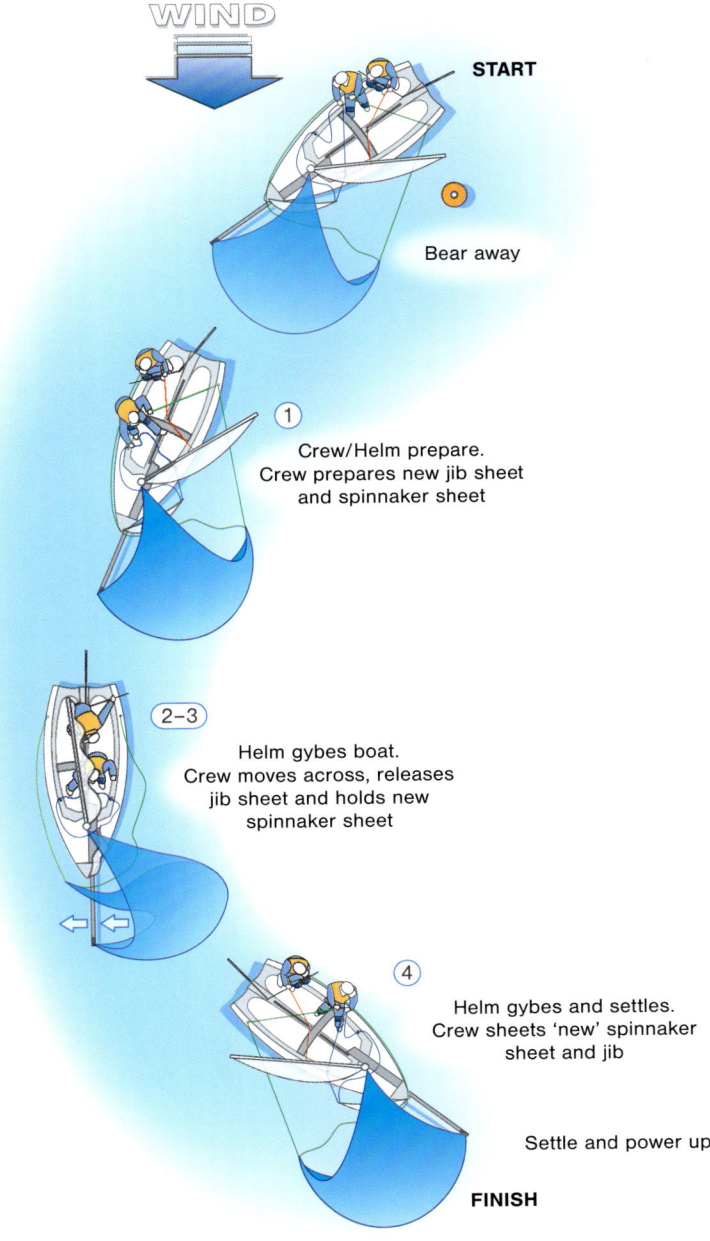

'M' Gybing

An 'M' gybe reduces the loads on the rig/sheets after the gybe, reducing the chance of capsize.

1. Helm and crew gybe the dinghy and sails as described on page 147.
2. Instead of luffing, the helm immediately bears away into the 'hoist/drop' zone again.
3. This provides the crew with the time and opportunity to set the spinnaker and jib on the new side.
4. When ready, and after communicating, helm luffs to seek 'power'.

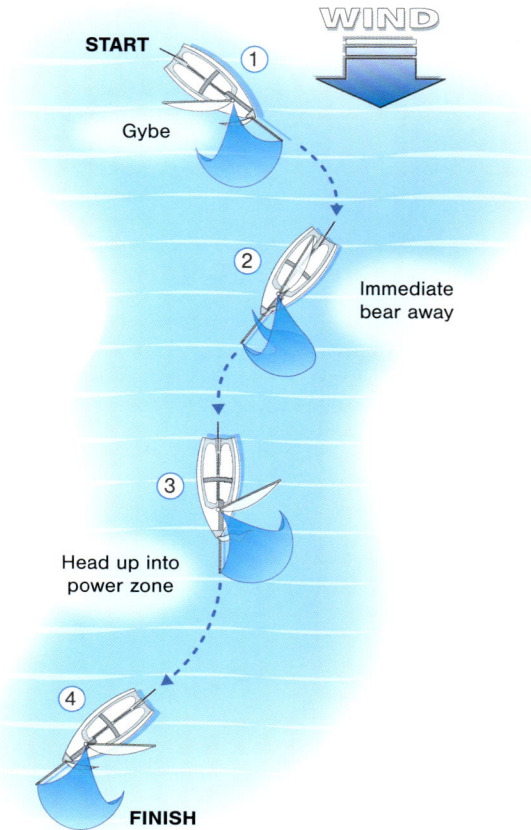

TOP TIP

Asymmetric spinnaker essentials for helm and crew:

- Communication between the helm and crew is essential for *all* sessions
- Centreboard remains down on *all* points of sail
- Crew informs helm of the pressure they are feeling on the spinnaker sheet and whether it is increasing or decreasing. This gives advance warning of what steering action might be needed

Asymmetric Spinnaker Capsize Recovery

1. Helm and crew check both are okay, especially if wearing a trapeze harness.
2. Helm swims to centreboard to stop inversion. Crew swims to spinnaker halyard.
3. Crew releases halyard and recovers spinnaker.

Then follow capsize recovery in previous session.

Session: Symmetrical Spinnaker

Aim

To rig a symmetric spinnaker, to be able to hoist and drop to windward and leeward, and set and gybe in various wind conditions. Set pole height and angle to the wind.

Session Considerations

- Instructor briefing ashore. Dependent on experience, consider a theory session. Introduce and explain Course Made Good (CMG) v. Velocity Made Good (VMG)
- Zones for hoist and drop
- Consider land drills for each technique
- Consider size of course required and courses for effective spinnaker session (windward/leeward or shallow triangle for gybing)
- Refer to G12 RYA Advanced Sailing Handbook for further information on symmetric spinnakers and the 'Power Zone'

Symmetric Spinnaker Hoisting

Leeward Hoist

Fit pole first – launch spinnaker – set spinnaker.

1. Helm bears away onto a run and cleats mainsheet.
2. Helm steers with the tiller between their legs and picks up spinnaker halyard.
3. Crew fits spinnaker guy to outboard end of pole, hook up.
4. Crew fits pole-height control, then fits inboard end of pole to mast, hook up, and pushes pole forwards.
5. Crew holds spinnaker sheets and informs helm, 'Ready to hoist.'
6. Helm calls 'Hoisting' and does so, using two hands for speed.
7. Crew sits to windward, fits guy into reaching cleat, and trims spinnaker.
8. Pole height can now be adjusted (if necessary).
9. Helm takes tiller extension, sits to balance boat, and steers correct course.

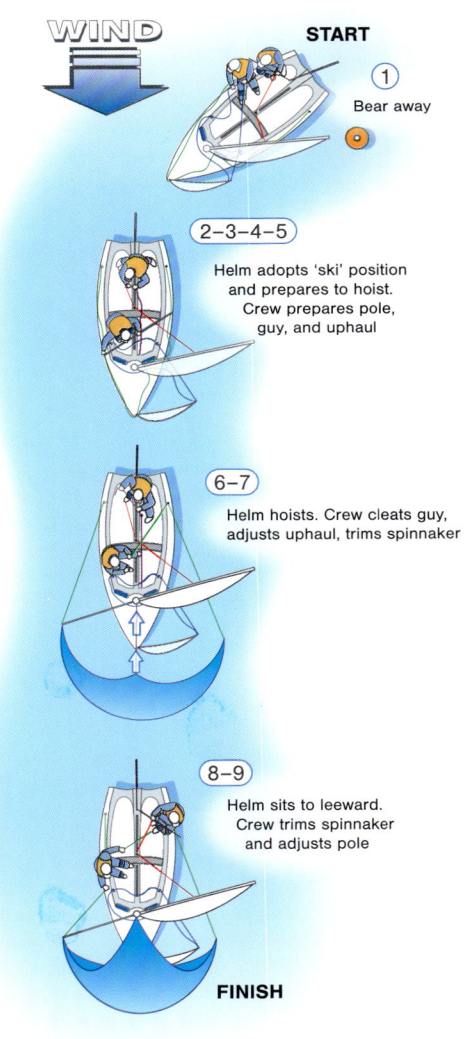

Windward Hoist

Manoeuvre:

Launch spinnaker, fit pole, and set spinnaker.

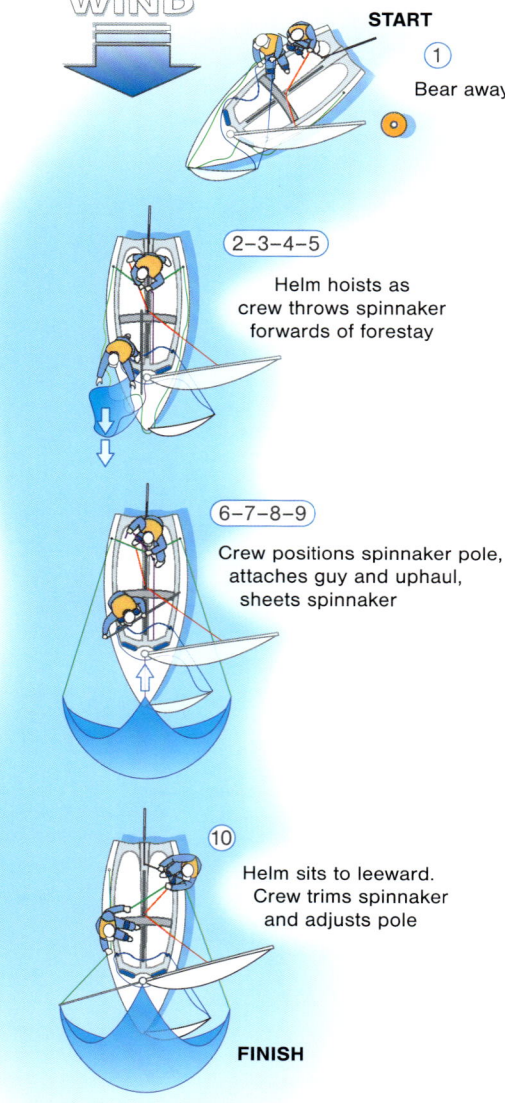

1. Helm bears away onto a run and cleats mainsheet.
2. Helm steers with tiller between their legs and picks up halyard.
3. Crew prepares pole and then gathers up spinnaker into a ball (unless it's in a chute).
4. Crew informs helm 'Ready for hoist.'
5. Helm responds 'Hoisting.' Crew throws spinnaker forwards, up, and to windward of jib luff.
6. Crew attaches pole-height control.
7. Crew fits inboard end of pole to mast (hook up). Helm assists by trimming spinnaker using sheet and guy.
8. Crew takes both lines and sits to windward. Helm takes back tiller extension and mainsheet, then sits to balance the dinghy.
9. Crew puts guy in reaching cleat and trims spinnaker. Pole height can now be adjusted (if necessary).
10. Helm steers best course and balances dinghy. Crew trims spinnaker and jib.

Windward Drop

Remove pole – drop spinnaker – gather under windward jib sheet.

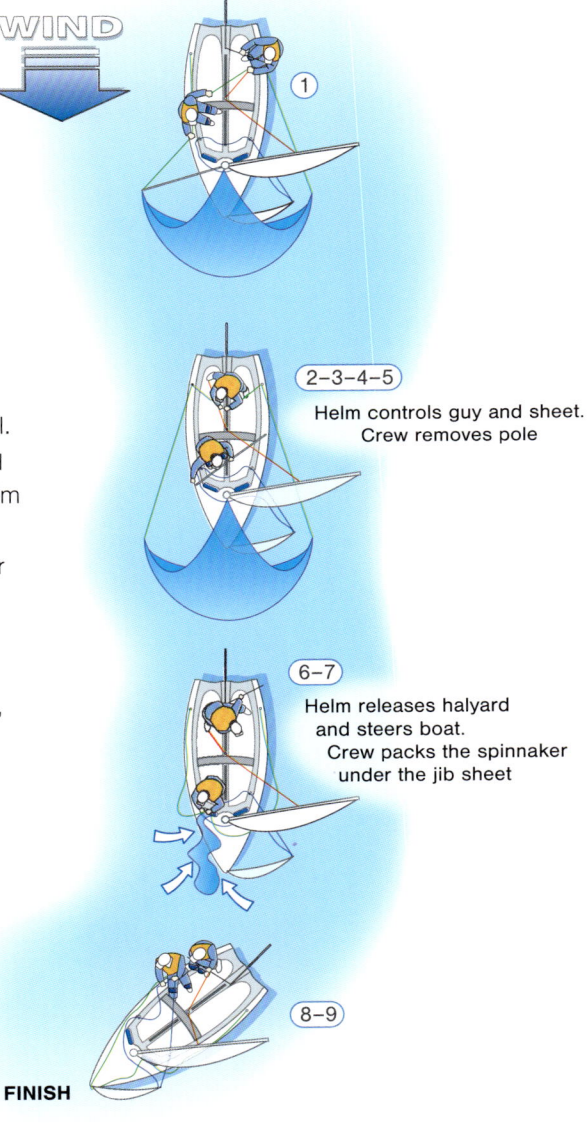

Manoeuvre:

1. Helm bears away onto a run and cleats mainsheet.

2. Helm steers with tiller between their legs and begins to trim the spinnaker using sheet and guy.
3. Crew removes the pole from the mast, and removes height control.
4. Crew removes guy from pole and stows pole away. They inform helm 'Prepare to drop.'
5. Crew begins to retrieve spinnaker by gathering down the leading edge (luff) of the spinnaker.

6. Helm releases spinnaker halyard, but controls the 'drop'.
7. Crew ensures that the windward jib sheet is aft of the windward spinnaker bag, before dropping spinnaker into it.

8. Helm and crew resume their positions on the windward side.
9. Helm and crew sheet in, balance boat, and sail away.

Symmetrical Spinnaker Gybing

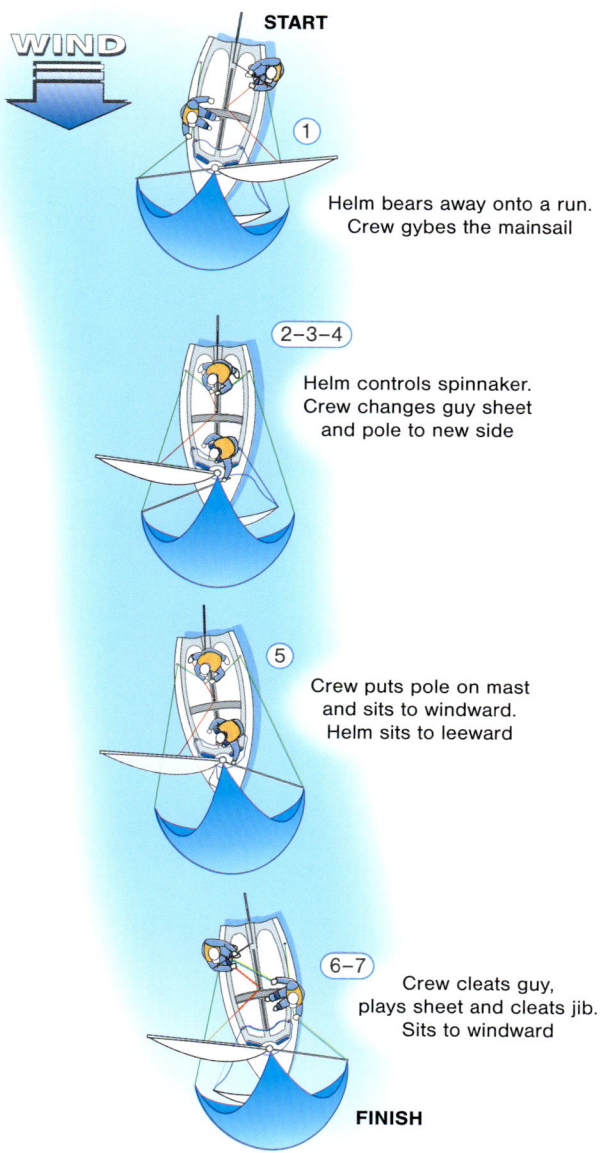

1. Helm bears away onto a run and cleats mainsheet.
2. Helm steers with the tiller between their legs, takes the sheet and guy from crew, and trims the spinnaker. Crew releases guy.
3. Crew gybes the mainsail.
4. Keeping their hands forward of the mast, crew removes pole end from mast and attaches new guy.
5. Crew then feeds the pole forwards and to windward, which allows the old guy to be removed and the pole to be attached to the mast.
6. Crew gybes jib, takes spinnaker sheet from helm, sits on windward side, fits new guy into reaching cleat, and trims spinnaker.
7. Helm and crew balance the dinghy, trim sails and sail away.

> **TOP TIP**
>
> When gybing a spinnaker, steering is key. Aim to follow the spinnaker round and balance the forces acting on the boat.

Adjusting Spinnaker Pole Height and Angle

Height
- Both clews are level
- Pole height should be set so both the spinnaker clews fly at the same height
- Set by using spinnaker pole height control (uphaul/downhaul)
- To check, ease the sheets – the luff should fold in the middle and peel towards the head and foot

Angle
- Ensure the pole is set at right angles to the apparent wind
- Set by using guy

Symmetrical Spinnaker Capsize Recovery

1. Helm and crew check both are okay (especially if wearing trapeze harnesses).
2. Helm swims to centreboard to stop inversion. Crew swims to mast.
3. Crew releases halyard and recovers pole and spinnaker.

Then follow capsize recovery in previous session.

Session: Roll Tack

Aim

To roll tack a double- or single-handed dinghy.

Session Considerations

- Instructor briefing ashore:
    - Background information (why and how)
    - Visual explanation and order of drill and technique
    - Consider a theory session
    - Cover light-wind technique and advanced technique for racing or improved tacking
- Provide a land drill and Instructor demonstration
- Allow students to have several attempts. For double-handed, this should be as both helm and crew

Double-handed Dinghy

Teaching Sequence

1. Helm and crew check area to windward and agree to tack using the recognised communication.
2. Helm (and crew) induce slight leeward heel and sheet in.
3. Helm allows dinghy to luff up, and allows the tiller to move slightly away, taking care not to over-heel or steer.
4. As dinghy passes through 'head to wind', helm and crew use their weight to roll the boat on top of them and ease their respective sheets.
5. When appropriate (usually as the gunwale reaches the surface of the water), having both feet under themselves, helm and crew smartly step up to windward, passing under the boom, sitting on the new side, and rolling the boat flat.
6. As the dinghy flattens, helm and crew 'squeeze' on power with their respective sheets.
7. Helm changes hands on controls and sails away on the new close-hauled course. Helm and crew balance dinghy.

Single-handed Dinghy
Teaching Sequence

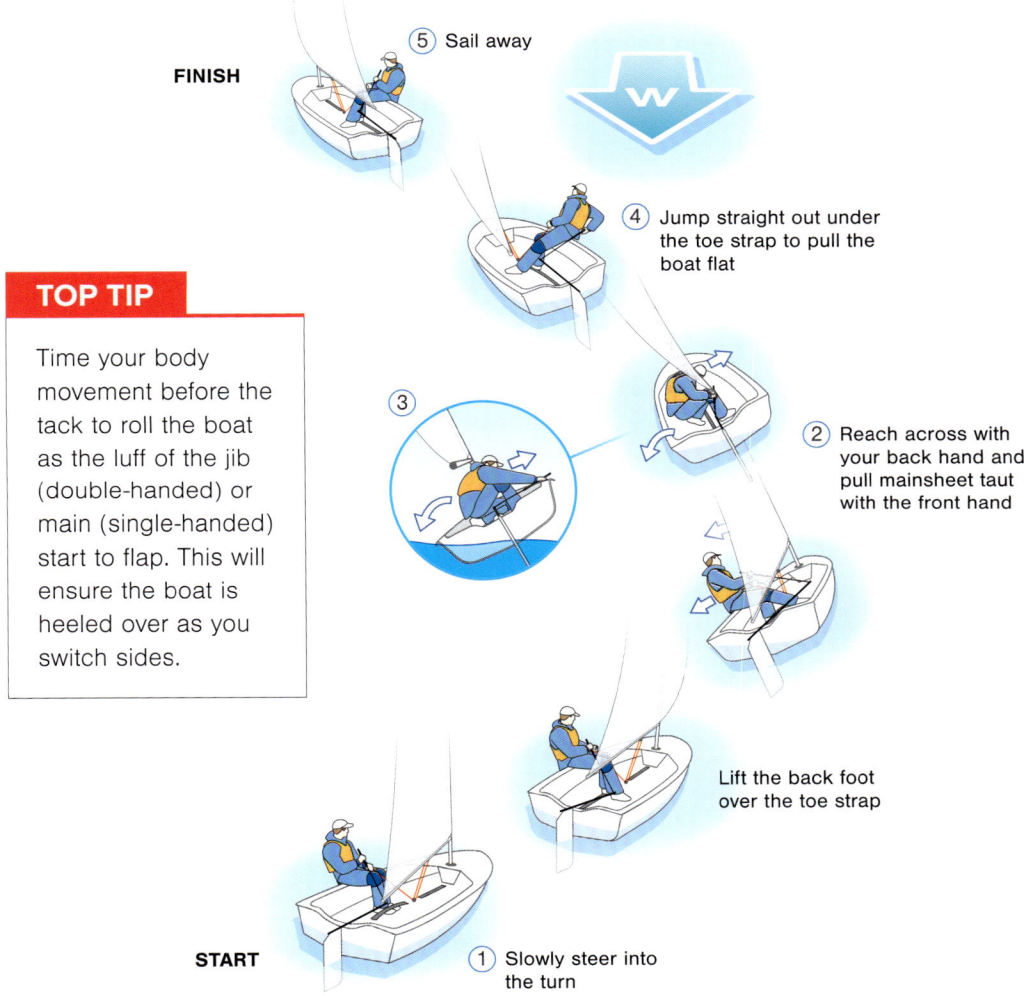

TOP TIP

Time your body movement before the tack to roll the boat as the luff of the jib (double-handed) or main (single-handed) start to flap. This will ensure the boat is heeled over as you switch sides.

1. Helm checks that the area to windward is clear.
   Helm causes dinghy to heel slightly to leeward by gently leaning in. Helm places the back foot over the toe strap.
2. As the dinghy luffs up, helm allows the tiller to move slightly away and sheets on hard.
3. As dinghy passes through head to wind, the helm uses their weight to heel the boat to windward. Helm eases the mainsheet to the required amount based on pressure in the rig. Dinghy will now be heeled to leeward.
4. When appropriate (usually as gunwale touches the water on the leeward side), helm steps smartly up to windward, resumes seating position on the new side, and hikes out.
5. As the dinghy flattens, helm 'squeezes' on power by sheeting in. Helm flattens dinghy, taking care not to roll the mast past its upright position, and sails away on a close-reach course.

Session: Roll Gybe

Aim

To roll gybe a double- or single-handed dinghy.

Session Considerations

- Instructor briefing ashore:
    - Background information (why and how)
    - Visual explanation and order of drill and technique
    - Consider a theory session
    - Cover light-wind technique and advanced technique for racing or improved gybing
- Provide a land drill and Instructor demonstration
- Allow students to have several attempts. For double-handed, this should be as both helm and crew

Double-handed Dinghy

Teaching Sequence

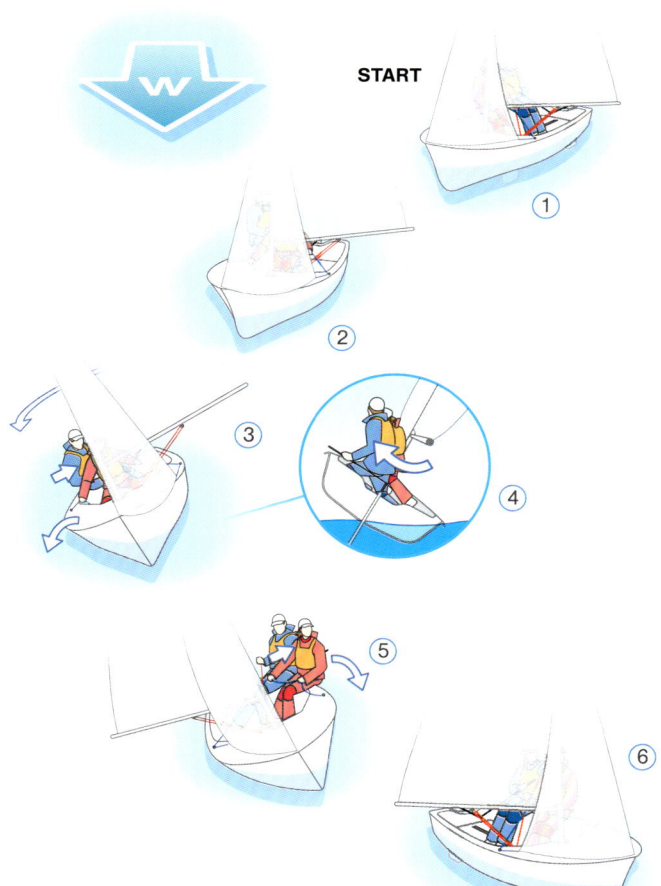

1. Check area to leeward is clear and that the boom is clear of the shroud.
2. Helm and crew heel the dinghy to windward to assist with the bear away. Helm takes the 'falls' with the front hand. Crew may need to assist with the 'heel'.
3. As the clew begins to lift, helm and crew step up smartly and cross the dinghy. They should be nearing the new side before the boom reaches the centreline.
4. Helm centralises the tiller.
5. Helm and crew hike to flatten the dinghy. Helm squeezes in some 'power' with the mainsheet.
6. Helm changes hands on controls and steers on new course. Helm and crew balance dinghy.

Single-handed Dinghy
Teaching Sequence

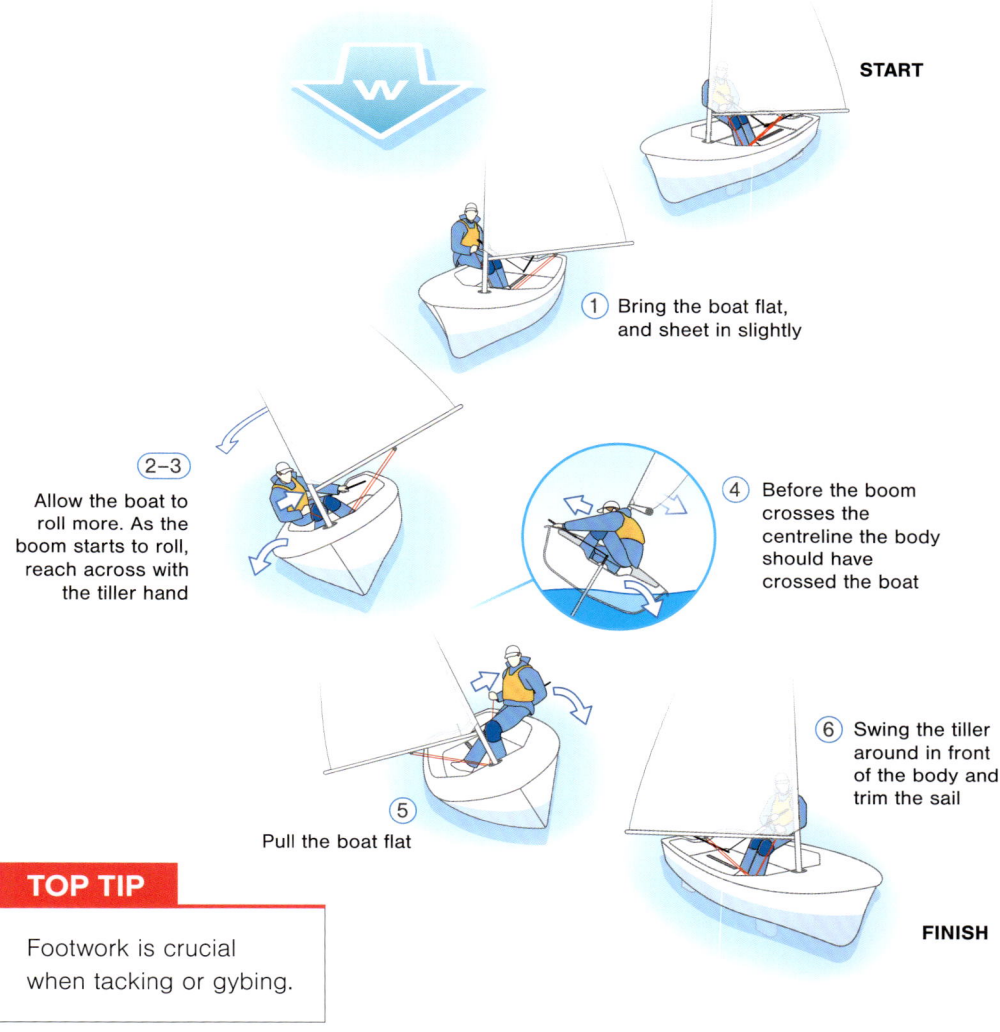

START

① Bring the boat flat, and sheet in slightly

②–③ Allow the boat to roll more. As the boom starts to roll, reach across with the tiller hand

④ Before the boom crosses the centreline the body should have crossed the boat

⑤ Pull the boat flat

⑥ Swing the tiller around in front of the body and trim the sail

FINISH

TOP TIP
Footwork is crucial when tacking or gybing.

1. Check the area is clear and flatten the boat.
2. Roll the boat to windward to assist bearing away. Sheet a few armfuls of mainsheet.
3. Pull one fast armful for mainsheet to gybe the main as the leach starts to lift.
4. Before the boom crosses the centre of the boat, helm must cross the boat swiftly and centralise the tiller.
5. Balance the boat by pulling the boat flat.
6. Sheet the sail and change hands on tiller and sheet.

Multihulls

Roll tacking a multihull is not very effective. However, moving the crew weight to the windward quarter and spinning the boat on the inside hull as the boat enters the no-go zone will make the boat tack more effectively.

Session: Trapezing

Aim
To fit a harness and get 'out' and 'in' on a trapeze line.

Session Considerations
- Instructor briefing ashore:
    - Consider a theory session
    - Provide a land drill ashore. Ensure a good, stable platform is used
    - Wearing the harness (including snug fit, hook facing down, centre of gravity should be near hook) – quick-release options and advantages, mechanics
- Allow students to have several attempts
- Consider fitting masthead flotation in case of entrapment

Teaching Sequence
Getting Out
1. Adjust trapeze wire 'ring' to the correct height (slightly higher than the harness hook,

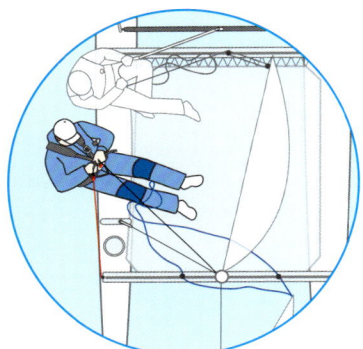

when learning). Grab handle with front hand and hook on with back hand.
2. Commit body weight to trapeze wire

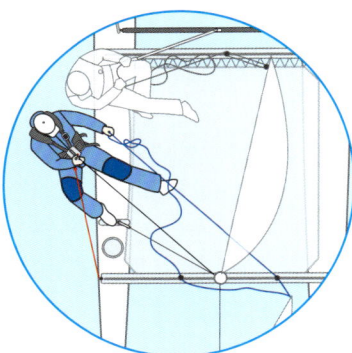

(pressing against the wire with the back hand will ensure that the hook doesn't disconnect from the 'ring') and ease hips out and over the gunwale. Flex front leg, placing foot against the gunwale. Pushing steadily with the front leg, ease body weight outwards until both feet are able to press against the gunwale. Trim jib accordingly.

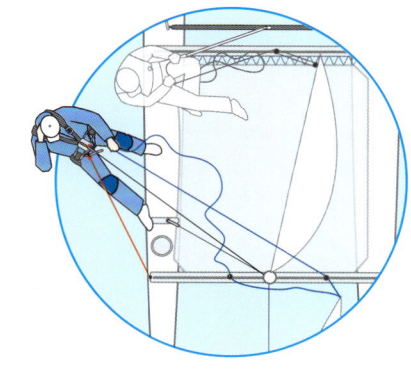

3. Follow with back foot, relax shoulders, place front hand behind head to reduce neck strain, look forward.

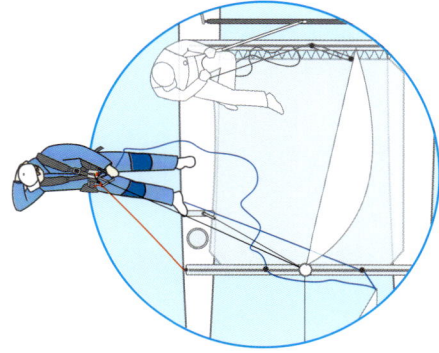

4. Set trapeze height. Front foot facing forward, feet together (if possible).

While on the Trapeze
1. Try to stay 'flat' for maximum leverage (depending on boat design and freeboard).
2. Teamwork is important in gusty conditions. Helm may move inboard to allow crew to stay on trapeze.
3. Communication is key.
4. Trimming downwind may mean crew needs to move backwards and can brace behind the helm.

Getting In
1. Bend the rear leg and hold sheet in rear hand.
2. Bring rear foot inboard, hold trapeze handle with front hand, and unhook using front hand.
3. Depending on length of trapeze, it may be necessary to stand to unhook.

Capsizing
1. If capsizing to windward, it will be very wet:
    a. Priority is to unhook.
    b. Move to the back of the boat.
2. If capsizing to leeward, try to unhook and either:
    a. Lower yourself into the water.
    b. Try to step over the gunwale onto the centreboard (dry capsize).
3. As soon as you are capsized, the priority is to unhook.
4. Carry out method capsize recovery.

Trapeze Harnesses
- A good harness should fit snugly and offer minimal opportunities for snagging
- The hook should be near your centre of gravity, with the hook facing down
- Some people wear a rash vest over the harness to reduce snagging
- To reduce the risk of entrapment there are a number of quick-release harnesses

BACKGROUND KNOWLEDGE & INFORMATION

RYA Organisations

RYA Training Centres

RYA Recognised Training Centres can issue RYA certificates in the disciplines for which they have been approved. These centres fall into three main categories:

- Sailing centres open to the public
- Sailing clubs providing tuition for their members and prospective members
- Organisations such as local education authorities, Scouts, and HM Services teaching their own groups or members

RYA Training Centre recognition is vested in the Principal. They are responsible for issuing RYA certificates and ensuring that the requirements of RYA recognition are maintained at all times.

Guidelines for the recognition of RYA Training Centres are available in a separate document on the RYA Training Support Site www.rya.org.uk/training-support.

RYA Affiliated Clubs

Affiliated clubs have been at the very heart of the RYA since its foundation in 1875 and a large part of RYA work is still devoted to their promotion and protection. Any club with an RYA-specified boating interest may apply to the RYA for affiliation, namely:

- Windsurfing
- Dinghy sailing (cruising and racing)
- Yacht sailing (cruising and racing)
- Motor cruising
- Sportsboats and RIBs
- Personal watercraft
- Inland waterways

RYA OnBoard

OnBoard is the RYA's grass roots programme for junior sailing and windsurfing. Its aim is to promote safe, fun, and equal access to sailing and windsurfing for anyone aged eight to 18 through structured and progressive sessions.

OnBoard is co-ordinated by the RYA and delivered across the UK by RYA Recognised Training Centres. It is supported by several Instructor resources.

OnBoard works alongside the RYA Youth Sailing and Windsurfing Schemes, operating in both coastal and inland locations. All the equipment to get started is usually provided, so all new participants need to bring is a willingness to learn.

Why?

Alongside teaching sailing and windsurfing, OnBoard develops a whole range of life skills. The programme focusses on six key character attributes: teamwork, communication, creativity, determination, confidence, and independence.

The idea of having a growth mindset is integral to the programme and having a positive attitude to learning is also becoming increasingly valued by schools and employers. Instilling a growth mindset into young children will in turn add to their resilience and therefore make them more likely to continue with the sport.

The programme compliments the National Curriculum, and with personal and social development moving to the forefront of education, OnBoard can be a fantastic way to connect with local schools and youth groups.

The inclusion of OnBoard in youth training can improve the experience of young people, develop the Instructor team, promote the sport to a much wider audience, and strengthen the offer from both clubs and centres involved with the programme.

CREATIVITY

Creativity involves having good ideas, dealing with uncertainty, and being able to make links between apparently unconnected things. Creative people have made great discoveries through seeing connections where others have not.

CONFIDENCE

Being confident involves being a can-do person and being able to act independently. We gain more self-belief when we understand that making mistakes is normal, and know that the smart thing to do is to put in extra effort to work hard to improve.

TEAMWORK

Being a team player requires the ability to listen, show kindness to others, and give and receive feedback well. Giving helpful feedback is a difficult skill, but once learned it is very useful in many situations and an essential element of effective teamwork.

COMMUNICATION

Communicating well is very important. A lot of unhappiness comes from accidental misunderstandings or careless explanations. Communication involves learning how to offer opinions. It also includes how to match language to the audience or person receiving the communication.

DETERMINATION

Determination involves coping with difficulty. When we get stuck, we need to have strategies for getting unstuck! Sometimes we also need to know how to bounce back after setbacks, rather than giving up.

INDEPENDENCE

Independence is not just about learning to do things yourself. It's also about knowing how to get the best out of those around you. Becoming independent is a fundamental part of growing up, and includes making decisions and dealing with responsibility.

British Youth Sailing Recognised Clubs

The British Youth Sailing (BYS) Recognised Club programme accredits and supports those clubs that have made a commitment to the development of junior training and racing-club activity.

They are safe and effective places to develop your skills and there will almost certainly be one in your area. Team15 clubs encompass the same values but focuses on the windsurfing rather than dinghy sailing.

The process is run by RYA Performance Managers. All details are listed on the RYA website. A BYS Recognised Club is required to:

- Provide a structured junior race-training programme
- Guide their promising youngsters into the recognised youth classes following their period in a junior class
- Have sufficient numbers of a recognised junior class of boat (member or club owned), equipment, and qualified personnel to achieve the aims of partnership

The Duke of Edinburgh's Award

The RYA is recognised as a National Operating Authority for The Duke of Edinburgh's Award (DofE).

The DofE is a voluntary, non-competitive programme of activities for anyone aged 14–24, giving the opportunity to experience new activities or develop existing skills.

There are three progressive levels of programmes which, when successfully completed, lead to a Bronze, Silver, or Gold Award.

Doing Your DofE

Achieving a DofE Award can be made an adventure from beginning to end. Within an RYA Recognised Training Centre or club there are already many activities young people can take part in which can count towards their DofE:

- **Volunteering:** Helping out at your local training centre, club, OnBoard or Team15 night on a regular basis. This could be as an assistant, in the kitchen, or maybe even on the committee!
- **Physical:** Regularly taking part in sailing or windsurfing activity. Why not set yourself a goal to gain a certain certificate in the RYA National Sailing or Windsurfing Scheme, or maybe participate in regular club racing?
- **Skill:** Develop your skills, whether practical, social, or personal. You may choose to sharpen up your powerboating, learn a new skill such as boat-repair work, become an Instructor, or perhaps increase your theory knowledge and learn all about meteorology!
- **Residential and Expedition:** You may never have been away from home before, let alone used your board or boat to go on an exciting adventure with friends, so now is the time!

Getting Involved as an Instructor, Coach, or Trainer

There is a considerable amount of interaction between the participants and the adults who are supporting them, with specific DofE roles such as Centre Co-ordinators, Leaders, Supervisors, and Assessors.

If you are interested in helping, further information on these roles or opportunities available can be found by visiting the RYA and DofE website.

- DofE website: www.dofe.org
- RYA website: www.rya.org.uk/go/dofe

Duke of Edinburgh Award Timescales

Bronze (14+ years)			
Volunteering	**Physical**	**Skills**	**Expedition**
Three months	Three months	Three months	Plan, train, and undertake a two-day, one-night expedition (At least six hours of planned activity each day)
All participants must undertake a further three months in the Volunteering, Physical, or Skills sections			

Silver (15+ years)			
Volunteering	**Physical**	**Skills**	**Expedition**
Six months	One section for six months and the other section for three months	One section for six months and the other section for three months	Plan, train, and undertake a three-day, two-night expedition (At least seven hours of planned activity each day)
Direct entrants must undertake a further six months in either the Volunteering or the longer of the Physical or Skills sections			

Gold (16+ years)				
Volunteering	**Physical**	**Skills**	**Expedition**	**Residential**
12 months	One section for 12 months and the other section for six months	One section for 12 months and the other section for six months	Plan, train, and undertake a four-day, three-night expedition (At least eight hours of planned activity each day)	Undertake a shared activity in a residential setting away from home for five days and four nights
If you didn't do Silver you must undertake a further six months in either the Volunteering or the longer of the Physical or Skills sections				

General Consideration: Advice and Guidance

Duty of Care

RYA Instructors and Coaches must always remember that they are usually teaching relatively inexperienced sailors, who may not be able to make a sound assessment of the risks inherent in the sport. Instructors, and particularly Senior Instructors, should not hesitate to make prudent decisions in unfavourable conditions to ensure the safety of the students in their care.

Instructor Health Declaration

I understand that in my capacity as an instructor I must be able to effectively deliver the relevant syllabus and to look after the safety of my students.

Accordingly, I confirm that at all times I can:

1. Communicate effectively with students, other water users and the centre, and acknowledge that RYA Training is delivered in English other than at those centres specifically recognised to teach in Mandarin.
2. Recover other craft.
3. Recover a person from the water without assistance.
4. Keep an effective lookout by sight and sound and monitor the safety of vessels and crew within the session.
5. Operate a powerboat independently.

If for any reason, health or otherwise I believe I may require support to fulfil the requirements above I have provided further details below, which the RYA will use to consider what reasonable adjustments may be necessary to enable me to continue to instruct. I acknowledge that adjustments identified on the training course may be taken into account.

I undertake to:

    a. Inform the RYA if my situation in relation to the above requirements changes on a permanent or temporary basis.

    b. Submit a health questionnaire to be reviewed by the RYA doctor, in some circumstances a medical assessment may also be required.

Student Health Declaration

In order to be informed as to any additional risk to students, RYA Recognised Training Centres are strongly advised to include a health declaration in their booking forms. The Principal/Chief Instructor must pass on such information to the individual Instructor responsible for the student.

The declaration should say that the student is, to the best of their knowledge, not suffering from epilepsy, disability, giddy spells, asthma, angina, or another heart condition and is fit to participate in the course. It should be signed and dated by the student and include details of any medical conditions or injuries and medication being taken. If there is doubt as to someone's fitness to take part then medical advice may be sought.

Swimmers

It is recommended that all those participating in the sport of sailing should be able to swim. No minimum level swimming ability is stipulated, but students should be able to demonstrate water confidence.

It is essential that the Instructor in charge of a course knows if any course members are non-swimmers. Non-swimmers may be required to wear life jackets instead of buoyancy aids.

RYA Instructor Code of Conduct

This is for RYA Instructors, Trainers, and Examiners.

The RYA values and respects the very talented people that make up our training network, and views them as important ambassadors of the RYA's brand and values. This document outlines the code of conduct to which all holders of RYA Instructor qualifications and RYA training appointments (hereafter referred to as Instructors) are required to comply. The code of conduct is intended to make clear to all participants, Instructors and RYA appointment holders the high standards to which all are expected to conform. Instructors must:

1. Behave in a manner that is consistent with the values of the RYA, particularly with regards to equality, diversity, inclusivity and sustainability.
2. Respect the rights, dignity and worth of every person and treat everyone equally within the context of their boating activity.
3. Place the wellbeing and safety of the student above the development of performance or delivery of training.
4. Encourage and guide students to accept responsibility for their own behaviour and performance.
5. Only develop relationships with students that are appropriate and legal (especially those under 18), whether face to face or in a digital context. Relationships must be consensual, based on mutual trust and respect and must not exert undue influence to obtain personal benefit or reward.
6. Ensure the activities they direct or advocate are student focused, and appropriate for the age, maturity, experience and ability of the individual. Always clarify with students (and where appropriate their parents or carers) exactly what is expected of them and what they are entitled to expect.
7. Behave appropriately to ensure the safety of Instructors, students and others under your direction.
8. Treat all RYA Instructors, appointment holders, staff and other stakeholders with respect.
9. Act with integrity in all customer and business to business dealings pertaining to RYA training.
10. Read, understand, and comply with the Safeguarding Children and Safeguarding Adults policies and guidelines as detailed on the RYA website at www.rya.org.uk/go/safeguarding.
11. Comply with the laws and regulations of the jurisdiction in which they are operating.

12. Follow all RYA guidance and standards with regards to specific training or coaching programmes.
13. Not do or neglect to do anything which may bring the RYA into disrepute, including through the use of social media.
14. Hold relevant, up to date governing body qualifications as approved by the RYA.
15. Only teach or provide RYA courses or RYA certification within the framework of an RYA Recognised Training Centre.
16. Notify the RYA immediately of any court-imposed sanction that precludes the instructor from contact with specific user groups (for example children or adults at risk) and be aware that certain sanctions may result in the automatic withdrawal of your qualification.
17. Notify RYA Training in the event of any health issues that may affect their ability to carry out their responsibilities, including the use of medication which may impact their role.
18. Not carry out RYA training, examining or coaching activities whilst under the influence of alcohol or drugs.

Failure to adhere to the RYA Instructor Code of Conduct may result in the suspension or withdrawal of RYA qualifications or appointments. Revised February 2023.

Instructor Training Assessment Standards

All RYA Instructors and Trainers are required to treat students and candidates with respect and fairness. They also have a duty of care to their candidates and are obliged to adhere to the RYA Instructor Code of Conduct.

All Instructor assessments in the use of boats and their equipment have implications for the safety of future sailing-scheme participants.

It is therefore essential that Trainers provide thorough assessment following current RYA assessment criteria for Instructor candidates, which results in fairness to candidates and provides assurance of quality to anyone they subsequently teach.

Realistic Aims

In some cases, it becomes clear to the Trainer at an early stage in the assessment process that the candidate has been overly ambitious in the course they have chosen to attend. In such instances the Trainer will discuss the situation with the candidate at the earliest opportunity and agree revised, achievable aims.

Grounds for Appeal

A candidate may have grounds for appeal if they believe:

- They have not been given a reasonable opportunity to demonstrate their competence, or
- The person carrying out the assessment has placed them under undue or unfair pressure, or
- The Trainer has reached the wrong conclusion on the basis of the outcome of the candidate's performance in the assessment

It is essential that all Instructor candidates are assessed on an impartial and objective basis. For this reason, RYA Dinghy Instructor courses are moderated by a second Trainer or, in the case of a Senior Instructor course, continual assessment by two Trainers.

To enable an appeal to move forward it would be necessary for the moderator or second Trainer to support the appeal.

It is crucial that a candidate understands that any appeal must be made on genuine grounds and supported by evidence, not simply on the basis that they have failed to demonstrate the level of competence required to achieve a successful outcome on the course.

The Procedure

The candidate should first raise the concern with the Trainer running the course as soon as possible to see if the matter can be amicably resolved. If it is inappropriate to consult the Trainer, or if there is no amicable solution, then the candidate should appeal in writing to the appropriate RYA Chief Instructor within 20 working days of the assessment.

The letter of appeal should contain the following:

- Full details of the assessment – when, where, involving whom etc.
- The grounds on which the appeal is being made
- Any supporting documentation relating to the assessment – outcome, action plans, reports etc.

On receipt of an appeal, an investigative process will commence, usually led by the RYA Chief Instructor for the relevant training scheme. Following investigation, the candidate will be informed of the outcome.

If the candidate is still unhappy about the decision, their final course of action would be to raise a formal complaint with the RYA Training Committee, outlining in full detail the grounds for their complaint.

RYA Equality Policy

Policy Statement

The Royal Yachting Association is committed to equality of opportunity and aims to ensure that all current and potential participants, members, instructors, coaches, competitors, officials, volunteers, and employees are treated fairly and on an equal basis, regardless of sex, age, disability, race, religion or belief, sexual orientation, pregnancy and maternity, marriage and civil partnership, gender reassignment, or social status.

Objectives

- To ensure boating is accessible and attractive to the widest audience
- To ensure that the RYA's services, including training schemes, are as accessible as possible, including to people with disabilities
- To increase the diversity of our Instructors, Coaches, and race officials
- To identify and promote more role models at all levels from under-represented groups, including women and girls, people with disabilities, people from Black, Asian, and Minority Ethnic backgrounds, and LGBT+ people
- To attract new participants from under-represented groups through targeted initiatives
- To maintain the Advanced level of the Equality Standard for Sport

Implementation

- The RYA encourages its affiliated clubs and organisations, Recognised Training Centres and other stakeholders to adopt similar policies, so that they offer an experience to participants that is friendly, welcoming, and open to all
- Appointments to voluntary or paid positions with the RYA will be made based on an individual's knowledge, skills, and experience and the competencies required for the role
- The RYA will tailor requirements in relation to RYA training schemes which may inhibit the performance of candidates with special needs, provided that the standard, quality, and integrity of schemes and assessments are not compromised
- The RYA will develop further policies for specific subject areas where appropriate (e.g. instructing, race officials)
- The RYA reserves the right to discipline any of its members, qualification holders, appointees, volunteers, or employees who practise any form of discrimination in breach of this policy, in line with the relevant articles, rules, codes of conduct and disciplinary procedures
- The effectiveness of this policy will be monitored and evaluated on an ongoing basis by the RYA Safeguarding & Equality Manager reporting to the RYA Board, the Sports Council Equality group, and related external charters

Avoiding Complaints

The best way to avoid complaints is to deliver training of the highest standard, covering the syllabus while offering excellent customer service.

Many complaints arise from a lack of communication.

After passing a course students often wish to attend further modules. They usually haven't done any practice in between, so may not have the skills to pass.

This should be recognised at the point of booking and appropriate alternatives offered. If not, the Instructor will need to do the adjusting and guiding. Fortunately, due to the scheme being modular, different skills, experience, and abilities can be catered for.

The purpose of the scheme remains to teach sailing and improve people's skills and techniques in a progressive manner. If the module is inappropriate the Instructor should discuss realistic aims and gain agreement using tact and diplomacy.

Struggling students are often relieved by this process, with performance often improving once the stress has been removed.

- Ensure students are kept informed with regular debriefs
- Try to spot 'serial' complainers early
- Counter them by running the course 'by the book'
- Regularly ask them if they are satisfied, would like any further input, and seek agreement
- The Principal or Chief Instructor should also give opportunities for feedback as the course progresses

Helpful Advice

If a student is unhappy and this results in a complaint, any complaints received should be referred to the SI, Chief Instructor, or Principal (in that order).

Begin with *'Thank you for bringing this to our attention. How can we resolve it?'* Often more tuition is all that's required. It can save a lot of correspondence afterwards.

If you do not inform people of their progress you are more likely to receive a complaint along the lines of *'I didn't achieve the certificate because I wasn't taught well.'*

The Instructors who receive the fewest complaints are those who:

- Are competent
- Take an interest in their students
- Ensure that even the difficult or weak students feel they are an important part of the group

The instructional skills required are well beyond those of just sailing or even just teaching.

Manual Handling

Manual handling is any transporting or supporting of a load (including the lifting, putting down, pushing, pulling, carrying, or moving thereof) by hand or bodily force.

As an Instructor it is worth being aware that workplace injuries can affect your life and recreation, as well as your work, particularly in later years. Injuries sustained while sailing can also affect your students.

This includes sudden injuries in the workplace as well as cumulative wear and tear commonly caused by poor positioning over a period of time. Common risks arise from:

- Excessive or awkward loads for one person
- Slippery or uneven surfaces
- Repetition or excessive duration of tasks
- Slipways, jetties, and dragging boats can all give rise to these circumstances.

Studies show that the overwhelming proportion of accidents in the workplace are sprains or strains due to manual handling. Of these, back injuries are three times more common than any other injury.

The Manual Handling Operations Regulations 1992 contain guidance suggesting that manual handling should be included in risk assessments and that employers, employees, and volunteers should take sensible steps to minimise the risks.

Finally, when it comes to moving boats, ensure you have sufficient people to carry out the task safely, e.g. pulling a heavy dinghy up a steep slipway.

TOP TIP

Handling tips for Instructors:

- Widen the base of support while lifting/carrying
- Keep the load inside the base of support whenever possible
- Avoid asymmetry, e.g. carrying a heavy fuel can
- In general before lifting:
  ASSESS: task, load, environment, individual(s)
  PLAN: task, route
  PREPARE: load, self, area

Safeguarding and Child Protection

Introduction

RYA Recognised Training Centres that teach children and young people aged under 18 are required to have a formal safeguarding and child protection policy which is checked as part of their annual inspection.

Your organisation is therefore strongly advised to take the following steps:

- Adopt a policy statement that defines the organisation's commitment to providing a safe environment for children.

- Produce a simple code of practice and procedures governing how the organisation runs.

The RYA publishes guidelines to help clubs, training centres, and Instructors to enable children and vulnerable adults to enjoy the sports of sailing, windsurfing, and powerboating in all their forms in a safe environment. The policy, guidelines, and other best practice guidance can be downloaded from the RYA's website www.rya.org.uk/go/safeguarding and adapted to meet the requirements of your organisation.

The RYA Policy Statement on Safeguarding is as follows:

For England, Wales, and Northern Ireland this policy refers to anyone under the age of 18 as defined by the Children Act 1989 and The Children (Northern Ireland) Order 1995 and anyone aged 18 or over who is an 'Adult at Risk', who is in need of care or support, and who, because of those needs, is unable to always safeguard themselves as defined by the Care Act 2014. For Scotland, the act defines adults at risk as those aged 16 years and over who:

- Are unable to safeguard their own wellbeing, property, rights, or other interests.
- And are at risk of harm.
- And because they are affected by disability, mental disorder, illness, or physical or mental infirmity, are more vulnerable to being harmed than adults who are not so affected.

The RYA is committed to safeguarding all children, young people, and adults at risk taking part in its activities from abuse and harm and ensuring their wellbeing. The RYA recognises that the safety, welfare, and needs of children, young people, and adults at risk are paramount and that any person, irrespective of their age, disability, race, religion or belief, marital status, sex, gender identity, sexual orientation, or social status, has a right to protection from discrimination and abuse.

The RYA takes all reasonable steps to ensure that, through safe recruitment, appropriate operating procedures, and training, it offers a safe and fun environment to children, young people, and adults at risk taking part in RYA events and activities. The RYA recognises that it has a legal responsibility to safeguard children, young people, and adults at risk, including due regard to the need to prevent people from being drawn into extremism and terrorism (the Prevent Duty).

The RYA is committed to minimising risk and supporting venues, programmes, events, and individuals to deliver a safe, positive, and fun boating experience for everyone by creating a welcoming environment, both on and off the water, where everyone can have fun and develop their skills and confidence. The RYA will treat everyone with respect, celebrate their achievements, listen to their views and experiences, and provide opportunities for all to fulfil their potential and be their authentic selves.

Through the RYA training scheme, the RYA is responsible for recognising Training Centres to deliver the RYA Training Scheme, and through its affiliation scheme, for providing advice and guidance for affiliated clubs and class associations. The RYA uses its position to require Recognised Training Centres to adopt and implement appropriate safeguarding policies and procedures and through its affiliation scheme encourages and supports affiliated organisations to do so by providing them with information, guidance and support.

The RYA:

- Recognises that safeguarding of vulnerable groups is the responsibility of everyone, not just those working directly with them.
- Carries out safe recruitment practices when recruiting all RYA employees, contractors and volunteers in roles involving close contact with vulnerable groups.
- Provides comprehensive training and personal development opportunities for all staff and volunteers, irrespective of their position, to ensure that any concerns are reported in a timely manner and to the right person.
- Responds swiftly and appropriately to all complaints and concerns about poor practice or suspected abuse, referring to external agencies as necessary.
- Provides signposting advice and guidance to anyone who needs it.
- Offers basic safeguarding advice and guidance to anyone within the boating community irrespective of if their club or centre is affiliated or recognised and gives full access to the safeguarding pages on the website to anyone wishing to access it.
- Regularly reviews safeguarding procedures and practices in the light of experience or to take account of legislative, social, or technological changes.
- Communicates changes and shares good practice with other NGBs, Recognised Training Centres, affiliates, and class associations.
- Encourages all RYA affiliates and class associations to adopt both a safeguarding children and young people policy and a safeguarding adults at risk policy.
- Ensures that all Recognised Training Centres have an in date Safeguarding and Protecting Children and Young People policy which is in line with the RYA's.
- Strives to achieve the highest level of safeguarding practices in line with the Child Protection in Sport Unit and Ann Craft Trust safeguarding standards and will undertake annual reviews of our policies and procedures to ensure full compliance with the standards.
- Provides mental health and wellbeing support to all staff through the colleagues' wellbeing programme.
- Will cooperate where necessary with multi-agency investigations and enquiries relating to serious case reviews involving children, young people, and adults at risk , if there is an association with the sport.

This policy will be reviewed by the RYA Safeguarding Steering Group annually and by the RYA Board at least every three years, or sooner if there are relevant legislative changes.

If you have a concern, allegation, or complaint please visit www.rya.org.uk/about-us/contact-us/comments-and-complaints.

Safe Recruitment and Criminal Records Disclosure Checks

The RYA is committed to ensuring that only those with the right motivations and suitability are recruited into positions involving regular contact with children, young people and adults at risk within its work and volunteer force. The RYA understands its legal responsibility within the Safeguarding Vulnerable Groups Act 2006, to ensure that all its recruitment practices are safe, fair, and equal and allows it to identify, deter, and reject applicants who may be at risk of abusing vulnerable groups.

The RYA will:

Ensure the best possible staff and volunteers are recruited based on their merits, abilities, and suitability for the position advertised.

Ensure that all applicants are considered equally and consistently, and that no applicant is treated unfairly based on any protected characteristics in compliance with the Equality Act 2010.

Comply with all relevant legislation, recommendations, and guidance including the statutory guidance published by the DfE (Keeping Children Safe in Education, the PREVENT Duty guidance) and any codes of practice published by any of the disclosure service providers used by the RYA (DBS, AccessNI, and PVG).

Meet its commitment to safeguarding and promoting the welfare of children, young people, and adults at risk by carrying out all necessary pre-employment checks.

The RYA uses the following safe recruitment practices when recruiting staff:

- Advertisements will make clear the commitment to safeguarding children, young people and adults at risk.
- Application forms are used which contain questions surrounding employment and academic history and a person's suitability for the role which includes the requirement to explain any gaps or discrepancies in the employment or academic history.
- The application form has a declaration regarding convictions and working with vulnerable groups and will make it clear if the post is exempt from the provisions of the Rehabilitation of Offenders Act 1974.
- CVs only will not be accepted.
- All job descriptions are clear and concise and accurately set out the duties and responsibilities of the job/volunteer role.
- Three references are requested alongside a job offer and a minimum of two must be received and reviewed before the candidate commences their role.
- All offers of employment will be subject to the receipt of a minimum of two references which are considered satisfactory by the RYA.
- Interviews are face-to-face where possible with a minimum of two interviewers and will cover the person's suitability for the role.
- All senior managers, recruiting staff/volunteers and HR personnel will undertake safe recruitment training which is refreshed every three years.
- All applicants invited to attend an interview will supply proof of their ID in the form of original documents and confirm their right to work within the UK.
- Where any position amounts to "regulated activity" an appropriate disclosure check will be carried out which will include the Children's Barred List where appropriate and an original certificate will be seen by the recruiting manager or HR personnel prior to the applicant commencing the role.
- Successful applicants in England and Wales will be encouraged to register with the DBS Update Service.
- Additional checks will be carried out if the applicant has lived or worked outside of the UK (certificate of good conduct, certificate of Sponsorship).

Criminal Records Disclosures

Organisations affiliated to or recognised by the RYA can access the DBS (previously CRB), Access NI, or PVG processes through the RYA which is a registered Umbrella/Intermediary Body. The procedure varies according to the home country and legal jurisdiction in which your organisation is located. Full information is available from the RYA website www.rya.org.uk/go/safeguarding or by contacting the RYA's Safeguarding and Equality Manager at disclosure@rya.org.uk.

Safeguarding Culture and Best Practice

The RYA considers the safeguarding of vulnerable groups to be the highest of priorities and, as such, is dedicated to ensuring that the RYA culture has safeguarding at its heart by incorporating policies, procedures, training, the use of best practice, and acting in accordance with RYA values to ensure that the most vulnerable groups are always protected. The RYA is committed to embedding safeguarding in everything it does, not only protecting vulnerable groups but also protecting its staff, volunteers, and contractors from putting themselves in potentially risky situations. There are many areas where best practice can be adhered to. Additional best practice can be found in the RYA Safeguarding and Protecting Children Policy and Guidelines for Clubs, Centres and Class Associations and the RYA Safeguarding Adults Policy and Guidelines for Clubs, Centres and Class Associations. Both of these policies can be accessed on the RYA website: www.rya.org.uk/about-us/policies/safeguarding.

Responsibilities of Staff and Volunteers

Staff or volunteers should be given clear roles and responsibilities. They should be aware of your organisation's safeguarding policy and procedures and be given guidelines on:

- Following good practice.
- Recognising signs of abuse.
- Reporting any concerns to the appropriate person.

Identifying and Recognising Abuse

Please refer to Appendix A: What is Child Abuse? within the RYA Safeguarding and Protecting Children Policy and Guidelines for Clubs, Centres and Class Associations. Please also refer to Appendix A: What is Abuse? within the RYA Safeguarding Adults Policy and Guidelines for Clubs, Centres and Class Associations. Both of these policies can be accessed on the RYA website: www.rya.org.uk/about-us/policies/safeguarding.

Dealing with a Safeguarding Disclosure and Information Sharing

Being the recipient of a safeguarding disclosure can be incredibly difficult, especially if the recipient is not a Safeguarding Lead. However, choosing not to respond to a disclosure can never happen, regardless of how uncomfortable the recipient is. The referral flowcharts found within the two policies: RYA Safeguarding and Protecting Children Policy and Guidelines for Clubs, Centres and Class Associations and the RYA Safeguarding Adults Policy and Guidelines for Clubs, Centres and Class Associations should be used as a guide to the physical steps that can be taken if a referral or disclosure is received. Both of these policies can be accessed on the RYA website: www.rya.org.uk/about-us/policies/safeguarding. Below is a list of dos and don'ts to support someone in the moment that they receive a disclosure.

Dos

- Keep calm and remain receptive and approachable.
- Assess the situation, has a crime been committed? Do you need to contact the emergency services?
- Listen carefully and patiently without interrupting if possible and let the victim recount the details in their own time.
- Use the victim's own words if you need to seek clarification.
- If you need more information, use TED: Tell me… Explain to me… Describe to me…
- Acknowledge how difficult it must have been to disclose.
- Reassure them that they have done the right thing in telling you and they are not to blame.
- Let them know that you will do everything you can to help them.
- Advise the victim what will happen next.
- Make a written record as soon as you can.
- Report the disclosure to the Safeguarding team.
- Adults: Always involve the adult in any decision making regarding the referral and gain consent from the victim to share the information. If you feel that the adult does not have sufficient capacity to make a decision about sharing information, you should consider if breaking confidentiality is in the best interests of the victim. Please see the Mental Capacity and Consent section of the RYA Safeguarding Adults Policy and Guidelines for Clubs, Centres and Class Associations. This can be accessed on the RYA website: www.rya.org.uk/about-us/policies/safeguarding.
- Children and young people: Gain consent from the parent/carer to share the information. Only speak with the parents/caregivers of the victim if this does not pose a risk to the child.
- Use a person-centred approach.

Don'ts

- Don't make promises to keep secrets.
- Don't ask leading questions or put words in the mouth of the victim.
- Don't repeatedly ask the victim to repeat their disclosure.
- Don't discuss the referral with anyone who does not need to know.
- Don't be judgmental.
- Never ignore what you have been told or pass it on.
- Don't confront or contact the Subject of Concern.
- Don't remove or contaminate any evidence that may be present.
- Never dismiss your concerns – even a gut feeling is worth reporting.

Confidentiality

The sharing of personal information within an organisation is not prevented by law. While appropriate confidentiality should be maintained, it is important to make sure the right people within the organisation are informed if the circumstances require this. If you are the recipient of a safeguarding disclosure, contact the Safeguarding Manager who will advise on the next steps, which may or may not include sharing that information with external agencies, however the following considerations should be taken into account.

Confidentiality: Children and Young People

Information sharing is essential for effective safeguarding and promoting the welfare of children and young people. It is a key factor identified in many Serious Case Reviews (SCRs), where poor information sharing has resulted in missed opportunities to take action that keeps children and young people safe.

There are seven golden rules to confidentiality and Information Sharing:

1. Remember that the General Data Protection Regulation (GDPR), Data Protection Act 2018, and Human Rights law are not barriers to justified information sharing but provide a framework to ensure that personal information about living individuals is shared appropriately.
2. Be open and honest with the individual (and/or their family where appropriate) from the outset about why, what, how, and with whom information will, or could, be shared, and seek their agreement, unless it is unsafe or inappropriate to do so.
3. Seek advice from other practitioners, or the RYA Data Protection Officer, if you are in any doubt about sharing the information concerned, without disclosing the identity of the individual where possible.
4. Where possible, share information with consent, and where possible, respect the wishes of those who do not consent to having their information shared. Under the GDPR and Data Protection Act 2018 you may share information without consent if, in your judgement, there is a lawful basis to do so, such as where safety may be at risk. You will need to base your judgement on the facts of the case. When you are sharing or requesting personal information from someone, be clear on the basis upon which you are doing so. Where you do not have consent, be mindful that an individual might not expect information to be shared.
5. Consider safety and well-being: base your information sharing decisions on considerations of the safety and well-being of the individual and others who may be affected by their actions.
6. Necessary, proportionate, relevant, adequate, accurate, timely, and secure. Ensure that the information you share is necessary for the purpose for which you are sharing it, is shared only with those individuals who need to have it, is accurate and up to date, is shared in a timely fashion, and is shared securely.
7. Keep a record of your decision and the reasons for it – whether it is to share information or not. If you decide to share, then record what you have shared, with whom, and for what purpose.

Confidentiality: Adults at Risk

Individuals may not give their consent to the sharing of safeguarding information for several reasons. For example, they may be frightened of reprisals, they may fear losing control, they may not trust social services or other partners, or they may fear that their relationship with the abuser will be damaged. Reassurance and appropriate support along with gentle persuasion may help to change their view on whether it is best to share information.

If a person refuses intervention to support them with a safeguarding concern, or requests that information about them is not shared with other safeguarding partners, their wishes should be respected. However, there are several circumstances where the practitioner can reasonably override such a decision, including:

- The person lacks the mental capacity to make that decision – this must be properly explored and recorded in line with the Mental Capacity Act.
- Other people are, or may be, at risk, including children.
- Sharing the information could prevent a crime.
- The alleged abuser has care and support needs and may also be at risk.
- A serious crime has been committed.
- Staff are implicated.
- The person has the mental capacity to make that decision, but they may be under duress or being coerced.
- In cases of domestic abuse, if the risk is unreasonably high and meets the criteria for a multi-agency risk assessment conference referral.
- A court order or other legal authority has requested the information.

If none of the above apply and the decision is not to share safeguarding information with other safeguarding partners, or not to intervene to safeguard the person:

- Support the person to weigh up the risks and benefits of different options.
- Ensure they are aware of the level of risk and possible outcomes.
- Offer to arrange for them to have an advocate or peer supporter.
- Offer support for them to build confidence and self-esteem if necessary.
- Agree on and record the level of risk the person is taking.
- Record the reasons for not intervening or sharing information.
- Regularly review the situation.
- Try to build trust and use gentle persuasion to enable the person to better protect themselves.

If it is necessary to share information outside the organisation:

- Explore the reasons for the person's objections – what are they worried about?
- Explain the concern and why you think it is important to share the information.
- Tell the person who you would like to share the information with and why.
- Explain the benefits, to them or others, of sharing information – could they access better help and support?
- Discuss the consequences of not sharing the information – could someone come to harm?

- Reassure them that the information will not be shared with anyone who does not need to know.
- Reassure them that they are not alone, and that support is available to them.

If the person cannot be persuaded to give their consent, then, unless it is considered dangerous to do so, it should be explained to them that the information may be shared without consent in some situations (as set out above). The reasons should be given and recorded. The safeguarding principle of proportionality should underpin decisions about sharing information without consent, and decisions should be on a case-by-case basis.

If it is not clear that information should be shared outside the organisation, a conversation can be had with the Data Protection Officer or the safeguarding partners in the police or local authority without disclosing the identity of the person in the first instance. They can then advise on whether full disclosure is necessary without the consent of the person concerned.

It is very important that the risk of sharing information is also considered. In some cases, such as domestic violence or hate crime, it is possible that sharing information could increase the risk to the individual. Safeguarding partners need to work jointly to provide advice, support, and protection to the individual to minimise the possibility of worsening the relationship or triggering retribution from the abuser.

SafeLives (www.safelives.org.uk – previously CAADA) provide resources for identifying the risk victims face including a Dash risk checklist, which is a risk assessment tool for practitioners who work with adult victims of domestic abuse. It offers a consistent approach to identifying those who are at high risk of harm and whose cases should be referred to a MARAC (multi-agency risk assessment conference) meeting in order to manage their risk. If there are concerns about a risk to a child or children, then a referral to ensure that a full assessment of their safety and welfare needs to be made.

What to Do if You Are Concerned About a Child or About the Behaviour of a Member of Staff

A complaint, concern, or allegation may come from a number of sources: a child, their parents, or someone within your organisation. It may involve the behaviour of a volunteer or employee, or something that has happened to the child outside the sport, perhaps at home or at school.

An allegation may range from mild verbal bullying to physical or sexual abuse. If you are concerned that a child may be being abused, it is NOT your responsibility to investigate further BUT it is your responsibility to act on your concerns and report them to the appropriate statutory authorities.

If you're not sure what to do and need advice, you can call the RYA Safeguarding Manager on 023 8060 4104 or the NSPCC's free 24-hour helpline on 0808 800 5000.

GLOSSARY

ABACK	The sail pressed backwards by the wind.
ABAFT	Behind the boat.
ABEAM	At right angles to the line of the boat.
ADRIFT	Afloat, but without a propulsive force.
AFT	Towards back of the boat.
AGROUND	On the ground and not afloat.
AHEAD	The area in front of the boat.
AMIDSHIPS	In the middle of the boat.
AWASH	The boat being full of water.
BACKING	The wind changing direction in an anti-clockwise direction (against the sun).
BALANCE	How level the boat is.
BEAM	The side of a boat.
BEARING AWAY	Changing direction away from the wind.
BELAY	Twist a rope around something to make fast.
BELLY OF THE SAIL	The fullness of the sail.
BIGHT	A loop.
BLANKETING	To take the wind from another craft which is to leeward.
BOTTLE SCREW	A means of attaching and adjusting shrouds.
BROACHING	To turn sideways on to the wind and heel over.
BURGEE	A flag.
BY THE LEE	Sailing with the wind on the same side of the boat as the mainsail.
CABLE	A nautical measurement being 200 yards or 100 fathoms.
CARS	Adjustable fairleads on tracks, to adjust sheet angle.
CASTING OFF	Leaving the moorings.
CATSPAWS	Ripples on the surface of the water showing a gust of wind.
CHAIN PLATE	Metal plate to which the shrouds are attached at their base.
CLAWING OFF	Sailing off a lee shore.
COAMING	The built up woodwork around hatches etc to exclude water.
CRINGLE	The metal ring used to reinforce any holes in the sail.
CROSS TREES	Horizontal spreaders which hold the shrouds away from the mast.
CUNNINGHAM	System for tensioning luff of sail.

DISPLACEMENT	The amount of water that a boat displaces (Archimedes' Principle).
DOWNHAUL	See Cunningham.
EASE, TO	To slacken.
EBB	A tide is on the ebb when it is falling.
EDDY	A current flowing in a different direction to the main stream.
FAIRLEADS	Permanent fixtures on a boat which are designed to guide a rope.
FAIRWAY	A clear passage for navigation.
FALL	The loose end of a rope.
FATHOM	A measurement of depth (1 fathom = 6 feet).
FLOOD	A flooding tide is a rising one.
FREEBOARD	The amount of boat above the waterline.
GHOSTING	To move when there is no recognisable wind.
GNAV	Lever above boom, function same as kicker.
HEADWAY	Forward momentum.
HEAT SEALING	Tidy end of rope by melting together.
HOUNDS	The fixture of the mast to which the shrouds are attached.
IN IRONS, STAYS	The boat lies head to wind, sails flapping.
JURY RIG	This is an emergency rig, having undergone temporary repair.
KICKER	(Kicking strap) pulley system between boom and mast designed to tension leech of sail.
LUFF	To change the boat's direction towards the wind.
MAKE FAST	To secure.
MAST STEP	The slot into which the mast heel fits.
OUTHAUL	System for tensioning foot of sail.
RACKS	Metal or carbon extensions to side of boat.
RAKE	Angle of mast to vertical.
ROCKER	Amount of curve on the longitudinal axis at bottom of boat.
SPLICE	To tidy end of rope by weaving through itself.
TELL-TALE	Wool or lightweight tape used to detect airflow.
TRIM	Fore and aft adjustment of weight in boat.
VANG	See KICKER.
VEERING	The wind changing direction in a clockwise direction (with the sun).
WARP	Rope used for anchoring or mooring.
WEIGHING	Raising the anchor.
WHIPPING	End of rope tidied by winding twine around it.

INDEX

Note: page numbers in *italics* refer to illustrations

A

adaptations to teaching techniques and environments	61–3
advice and guidance	165
anchoring (dinghy, keelboat, or multihull)	11, 134–5, *134–5*
assistant instructor	7, 8, 28, 29
asymmetric spinnaker	144–8
capsize recovery	148
drop	146, *146*
gybing	147–8, *147*, *148*
hoisting	144–5, *145*
avoiding complaints	170

B

basic boat controls	76–7
bearing away	83, 104–5, *105*, 141, 157
briefing and debriefing	12, 21, 48–52, 59
British Youth Sailing recognised clubs	163

C

capsize recovery	99, 100, 114–19
asymmetric spinnaker	148
dinghy inversion	116
multihull	118
multihull inversion	119
symmetrical spinnaker	153
trapezing	159
CAS (coming alongside)	113, 127–30, *127–30*, 138
CAT (Crew weight, Airflow, Technique)	68, 77
communication skills	23, 37–8, 59, 162

D

day sailing	9, 14, 28, 142–3
planning and pilotage	142
teaching sequence	143
dinghy/keelboat/multihull instructor	9, 20, 28, 29

double-handed dinghy	70, 154, 156
double-handed teaching method	68, 69–91
adaptations	88–91
basic boat controls	76–7
gybing	84–6, 90, 91
launching and familiarisation	73, *73*–5
personal equipment, boat orientation, and basic rigging	70–72
sailing a triangular course/first solo sail	87
sailing downwind	83
sailing to windward	81–2
step by step	69
tacking/going about	78–80
Duke of Edinburgh's Award	163–4
duty of care	165

E

EDICTS (Explanation, Demonstration, Imitation, Correction, Training, Summary)	40, 41
effective instructing	39–41
emotional intelligence	42
equality policy	169

F

feedback	15, 18, 22, 34, 36–8, 40, 48, 58, 78, 92, 106
models	49–52
TED	52
the 'hamburger'	49, 50, 52
the 'tell' or 'hairdryer'	49, 50, 51, 52
the 'traffic light'	51, 52
five essentials	10, 11, 15, 66–8, *66–8*, 76, 102, 136
double-handed teaching method	69
follow my leader	109
sailing a triangular course	108
sailing downwind	83, 106
sailing rudderless	140
sailing to windward	81, 104
teaching in keelboats	68
teaching in multihulls	68
follow my leader	96, 109, *109*, 111

G

group control	21, 22, 24, 25, 58–9, 87, 92, 93
GROW (Goal, Reality, Options, Will)	60
gybing	41, 58, 69, 84–6, *85*, 96, 106–7, *107*, 108, 109
keelboat	91, *91*
long tiller extension adaptation	84, 90, 106
'M' gybing	148, *148*
multihull	86, *86*
roll gybe	156–7, *156–7*
sailing rudderless	140–41
without a centreboard	137

H

'hairdryer'	49, 50, 51, 52
'hamburger'	49, 50, 52
heaving to	76, 77, *77*, 112

I

instructor code of conduct	166–7
instructor endorsements	14–17
advanced instructor endorsement	15, 28, 29
dinghy, keelboat, or multihull	14, 28, 29
foiling endorsement	16, 28, 29
race coach level 1 (RCL1)	17, 28, 29
instructor health declaration	165
instructor pathway	7, 7
instructor training assessment standards	167–8
instructor training awards	7–29
assistant instructor	8, 28, 29
trainer	23–6, 28, 29
appointment revalidation	26
selection days	24
training course	25
dinghy/keelboat/multihull instructor	9, 28, 29
instructor endorsements	14–17
instructor training course	12–13
pre-entry sailing assessment	10
tasks	10–11
progression	7
race coach level 2 (RCL2)	18, 28, 29
senior instructor	19–22, 28, 29
teaching/training ratios	29
useful publications	7
who teaches what	28
instructor training course	12–13
afloat	12
ashore	12–13
instructor endorsements	14–17
moderation and course outcome	13
instructor training ratios	29

K

keelboat	
anchoring	134–5
coming alongside	*130*
gybing	91, *91*
instructor	9, 20, 25, 28, 29
instructor endorsement	14
man overboard	131–3, *133*
reefing afloat	120–21
rigging and launching	72, 75
seamanship skills	113
tacking	89, *89*
teaching the five essentials	68

L

land drills	12, 41, 94, 99, 144, 149
launching	73–5, *73*, *74*, 93, 112, 122
learning	
barriers	33–4
conditions	61
motivators	33
styles	31–2, 33, 56, 62
lying to	12, 76, 77, 99, 100, 132

M

manual handling	171
MOB (man overboard recovery)	131–3
keelboats	133, *133*
multihull	133, *133*
teaching sequence	132, *132*
multihull	
anchoring	134–5
capsize recovery	118
gybing	86
instructor	9, 20, 25, 28, 29
instructor endorsement	14
inversion	119
leaving and returning to shore	122–4
man overboard	133, *133*
orientation/basic boat controls	77
reefing afloat	120–21
rigging and launching	72, 74, *74*
tacking/going about	80, 157
teaching the five essentials	68

P

people skills	25, 39
personal equipment	70, *70*, 97, *97*, *142*
planning and pilotage	142
pre-entry sailing assessment	9, 10
tasks	10–11
presentation skills	43–6
content	44–5
handling questions	45
visual aids	46
PUM (Pick Up A Mooring)	125–6

R

race coach level 2 (RCL2)	18, 28, 29
rigging	70, 98, *98*, 144
rigging a multihull and keelboat	72, 74, 75
rule of three	49
RYA affiliated clubs	161
RYA OnBoard initiative	162
RYA teaching method	65–9
becoming an RYA instructor	65
double-handed teaching method	69–91
single-handed teaching method	92–109
five essentials	66–8
teaching in keelboats	68
teaching in multihulls	68
further sessions	110–60
additional practical sessions	112
anchoring (dinghy, keelboat, or multihull)	134–5, *134*, *135*
capsize recovery	114–19
asymmetric spinnaker	148
dinghy inversion	116
multihull	118
multihull inversion	119
teaching sequence	114–15, *114–15*
CAS (coming alongside)	127–30, *127–30*
leaving and returning to shore	122–4, *122*
lee shore landing (downwind approach)	123, *123*
windward shore landing	124, *124*
MOB (man overboard recovery)	131–3
PUM (pick up a mooring)	125–6
reefing afloat	120–21
sailing backwards	138–9, *139*
sailing rudderless	*140*, 140–41
sailing without a centreboard (dinghy only)	136–7
seamanship skills in keelboats	113
session considerations	111
teaching day sailing	142–3
teaching performance sailing	144–60
asymmetrical spinnaker	144–8, *144–8*
symmetrical spinnaker	149–53, *149–52*
roll gybe	156–7, *156–7*
roll tack	154–5, *154–5*
trapezing	158–60, *158*, *159*
RYA training centres	161
RYA youth sailing scheme	6, 8, 9, 12, 14, 17, 23, 26, 28, 65

S

safeguarding and child protection	171–9
criminal records disclosure	173–175
good practice guidelines	175
good recruitment practice	173–175
handling allegations	175–179
identifying child abuse	175
policy statement	172–173
safety signals	59, *59*
sailing a triangular course	96, 108, *108*
sailing across the wind	76, 96, 99–101, *100*
sailing backwards	138–9, *139*
sailing downwind	69, 83, 104, 141
sailing rudderless	140–41
sailing to windward	81–2, *82*, 102, 104–5, *105*, 141
senior instructor	8, 14, 18, 19–22, 23, 28, 29, 114, 142, 165
session planning	53–6
choosing the right session	55
example plan	54
single-handed dinghy	154, 155, 156, 157
single-handed teaching method	92–109
capsize	95
communication	94, *94*
downwind and gybing	106–7, *107*
follow my leader	109, *109*
group control	93
improving sailing to windward/bearing away	104–5, *105*
improving steering	102–3
land drills	94
personal equipment and boat orientation	97
rigging	98, *98*
sailing a triangular course	108, *108*
sailing across the wind	99–101
tacking sequence	101
teaching sequence	100
step by step	96
teaching equipment/sailing area	93, *93*
stages of learning	36, 56

student health declaration	165
swimmers	166
symmetrical spinnaker	149–53
capsize recovery	153
drop	151, *151*
gybing	152–3, *152*
hoisting	149–50, *149*, 150

T

tacking/going about	*78*, 78–80
aft mainsheet adaptation	88, *88*
longer tiller extension adaptation	79, 101
roll tack	154–5, *154–5*
sailing rudderless	141
single-handed sequence	101
without a centreboard	137
teaching/training ratios	29
techniques for instructing and coaching	30–60
adaptations to teaching techniques and environments	61–3
learning conditions	61
'transitional booklet'	62
assessing students' abilities	64
being an effective instructor	39–41
briefing and debriefing	48–52, 59
feedback effectiveness	52
reviewing and feedback	49
rule of three	49
the brief	48, 59
the 'hamburger'	49, 50, 52
the 'tell' or 'hairdryer'	49, 50, 51, 52
the 'traffic light'	51, 52
communication skills	37–8, 59
discussion	47
emotional intelligence	42
group control	58–9, 93
factors	58
principles	58
how and why people learn	31–2
methods, motivators, and barriers	33–4
presentation skills	43–6
session planning	53–6
stages of learning	36
successful learning	60
TED (Tell, Explain, Describe)	52
'tell' or 'hairdryer'	49, 50, 51, 52
'traffic light'	51, 52
trapezing	158–60, *158*, *159*

W

Whole – Part – Whole teaching structure	12, 41, *41*, 56, 65, 78, 94, 99, 106
WWWWWH question style	51, 52

INSTRUCTOR LOG

Date	Location	Hours' Experience		Activity and Weather Conditions		Authorisation
		Role	Hours	Type of Course or Activity	Max. Wind Speed	Signature/Name

Date	Location	Hours' Experience		Activity and Weather Conditions		Authorisation
		Role	Hours	Type of Course or Activity	Max. Wind Speed	Signature/Name

Date	Location	Hours' Experience		Activity and Weather Conditions		Authorisation
		Role	Hours	Type of Course or Activity	Max. Wind Speed	Signature/Name

Date	Location	Hours' Experience		Activity and Weather Conditions		Authorisation
		Role	Hours	Type of Course or Activity	Max. Wind Speed	Signature/Name

Date	Location	Hours' Experience		Activity and Weather Conditions		Authorisation
		Role	Hours	Type of Course or Activity	Max. Wind Speed	Signature/Name

RYA Audiobooks

A range of our titles are available to listen to now on Spotify, Apple, Google, and Audible

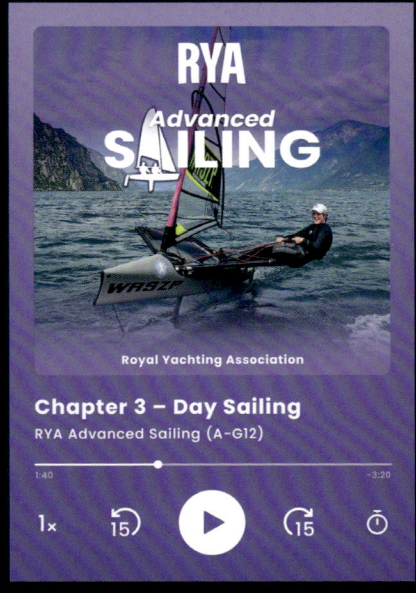

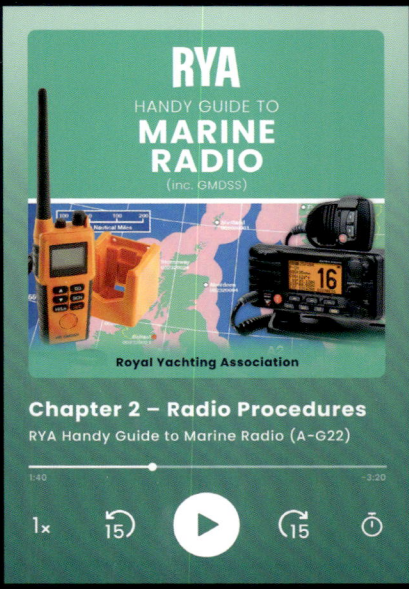

www.rya.org.uk/audiobooks

RYA

eBooks

There are several quick and easy ways to purchase your RYA eBook:

- in-app (iOS and Android only)
- www.rya.org.uk
- Apple Books
- Google Play Books

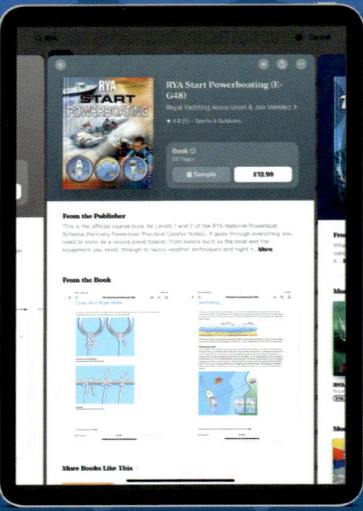

www.rya.org.uk/ebooks